# Sexual Intimacy and Gender Identity 'Fraud'



This book is a legal and political intervention into a contemporary debate concerning the appropriateness of sexual offence prosecutions brought against young gender non-conforming people for so-called 'gender identity fraud'. It comes down squarely against prosecution. To that end, it offers a series of principled objections based both on liberal principles, and arguments derived from queer and feminist theories.

Thus prosecution will be challenged as criminal law overreach and as a spectacular example of legal inconsistency, but also as indicative of a failure to grasp the complexity of sexual desire and its disavowal. In particular, the book will think through the concepts of consent, harm and deception and their legal application to these specific forms of intimacy. In doing so, it will reveal how cisnormativity frames the legal interpretation of each and how this serves to preclude more marginal perspectives.

Beyond law, the book takes up the ethical challenge of the non-disclosure of gender history. Rather than dwelling on this omission, it argues that we ought to focus on a cisgender demand to know as the proper object of ethical inquiry. Finally, and as an act of legal and ethical re-imagination, the book offers a queer counter-judgment to *R v McNally*, the only case involving a gender non-conforming defendant, so far, to have come before the Court of Appeal.

**Alex Sharpe** is Professor of Law at Keele University. She is also a Barrister at Garden Court Chambers, London.

# Sexual Intimacy and Gender Identity 'Fraud'

## Reframing the Legal and Ethical Debate

Alex Sharpe

Routledge
Taylor & Francis Group
LONDON AND NEW YORK

First published 2018 by Routledge

2 Park Square, Milton Park, Abingdon, Oxfordshire OX14 4RN
52 Vanderbilt Avenue, New York, NY 10017

A GlassHouse book

*Routledge is an imprint of the Taylor & Francis Group, an informa business*

First issued in paperback 2019



*British Library Cataloguing in Publication Data*
A catalogue record for this book is available from the British Library

*Library of Congress Cataloging in Publication Data*
Names: Sharpe, Alex, (Law teacher), author.
Title: Sexual intimacy and gender identity 'fraud' : reframing the legal and ethical debate / Alex Sharpe.
Description: New York, NY : Routledge, 2018. | Includes bibliographical references and index.
Identifiers: LCCN 2017037155 | ISBN 9781138502550 (hbk)
Subjects: LCSH: Gender identity--Law and legislation--Great Britain. | Transgender people--Legal status, laws, etc.--Great Britain. | Sex crimes--Great Britain. | Sex and law.
Classification: LCC KD7975 .S53 2018 | DDC 345.41/02536--dc23
LC record available at https://lccn.loc.gov/2017037155

ISBN: 978-1-138-50255-0 (hbk)
ISBN: 978-0-367-28024-6 (pbk)

Typeset in Galliard
by Taylor & Francis Books

In loving memory of my mother and father

# Contents

# Foreword

At a time when transgender hate crime is on the rise (though still under reported), UK jurisdictions are prosecuting young transgender men for sexual assault, based on their failure to disclose their gender history to sexual partners. In *Sexual Intimacy and Gender Identity 'Fraud': Reframing the Legal and Ethical Debate*, Alex Sharpe continues her ground-breaking work on transgender and queer jurisprudence, undertaking a forensic analysis of these recent cases, and highlighting the normative construction (and refusal) of intimacy, desire, sex and gender identity.

Building on twenty years of work that has marked out new territory and new terms of reference by which transgender equality is now understood, Alex Sharpe's latest volume focuses on criminal law questions of harm, fraud and consent, and ethical questions of deception, autonomy and agency. As the leading scholar in this field, Sharpe forces us to rethink our intuitive legal and ethical responses to questions of trust, authenticity and consent, specifically by rejecting the criminalisation of LGBTQI defendants whose identities are not legally or socially recognised as 'real'. In particular, and inspired by the feminist judgments projects that are happening across the globe, Sharpe presents a queer re-writing of the judgment in the case of *McNally*, offering an ethical and legal re-imagination of the 'othering' of those whose lived experiences and choices do not meet cis-heteronormative expectations. It is deeply inspiring – and instructive – for students, teachers, lawyers and judges to see how decision-makers might approach these kinds of cases differently were they minded to do so.

This book might be difficult reading for those who think that the truth about one's gender is a core matter upon which sexual consent is contingent. It will undoubtedly also be considered provocative by those who (rightly) call for sexual assault to be taken more seriously by the criminal law. However, through principled, pragmatic, public interest and rights based arguments, Sharpe makes a persuasive case against the use of state power in this context, and exhorts us to rebalance the ethical burdens imposed upon gender non-conforming individuals. It is not only a rigorous, innovative and comprehensive analysis, but as all pioneering work should be, challenging, stimulating and passionate. I was excited to read this timely and absorbing book, and I hope you are too.

Sharon Cowan
Professor of Feminist and Queer Legal Studies
University of Edinburgh
June 2017

# Acknowledgments

In thinking about legal and ethical issues relating to gender identity 'fraud,' and in writing this book, I have received the support, encouragement and constructive criticism of many friends and colleagues. In particular, I would like to thank Neil Cobb, Sharon Cowan, Angus Dawson, Aeyal Gross, Les Moran, Anthony Wrigley and Aleardo Zanghellini. I would also like to thank Matilda Arvidsson, Matt Ball, Kerry Carrington, Rachel Clement, Thomas Crofts, Ange Dwyer, Katherine Franke, David Gurnham, Gina Heathcote, Anne Hellum, Russell Hogg, Jonathan Herring, Leila Khademi, Jane Krishnadas, Dru Levasseur, Desmond Manderson, Gail Mason, Daniel Monk, Wayne Morgan, Diane Otto, Colin Perrin, Nigel Power, Amit Pundik, Helen Reece, Ruthann Robson, Anniken Sorlie, Hedi Viterbo, Steve Wilkinson and Rebecca Williams. I would also like to thank the *Centre for Law, Ethics and Society* at Keele University and, more generally, my Keele Colleagues for their collegiality and generosity of spirit.

The book has also benefited from the comments of audiences at numerous conferences and symposiums. These include the *Queer Perspectives on Law* conference at SOAS (2014), the *LGBT/Queer Studies* Conference at Tel Aviv University (2014), the *Transgender Bodies of Law* conference at the Centre for Law and Public Affairs, Prague (2014), the *Sexual Freedom, Equality & the Right to Gender Identity as a Site of Legal & Political Struggle* conference at the University of Oslo (2014), the *Challenging Rape Orthodoxy* Symposium at the University of Nottingham (2015), the *Trans Justice* conference held at Garden Court Chambers (2016) and the launch of the *Transgender Equality Legal Initiative* (TELI) in London (2016). The book has also benefited from audience comments at law seminars at the ANU, Columbia, CUNY, Durham, Keele, Kent, Lund, Macquarie, Oxford, Manchester and Warwick universities, as well as at LAMBDA Legal, New York. I would also like to acknowledge the assistance of visiting fellowships at the Institute of Criminology, the University of Sydney (2014) and the Crime and Justice Research Centre, QUT (2014 and 2016), as well as the considerable benefit derived from a Leverhulme Trust Research Fellowship (2016–2017).

Finally, I acknowledge the following copyright © permissions. An earlier version of portions of chapters 3 and 6 appears as 'Transgender Marriage and the Legal Obligation to Disclose Gender History' in the *Modern Law Review* (2012) reprinted by permission of Wiley-Blackwell; an earlier version of portions of chapters 3 and 4 appears as 'Criminalising Sexual Intimacy: Transgender Defendants and the Legal Construction of Non-Consent' in the *Criminal Law Review* (2014) reprinted by permission of Sweet & Maxwell; an earlier version of portions of chapters 3 and 4 appears as 'Sexual Intimacy, Gender Variance and Criminal Law' in the *Nordic Journal of Human Rights* (2015) reprinted by permission of Taylor & Francis Ltd on behalf of the Norwegian Centre for Human Rights; an earlier version of portions of chapters 4 and 5 appears as 'Expanding Liability for Sexual Fraud through the Concept of 'Active Deception': A Flawed Approach' in the *Journal of Criminal Law* (2016) reprinted by permission of Sage, an earlier version of chapter 7 appears as 'Queering Judgment: The Case of Gender Identity Fraud' in the *Journal of Criminal Law* (2017) reprinted by permission of Sage, and an earlier version of chapter 6 appears as 'The Ethicality of the Demand for (Trans) parency in Sexual Relations' in the *Australian Feminist Law Journal* (2017) reprinted by permission of Taylor & Francis Ltd www.tandfonline.com.

# Table of cases

# Table of legislation

## UK Primary Legislation

## Australian Primary Legislation



## International Law

# Part I

# Preliminaries

Chapter 1

# Introduction

This book is concerned with questions of intimacy, desire and the liberal state. More specifically, it is concerned to interrogate sexual offence prosecutions brought in the UK based on a claim of fraud. Thus, in writing this book, I am not interested in sexual coercion, or behaviour that might be described as borderline coercive. There is an abundance of criminal law, philosophical and feminist literature that concerns itself with such important questions (Estrich, 1987; West, 1996; Lacey, 1998; Archard, 1998; Schulhofer, 1998; Gardner and Shute, 2000; McGregor, 2005). Rather, I am concerned with acts or omissions that might legally be classified as deceptive. In recent years, there has been an increase in prosecutions in circumstances where sexual intimacy is alleged to have been occasioned by deception, a fact, no doubt, related to judicial expansion of the fraud category within sexual offences law. However, I am not interested in deception at large. Rather, I am interested only in cases where claims of deception hinge on the identity of the defendant.

Moreover, an analysis of these cases enables not only consideration of a set of liberal-legal concerns: the setting of appropriate limits to the operation of criminal law; the trumping of apparent consent to desire-led intimacy; pragmatic difficulties in establishing defendant knowledge in relation to facts designated legally material; clashes of rights between the parties to intimacy; and the threshold of harm necessary to trigger prosecution. It also permits examination of the ways in which identities are constituted and refused through legal struggle. For the purposes of the book, I will focus on gender identity. This is because prosecution claims of deception as to identity have, at least in the UK, been confined to this type.[1] It is

1 In the UK, prosecutions based on identity fraud have, so far, been limited to gender: *R v Gemma Barker* 5/3/12 (Unrept, Guildford Crown Court, Judge Moss); *R v Chris Wilson* 7/3/13 (Unrept, Edinburgh High Court Lord Bannatyne); *R v Justine McNally* [2013] EWCA Crim 1051; *R v Gayle Newland* 15/9/15 (Unrept, Chester Crown Court, Judge Dutton); *R v Kyran Lee (Mason)* 16/12/15 (Unrept, Lincoln Crown Court, Judge Heath); *R v Jason Staines* 24/3/16 (Unrept, Bristol Crown Court, Judge Cotter); *R v Newland* 29/6/17 (Unrept, Manchester Crown Court, Judge Stockdale). There was also an earlier case (*R v Jennifer Saunders* 12/10/91 (Unrept, Doncaster Crown Court, Judge Crabtree)). For a discussion of this latter case

true that there have been successful prosecutions for fraud on the basis of deception as to ethnicity/nationality in Israel.[2] However, such prosecutions, ones unlikely to be prosecuted in the UK, find their 'intelligibility' in the very specific context of the Israeli State and Jewish/Arab relations. As Aeyal Gross has put it, commenting on the case of *Kashur*, it is 'relatively unique, in both context and form, to Israel, reflecting its ethno-nationalistic character' (Gross, 2015, p. 32; see also Gross, 2000).[3] In any event, this book's focus will be on gender identity fraud and its legal construction primarily within English common law. The prosecution of young gender non-conforming people will nevertheless provide a case study

see Smith, 1995, pp. 164–179. There have also been prosecutions for gender identity fraud in Israel and the US. In relation to Israel see *Israel v Alkobi* [2003] IsrDC 3341 (3); *Israel v Jane Doe* [2007] Indictment, CrimC (Kfar Saba) 2372/07 Unpublished. Hen Alkobi, then aged 20, was convicted of *false impersonation of a man* and *attempting to penetrate the complainant's genitalia with an object* and was sentenced to six months in prison, commuted to six months community service and 24 months probation. Jane Doe, then aged 20, was convicted of indecently assaulting a female minor where consent had been obtained by deception, and with statutory rape of a minor. After a guilty plea, the sentencing court handed down a sentence of six months in prison to be served as community service, followed by a 12-month suspended sentence, along with a fine and payment of financial compensation to the complainant. For a discussion and critique of these cases, see Gross, 2009; Gross, 2015. In relation to the US see *People v Sean Clark*, No. 1994CR003290 (Colo. Dist. Ct. Feb 16, 1996); *State v Wheatley*, No. 97-1-50056-6 (Wash. Superior Ct. May 13, 1997). In *People v Clark*, Sean O'Neill, whose birth name was Clark, was tried in the State of Colorado and convicted of the rape of four young women, each of whom he had dated. He received a custodial sentence of three months and a period of probation (Green, 1996). For discussion of the case see Nye, 1998; Califia, 2003, pp. 234–237. Christopher Wheatley, then aged 20, was convicted of third degree rape in the State of Washington. He was sentenced to prison for 27 months (see Gross, 2009, p. 172).

2 The Israeli courts have convicted Arab men who lied about their ethnic background or failed to disclose it prior to sexual intimacy with Jewish women, although only *Kashur* was convicted of a sexual offence (*Sabbar Kashur v State of Israel* [2012] CrimA 5734/10 Takdin (Isr.), Nevo Legal Database). For a discussion of *Kashur* and the other cases see Gross, 2015.

3 It should be noted that there has been one recent prosecution in Australia for deception as to ethnicity. A man of Indian decent, Deepak Dhankar, was convicted by a court in the state of Victoria of 'procuring a person to take part in an act of sexual penetration by fraudulent means' (s. 57 Crimes Act 1958 Victoria). His deception lay in claiming to be a muscular blond-haired caucasian ('Indian-Born Man who Duped Woman into Sex by Pretending he was Caucasian Avoids Jail' news.com.au 25/2/15 available at www.news.com.au/national/victoria/indianborn-man-who-duped-woman-into-sex-by-pretending-he-was-caucasian-avoids-jail/news-story/3defd87c9b97f40bf53dd789a8114570 (last accessed: 3/2/17)). The complainant apparently remained oblivious to the obvious facts that Mr Dhankar is not caucasian, blond or muscular because the parties had agreed in advance to act out a dominant/submissive scene which required the complainant to leave her house door open, lie face down on the bed and not look at the defendant once he arrived. He received a two year suspended sentence and a community service order of 200 hours. At the time of writing, and as far as I am aware, this is the only ethnicity-based identity prosecution brought outside Israel, and before a common law court.

offering valuable insights for wider public and academic debate both within the UK and internationally concerning the expansion of the fraud category generally within sexual offences law and specifically in relation to the criminalisation of identity-based fraud.

It is necessary from the outset to clarify that in referring to *gender identity* fraud, I am placing emphasis on, and intend to refute, at least in some cases, the legal claim that defendants' gender identities are false. This is the central claim made by the prosecution in the cases to be considered. It might be said that gender fraud relates to things other than identity. Thus, it might be said that all sorts of facts pertaining to gender, that is, to gendered lives or experiences, could provide the basis for a deception claim. For example, a woman who lied about having had an abortion prior to intimacy might be argued to have committed gender fraud if she knew her partner would not have consented if aware of this fact. Of course, a prosecution would not be brought in such a case. This is because the fact of abortion, while a gendered fact, would be considered immaterial to the question of consent as a matter of law. This issue of fact materiality, and its legal construction, is one we will consider throughout the book. The point here is to recognise that while gender fraud could in theory encompass all kinds of gendered facts, it does not do so legally speaking. Rather, prosecutions brought have been confined to claims about gender identity and, so far, have been limited to defendants designated female at birth. Accordingly, the question that has preoccupied the courts has been as to whether the defendant is or is not a man.

In the context of transgender,[4] genderqueer[5] and/or other gender non-conforming people however, this issue of the scope of gender for the purposes of fraud prosecutions assumes particular and additional significance. This is because, in these contexts, legal concern extends beyond the fact of present gender identity to include other facts about the present and/or past (for example, facts relating to legal gender, anatomical status and/or gender socialisation). In this book, I will use the phrase *gender identity* when describing the object of fraud prosecutions. This is for two reasons. First, gender identity is, at least ostensibly, the state's object. Second, if we conclude there has been deception regarding gender identity, then any issue concerning gender history or other present gendered facts, as a separate matter, effectively disappears. Conversely, if we conclude that there has

4 The term *transgender* has become something of an umbrella term for all trans identified people (see Bornstein, 1994; Feinberg, 1996). For the purposes of this book, it is used in a more limited sense to refer to people who feel incongruence between their gender identity and their anatomy. The term *transsexual* is often used in this respect. However, the term *transsexual* fails to exhaust this group because many transgender people refuse the *transsexual* label because of its medical history and pathologising effects, and because not all transgender people seek to resolve the conflict through surgical intervention (see Sharpe, 2002, Chapter 2).

5 The term *genderqueer* denotes a person who does not subscribe to conventional gender distinctions but identifies with neither, both, or a combination of male and female genders (Nestle et al, 2002). However, throughout the book, I will, in general, use the broader term of *gender non-conforming people*.

been no deception regarding gender identity, then we ought to insist on the immateriality of other facts pertaining to gender, a normative claim I will develop in subsequent chapters. Nevertheless, because gender history provides a subtext to understanding fraud prosecutions, and because at least some criminal legal commentators take the view that deception regarding the past ought to vitiate consent (Herring, 2005, pp. 522–523) or can be viewed as doing so (Williams, 2008, p. 149), this phrase will be used where appropriate.

In considering legal affirmation or, more typically, negation of defendant gender identity, the book aims to tease out the ways in which fixed identities are legally required. That is, a defendant either is the man or woman s/he claims to be (and therefore is not legally deceptive) or s/he is not (and therefore is legally deceptive). In other words, the possibility of being both or of moving between categories is both precluded and taken as proof of deception. And yet, such fluidity is not only an empirical reality, but one that appears to have assumed increased relevance in contemporary society. Thus, the number of people living transgender or otherwise gender non-conforming lives has increased exponentially in recent decades.[6] To the extent that the notion of coherent fixed gender identity, around which legal decisions coalesce, belies fluidity or ambiguity, the book will take to task claims of deception and therefore the appropriateness of prosecution, while at the same time drawing attention to the way in which prosecutions based on the idea of fabricated gender identity serve to bolster more hegemonic, though no less socially constructed, gender identity categories, and thereby contribute, among other things, to complainant trauma.

## 1.1 Queering law

In approaching legal and ethical issues surrounding gender identity fraud, this book will adopt a queer approach. That is, it will draw explicitly on queer theory (Butler, 1990; Sedgwick, 1990; Butler, 1993; Halberstam, 1998; Warner, 1991; Stychin, 1995b; Warner, 2000) and, to the extent there is common cause, trans (Bornstein, 1994; Feinberg, 1996; Cromwell, 1999; Namaste, 2000; Stryker, 2004; Stone, 2006; Serano, 2007)[7] and pro-sex feminist theories (Rubin, 1984; Rubin, 2006; Vance, 1984; Nestle, 1992; Segal, 1994). In adopting this

6 Transgender and other gender non-conforming people have become increasing visible since the 1990s. In relation to transgender people, while many have no need for medical services, the number of patients going through Gender Identity Clinics in the UK has quadrupled over the last ten years. See K. Lyons, 'Gender Identity Clinic Services Under Strain as Referral Rates Soar', *The Guardian*, 10/7/16 available at www.theguardian.com/society/2016/jul/10/transgender-clinic-waiting-times-patient-numbers-soar-gender-identity-services (last accessed: 3/2/17).

7 It is recognised that there are some tensions between queer and trans theories, and that some trans scholars have been critical of queer theory. In particular, and by way of example, Jay Prosser has offered a sustained critique of Judith Butler's work around gender performativity, and what he considers its failure to attend to the materiality of transsexual bodies, that is, to flesh (Prosser, 1998, especially Chapter 1).

approach, the book takes as axiomatic the idea that sex, gender and sexuality are socially constructed, that is, they are the products of time (history) and place (culture). As Biddy Martin puts it, queer theory challenges 'hegemonic assumptions about the continuities between anatomical sex, social gender, gender identity, sexual identity, sexual object choice, and sexual practice' (Martin, 1994, p. 105). Law will be seen to reify or naturalise these categories in ways that reproduce what Judith Butler has described as 'the heterosexual matrix' (Butler, 1990, p. 35).

Thus, in the present context, the prosecution claim, one which this book will challenge, is set up in the following terms: a heterosexual cisgender woman has sex with a transgender man or gender non-conforming person designated female at birth; she does so on the basis of a 'false' belief that the latter is a heterosexual cisgender man; the transgender man or gender non-conforming person is aware of her 'mistaken' belief; and the combination of these facts serves to vitiate consent. Putting to one side the credibility of complainant ignorance, an issue that the book will take up, especially in Chapter 5, and in relation to which it will adopt a position of scepticism, this type of prosecution assumes the naturalness and stability of the categories of sex, gender and heterosexuality. Thus, and in the context of gender identity fraud prosecutions, the deployment of the trope of innocence is not confined in its effects to complainant naivety, and therefore to defendant fate, but rather extends to and reinforces the idea and fallacy of original and pure categories (Shiner, 1982, p. 387). The effect is to bolster the sexual and gender identities of complainants, while at the same time negating the sexual and gender identities of defendants. Thus, what is at stake are the proper boundaries of 'authentic' and legitimate sexuality and masculinity, as well as who has the interpretive power to decide such questions.

However, this book is not only, or even primarily, interested in questions of legal representation, important though they are. While it will highlight the discursive fallout for those at the sexual and gender margins produced by gender identity fraud prosecutions, the book is explicitly concerned to express normative commitments and to make normative arguments. Thus, the book proceeds on the basis that queer legal theoretical scholarship must transcend a preoccupation with the 'conceptual', and worse still a fixation with transgression for its own sake (Seidman, 1997; Kirby, 2015), at the expense of the 'normative' in mapping out jurisprudential space (Zanghellini, 2009). As Aleardo Zanghellini explains, while counter-normativity, 'the repudiation of dominant norms', is important, it should not succumb to antinormativity, which would commit us to a 'renunciation of prescriptive projects' (Zanghellini, 2009, p. 1. See also Jagose, 2015). Rather, 'the primary motor of queer incursions into conceptual jurisprudential ground … must be political in nature – in the sense of its connection with a concern for justice for sex and gender outsiders' (Zanghellini, 2009, p. 4).

While some might view such an approach to be anything but queer, it remains a truism to say that it is 'the normative commitments from which they proceed' that make queer critiques 'ultimately worthwhile' (Zanghellini, 2009, p. 6). Thus, while it is important to chart disciplinary power and its normalising effects, it is equally, if not more, important to recognise how they 'constrain personal autonomy' (Zanghellini, 2009, p. 6) and counter diversity. Moreover, and importantly, despite queer's anti-humanist rhetoric, one tends to find, as Zanghellini contends, 'a general commitment to liberal humanist values ... such as ideas of respect, value pluralism and personal autonomy' (Zanghellini, 2009, p. 8. See also Seidman, 1997, p. 157; Turner, 2000, p. 17; Ball, 2002, pp. 457–458). Thus, while queer, influenced by poststructural thought as it is, conceives of the concepts of power, epistemology and ontology and their interrelationship differently from liberalism, broader values of tolerance, pluralism and respect for agency (a queer and feminist version of liberal autonomy) belie some common and worthwhile ground.

In this book, I intend to take up Zanghellini's challenge both because I am persuaded as to the necessity for queer legal theory to engage with normative questions, and because such questions are urgent ones in the context of gender identity fraud, given the recent spate of successful sexual offence prosecutions brought in the UK, and the fact that nearly all convicted gender non-conforming defendants have received (often lengthy) prison sentences and have been placed on Sex Offenders Registers (usually for life). In attempting to challenge such prosecutions from a queer perspective, the book will engage with liberal arguments around autonomy, consent, privacy, harm, equality and diversity. It will do so, while recognising tensions between liberalism and queer theory, but in the spirit that some normative idea (some alternative vision) of each of these terms is implicit within queer theory and is precisely what animates and drives it forward. The prescriptive project of this book is a limited affair, the prevention of gender identity fraud prosecutions. It is however, an important one and, as with other possible queer legal projects, failure to imagine and articulate alternative ways of describing the fraud scene, serves only to vacate the space for knowledge construction and action, a space which will otherwise, and inevitably, be filled by more dominant and antithetical legal discourses and practices.

## 1.2 Themes

In considering issues of desire, intimacy and fraud, the book will explore a series of interrelated themes. These include ideology, agency, ignorance/knowledge, act/identity, resistance, law's bodily aesthetics, act/omission, and three key legal and philosophical concepts central to criminal law, ones especially relevant to sexual offences: *consent, harm* and *deception.*

### *(i) Ideology*

In relation to ideology, the book will foreground particular kinds of judicial 'common sense'. In relation to gender identity fraud claims, the forms of ubiquitous wisdom that require naming and challenging are heteronormativity (Warner, 1991) and cisnormativity (Serano, 2007). Accordingly, the book will draw on queer (Butler, 1990; Sedgwick, 1990; Butler, 1993; Halberstam, 1998; Warner, 1991; Stychin, 1995b; Warner, 2000)[8] and trans theories (Bornstein, 1994; Feinberg, 1996; Cromwell, 1999; Namaste, 2000; Stryker, 2004; Serano, 2007; Serano, 2013). *Heteronormativity* assumes heterosexuality to be the normal or preferred sexuality through which society ought to be organised, and in the absence of clarity, the default sexuality. *Cisnormativity* operates in a similar fashion, assuming people to experience harmony between their gender identity and their anatomy, and privileging those who do. The related term, *cissexism*, refers to the belief that transgender people's gender identities 'are inferior to, or less authentic than, those of cissexuals' (Serano, 2007, p. 12).

The term *cissexual* refers to people 'who have only ever experienced their subconscious and physical sexes as being aligned' (Serano, 2007, p. 33). It is used in preference to terms like *natural, real, biological, genetic* or other terms which presuppose and reinforce the primacy of cissexual people. The term *cisgender* refers to those cissexual people who are comfortable with gender expectations that are socially constructed to follow from the fact of cissexuality. In this book, I will use both *cisgender* and *cissexual* depending on the context. However, I will typically use *cisgender* because cisgender people are also cissexual, while the reverse is not necessarily so (for example, queer identified people do not identify as cisgender) and it is cisgender, rather than cissexual, complainant status that is likely to be the better indicator of whether a gender identity fraud complaint will be made and whether the ethicality of gender non-conforming people will be challenged.[9]

It will be argued that these powerful ideologies not only shape discussion of legal and ethical issues arising, but frame them from the outset, thereby rendering unintelligible and unimaginable alternative ways of thinking about and experiencing forms of embodiment, identity and desire. Thus, and while approaching these issues from a social constructionist perspective, it is, as Judith Butler has pointed out, 'not enough to claim [only] that human subjects are constructed, for the construction of the human is a differential operation that produces the more and the less "human", the inhuman, the humanly unthinkable' (Butler, 1993 p. 8). Moreover, these less than human figures 'come to bound the "human" as its constitutive outside' (Butler, 1993, p. 8). That is, they serve to shore up the ontological status and primacy of those considered fully human. In terms of the issues to be explored in this book, we will see that it is transgender and other gender non-conforming people and their 'dubious' sexualities that provide an outside to law's fully human subject, the heterosexual cisgender person. Gender identity fraud prosecutions therefore should not be viewed only as an exercise in 'repressive power' (Foucault, 1981), in the sense of sanction and/or the sublimation of desire. Rather, they are

8 For a general introduction to queer theory see Jagose, 1997; Sullivan, 2003.

9 I recognise that the cis/trans binary distinction might itself be subject to critique. However, the distinction is both analytically useful in the present context and meaningful for most people. Ultimately however, the distinction may need to yield to new terms, ones that avoid reproducing an 'us' and 'them'.

also exercises in 'productive' power in terms of the work they do in maintaining and reproducing gender and sexual hierarchies, in rendering identities, bodies and desires normal/abnormal (Foucault, 1980b; Garland, 1990, pp. 252–253), in producing subjects of the law, and those not fully human (Butler, 1993, p. 22).

The exploration of such issues will function as a ground clearing exercise, a necessary prelude to any serious engagement with doctrinal issues. Indeed, the unmasking of ideology, in the context of prosecutions around gender identity, is not only important in revealing the embedded politics of sexual offences law, but also in understanding emotional responses to 'discovery' of facts complainants consider material. This latter point relates not only to the experience of harm but also to empathy afforded (or not afforded) to other sexual parties. In other words, in addressing the question of ideology, the book will throw light on law's effects (both instrumental and discursive), as well as its role in establishing and regulating affective relations at sites of desire. Thus, while the book expresses concern over the liberty of gender non-conforming people, it also sets itself against prosecution for a variety of other reasons.

### *(ii) Agency*

This theme is clearly an important one in the context of gender identity fraud prosecutions. Within liberal legal discourse, emphasis is placed on sexual autonomy which, it is argued, is undermined by non-disclosure of material facts and/or active deception pertaining to those facts prior to sexual intimacy (Herring, 2005; Herring, 2007). While the concept of agency is preferred, given its recognition of the socially constructed nature of identity and its more sophisticated theorisation of complex configurations of structural, cultural and psychological constraints that shape action, it is recognised that liberal scholars recognise limits to choice (Sherwin, 1996). In the gender identity fraud cases to be considered in this book, a central difficulty both with prosecutions and attendant wider legal and media discourses, is the fact that complainants are routinely depicted as powerless and passive. This view of women, one contributed to by 'carceral' or 'governance' feminism (Estrich, 1986; Chamallas, 1988; MacKinnon, 1989; Falk, 1998; Gotell, 2015), is, as argued by Bernstein (2007, 2012) and Halley et al (2006), both politically problematic and ethically suspect.

In relation to politics, it does women a disservice because it contracts the space for possible action as well as the possibility of imagining action as possible. This problem connects to the previous theme of ideology. In the present context, it is the ideology of 'hegemonic masculinity', one subjected to sustained critique (Connell, 1995; Hollway, 1996), especially within criminology (Messerschmidt, 1993; Jefferson, 1997; Carmody and Carrington, 2000), that reinforces the idea that female complainants are necessarily passive victims, while men charged with sexual offences are necessarily active and coercive or, in the present context, deceptive. These totalising concepts of masculinity and femininity '[rob] women of agency or [the] ability to exert power, express desire, take control, resist, prevent or avoid their victimisation in intimate sexual encounters with men' (Carmody, 2004, p. 47). The ideology of hegemonic masculinity might be thought to lack pertinence in relation to gender identity fraud cases given judicial findings that the defendants are women. Yet, the opposite is true. First, abuse between women weakens its universalising claims (Istar, 1996; Burke and Follingstad, 1999). Second, and more importantly for our purposes, some of the defendants are men and all presented as men. Moreover, their performance of masculinity remains central to legal outcomes, as well as their status as gender and sexual 'deviants'. That is, the playing out of gender identity fraud cases can neither be reduced to, nor easily separated from, an encounter between masculinity and femininity and the cultural frames through which such an encounter 'makes sense'.

Turning to ethics, a view of complainants as passive in their sexual encounters with gender non-conforming people serves to elide mutual desire and pleasure, as well as apparent consent. It contributes to the 'intelligibility' of the disavowal of complainant desire. And yet, while complainants may have been ignorant of the defendants' gender identities, they were nevertheless attracted to the 'men' who stood before them. Moreover, if some of these men had ambiguous genders then perhaps this might be viewed as constitutive of complainant desire, rather than as evidence of its absence (Butler, 1990, p. 123). Further, the relationship between desire and agency bears another relation to ethics. For not only does a refusal of desire present a problem. There is also the ontological problem that it is, in the present context, inseparable from an insistence that the gender identity of the defendant is false. In other words, discussions of female agency cannot be thought apart from the self-determination of gender non-conforming people.

### *(iii) Ignorance/knowledge*

This theme connects to the theme of agency. In thinking about gender identity fraud cases there is a tendency to think about being ignorant of facts (not knowing) and having knowledge (knowing) as polar opposites. Of course, this tendency is not confined to gender identity fraud cases. The tendency is problematic in a number of respects. First, it serves to elide the complexity of the relationship ignorance has to knowledge, and relatedly, it insulates the concept of non-consent from a more nuanced and throughgoing critique, one which reaches into cultural and psychological territory. Thus, if we accept that complainants genuinely believed their object of desire to be a man, a conclusion arrived at in the only case, so far, to go before a jury,[10] we should not conclude that complainant ignorance necessarily equates with non-consent. While some complainants may have lied, the point here is to emphasise how ignorance may be related to agency, and therefore consent.

This idea that we might view ignorance as a form of knowledge, rather than its absence, is one developed by Eve Sedgwick in the context of queer sexuality

10 *Newland* 15/9/15, *Newland* 29/6/17 above note 1.

(Sedgwick, 1988,; Sedgwick, 1993). In coining the phrase, 'the privilege of unknowing', she is referring to a cultural and psychological process whereby privileged people learn not to see, to a kind of 'careful education' (Sedgwick, 1993, p. 24) which erases difference from view. That is, difference is in plain view, yet remains unrecognised by privileged onlookers. Accordingly, ignorance should not be placed beyond critique. Rather, we should ask after the erotics of its 'human production and distribution' (Sedgwick, 1993, p. 25), which include the 'psychological operations of shame, denial [and] projection' that surround it (Sedgwick, 1993, p. 25). As she notes, knowledge does not exhaust power, rather '[i]gnorance and opacity collude and compete with it' (Sedgwick, 1988, p. 102). '[T]hese ignorances far from being pieces of the originary dark, are produced by and correspond to particular knowledges and circulate as part of particular regimes of truth' (Sedgwick, 1988, p. 104).

In the context of sexual fraud cases, complainant ignorance of facts, in relation to which a 'deception' is said to have been perpetrated, is readily translated into non-consent. In exploring the relationship between ignorance and knowledge through gender identity fraud cases, the book will, following Sedgwick, suggest that ignorance might be viewed as a form of knowledge, one that requires labour, not passivity, a psychological and cultural participation in learning not to know. Once acquired, ignorance might operate so as to refuse contrary facts, including those that come through our bodies, and our lovers' bodies, wave after wave. In other words, in a hetero and cisnormative society we may have learned not to recognise difference, especially trans and genderqueer differences, ones which might produce crisis at the level of sexual identity. Thus, while belief that one's sexual partner is male may be genuinely held, it might also be based on learned ignorance regarding the existence of trans and other gender non-conforming people, and be an effect, at least in part, of repudiation, disavowal or wilful blindness, especially perhaps regarding information that passes between bodies during intimacy. Repudiation can occur through repression or, in Lacanian terms, where 'the ego rejects (*verwirft*) the incompatible representation' and 'behaves as if the representation had never occurred to the ego at all' (Laplanche and Pontalis, 1972, p. 187). These matters, and their implications for how we think about the important issue, and actus reus element of non-consent, are ones that ought to register within feminism and wider criminal justice debates.

### *(iv) Act/identity*

Turning to identity, I begin from the premise that gender identity is socially constructed in a number of important senses and in doing so recognise a significant and well-established literature on the question of identity within sociology (Goffman, 1959; Berger and Luckman, 1966; Plummer, 1981; Weeks, 1985; Weeks, 1991) and poststructuralism (Foucault, 1981; Butler 1990; Sedgwick, 1990; Butler, 1993). No matter how fixed some people may experience sex and gender to be, they are not fixed categories. While sex is often seen as the clearest example of categorical certainty, the male/female dyad does not stand close scrutiny (Laqueur, 1990). Medical science recognises the complexity of sex and the fact that not all people fall easily within a binary understanding. Indeed, the existence of intersex people gives the game away (Dreger, 2000). Sex is a category underwritten by the ideology of gender (Butler, 1990, p. 7; Butler, 1993, p. 5). That is, gender may be binary, as a set of regulatory practices, but sex is not. Similarly, the categories of homosexuality and heterosexuality, categories that loom large in gender identity fraud cases, are nineteenth-century sexological constructs (Foucault, 1981; Greenberg, 1988; Weeks, 1991). Their relationship to the sexual life-world can, as queer theory contends, be viewed as reductive.[11]

In terms of Judith Butler's theory of *gender performativity*, gender is understood as a process, one that precedes the subject but in which the subject is caught up (Butler, 1993, p. 9), and therefore in relation to which she can exercise limited agency (Butler, 1993, p. 15). This understanding of identity, one that can be traced back through Foucault to Nietzsche, problematises legal attempts to impose 'the ideal of [gendered] Being on the fact of becoming' (Booth, 1985, p. 132). Rather, on this account, there is no gendered being which precedes the assignation of gender. Moreover, as Butler stresses, the assignation of gender 'is never quite carried out according to expectation', its addressee 'never quite inhabits the ideal s/he is compelled to approximate' (Butler, 1993, p. 231). Indeed, 'the paternal law ought to be understood not as a deterministic divine will, but as a perpetual bumbler, preparing the ground for the insurrections against him' (Butler, 1990, p. 28). In other words, gender always 'fails', sometimes spectacularly, as in the case of gender non-conforming people with whom this book is concerned, but always to some degree. Indeed, it is precisely gender 'failure' that points to the possibility of agency (Butler, 1990, p. 28). As already noted, gender is not a pre-discursive given or essence. It is the product of acts, not 'a singular and deliberate "act"', of course, but rather the effect of 'reiterative and citational practice[s]' over time (Butler, 1993, p. 2).

Accordingly, Butler's theory of gender identity, and social constructionist approaches more generally, beg some important questions concerning the idea of gender identity fraud. After all, fraud presupposes discrepancy between the representation of gender and some ontological 'truth' in which it is notionally grounded. Yet, how can there be fraud if represented gender has no ontological referent, and

11 The approach of social constructionism, which is adopted in this book, also applies to other identity categories. Thus, for example, in relation to race, the category has no proper scientific basis, but rather is an idea having its origins in a racist and colonial past. The 'scientific' study of race commenced in the mid-eighteenth century with Carl von Linneaus' taxonomic study of human beings in *Systema Naturae* published in 1735. In the text he presented five 'racial' groups: (i) the Americanus, (ii) the Asiaticus, (iii) the Africanus, (iv) the Europeanus, and (v) the Monstrosus (see Anderson, 1997; Blunt, 2001; Polaszek, 2010). The view that racial categories are socially constructed and lack a biological basis has been reinforced by the advent of, and advances made in the study of, DNA (Marks, 1995).

if performed gender always falls short of its idealisation? This is not to deny that courts readily find fraud and act on this finding with impunity. Rather, it is to highlight how such legal practices reproduce a contestable understanding of gender identity, one which operates to the obvious detriment of defendants in gender identity fraud cases. In emphasising law's fixation with gender identity in these cases, it is necessary to elaborate the precise relationship of prosecution to the act/identity distinction, a distinction that has proved important, and one that sometimes unravels, thereby producing queer effects, in the context of the regulation of gender and sexuality (Stychin, 1995a; Moran, 1996, Chapter 2; Sharpe, 2002).[12]

To begin with, criminal prosecutions are brought on the basis of conduct (or omission). That is, some actus reus, no matter how minimal, must be established. In the context of adult sexual offences, the state is concerned to prove sexual acts, the absence of consent and the guilty mind of the defendant. It is not, at least ostensibly, concerned with the identity of the defendant. However, in cases of gender identity fraud this account becomes more complicated because claims of non-consent and deception only make sense if the defendant has perpetrated a fraud concerning his/her gender identity. That is, while the actus reus can only be established through proof of false representation or deed, and therefore action (or as we will see in Chapter 5, omission), the false representation or deed in question necessarily pertains to identity. In this sense, gender identity fraud prosecutions implicate both sides of the act/identity distinction, but crucially remain tied to identity. That is, it is legal challenge to the defendant's ontological position that best characterises state prosecutions. This is also important to emphasise because most of the cases to be considered involve vaginal penetration by means of a prosthetic device. This might lead to an argument, one perhaps entirely consistent with legal doctrine, that prosecution and conviction are justified on the basis of proof of non-consensual sex, and irrespective of questions of the defendant's gender identity (Sharpe, 2014, p. 214). However, as we will see, identity remains central to understanding these cases because it is highly unlikely that complaints would have been made, and therefore prosecutions brought, had the object of complainant desire been a cisgender man. In this sense, an emphasis on identity functions not to deny the legality of prosecution,[13] but to draw attention to the selective enforcement of the law against gender non-conforming people.

12 For example, when the offence of buggery was partially decriminalised by the Sexual Offences Act 1967, and replaced by so-called 'homosexual offences', legal regulation shifted from an ostensible concern with sexual acts (the buggery law, while gender neutral, had always been used in practice to target gay men) to a concern over homosexual identity. However, because the 'homosexual' proved elusive as a legal category and because criminal offences require, in any event, proof of actus reus, prosecution necessarily involved a focus on sexual acts (see Moran, 1996). For other examples of how law struggles with the act/identity distinction see the US Supreme Court decision in *Bowers v Hardwick* 478 US 186 (1986) (Stychin, 1995b, p. 150) and the decision of the House of Lords in *R v Brown* [1994] 1 AC 212 (Stychin, 1995a).

13 However, in Chapter 4 we will see that a prosthetic penis is, for at least some transgender men, experienced as an extension of embodied self, as no different

Ultimately, the central legal and ethical issues arising in the context of gender identity fraud claims are best understood in terms of a disjunction between complainant understandings of identity as fixed and defendant understandings of identity as shifting, or as less fixed. Legal insistence on an established set of sexes/genders, from which there can be no or limited movement, and therefore the privileging of complainant perspectives, amounts to a refusal to acknowledge the messiness of identity as well as the spontaneity of desire. Moreover, in foregrounding binary sex/gender positions, law emphasises body parts, as though desire is somehow unconnected to 'the entirety of gender behaviour' (Gross, 2009, p. 199). In opposition to liberal law, this book invokes insights from pro-sex feminism (Rubin, 1984; Rubin, 2006; Vance, 1984; Nestle, 1992; Segal, 1994) and draws on queer and trans theories in order to hold onto the possibility that lack of knowledge, confusion with regard to gender, and gender incongruence can sometimes animate desire (Butler, 1990, p. 123).

Finally, in adopting a social constructionist understanding of identity, it is not intended to deny the importance of lived reality, of people's experiences of identity. Identities, whatever else they may/may not be, are hardly trivial. As Butler observes, asserting gender identity is 'certainly not a question of taking on a mask' (Butler, 1993, p. 7). Moreover, there should be no hierarchy of identities. While this might seem an obvious and uncontentious point, it is an important one to make as there is certainly a danger in the context of transgender and other gender non-conforming people, of effecting hierarchies whereby cisgender people's gender performances become understood as more 'real'. This tendency, one clearly evident in law, and also in some feminist scholarship (most noticeably, Raymond, 1979; Greer, 1999; Jeffreys, 2014), is to be resisted. Indeed, the particular vulnerability of transgender and other gender non-conforming people in this respect, and especially in the context of criminal prosecution, points perhaps to a need to, and the legitimacy of, adopting some form of what Gayatri Spivak has described as 'strategic essentialism' (Spivak, 1990, p. 51). This is a strategy we will consider under the rubric of the following theme.

### *(v) Resistance*

In resisting gender identity fraud prosecutions, attention needs to be paid both to actual litigation strategy and to the discursive and cultural effects likely to be generated. In relation to the former, the book will offer a series of arguments against prosecution. In addition to these arguments, which will take the form of both internal and external critique, three Articles of the European Convention on Human Rights (Articles 3, 8 and 14)[14] will be identified as potential legal avenues

phenomenologically from the fleshy kind (Hale, 2003; Davy, 2011, Chapter 3; Latham, 2016, pp. 355–356). Accordingly, even in scenarios involving a prosthetic penis, claims of deception should not be considered to be unproblematic.

14 Article 3: No one shall be subjected to torture or to inhuman or degrading treatment or punishment; Article 8: Everyone has the right to respect for his private and family life, his home and his correspondence; Article 14: The enjoyment of the rights and

for challenging this type of prosecution. To the extent that these arguments, and possible resort to Convention rights, rely on strong claims about gender identity, this might be thought to be incompatible with the social constructionist model of gender identity endorsed above. However, if 'essentialism' is to be pursued, it is an essentialism of a 'strategic' kind (Spivak, 1990, p. 51). Moreover, this may prove both an effective and a legitimate option in the context of transgender and other gender non-conforming defendants.

This strategy 'empowers previously subordinated groups by providing them a means to self-define, as opposed to being defined by those who would oppress them' (Karaian, 2009, p. 378). As Judith Butler has observed, it can be both theoretically and politically necessary 'to invoke [a] category, and hence, provisionally to institute an identity' (Butler, 1993, p. 222). In other words, social constructionism does not remove a political imperative to 'mobilise the necessary error of identity', though ethically it remains 'necessary to confirm [its] contingency' (Butler, 1993, p. 229) lest this strategy contribute to the exclusion of others, including those to come. Moreover, it is difficult in practice to escape essentialism at least in some form (Karaian, 2009, p. 378). As Diana Fuss explains, even within social constructionism, '[the] notion of "where I stand", of what has come to be called … "subject-positions"' (Fuss, 1990, p. 29), appear unavoidable. And as Butler notes, in thinking through the predicament of transgender people, a liveable life requires some degree of stability (Butler, 2004, p. 8). Thus, and while recognising that law is always a risk or wager, the assertion of a male or female identity by those marked 'opposite' gender at birth, or indeed the assertion of a genderqueer identity, may be necessary, especially given the fact that prosecution proceeds on the basis of a fundamental denial of the authenticity of these particular gender identities.

However, we must insist that the notion of 'authenticity' remains compatible with the assertion of different gender identities at different times. For gender identity can be fluid for some people. It can change over time. Thus, in asserting gender identity, emphasis should perhaps be placed on the genuineness or sincerity of present gender identity evidenced by gender practice or performance, as opposed to being grounded in claims proceeding from biology, psychological assessment or present anatomical or legal status. In the absence of some strong reason to disbelieve an assertion of gender identity, it is argued that self-declaration ought to prevail. Of course, some transgender people will have been diagnosed with gender dysphoria, be currently taking cross-sex hormones, have undertaken gender reassignment surgeries, and/or been granted a Gender Recognition Certificate,[15] and these facts may assist in persuading a court.

However, the key thing, in the present context, is to endorse the notion that transgender men are men because they assert and live it. They are best placed to

freedoms set forth in this Convention shall be secured without discrimination on any ground such as sex, race, colour, language, religion, political or other opinion, national or social origin, association with a national minority, property, birth or other status.

15 s. 4 Gender Recognition Act 2004.

articulate their own (dis)embodied, psychic and experiential truth. Such an argument not only creates a space for the recognition of gender variance within law, as well as insulating gender non-conforming people from inappropriate and unnecessary criminal law intervention into their sexual lives. It also serves to enable the queering of law from within. To the extent that contradictions arise, this presents less of a problem for queer than it does for liberal law because their respective self-images bear different relationships to economies of order, predictability, determinacy and consistency. To the extent that the idea of gender fluidity can be given a legal life, the 'logic' of heteronormativity and cisnormativity can be challenged.

Of course, we must recognise tensions that may lie between litigation strategy and broader cultural struggle. That is, the needs of individual defendants are not necessarily synonymous with those of wider constituencies to which they may belong. Beyond her obligation to the court, a lawyer must fight for her client, and, of course, the stakes can be high, as the gender identity fraud convictions demonstrate. However, to the maximum extent possible, criminal lawyers concerned with social justice should seek to advance arguments that not only assist their clients, but which anticipate future clients and the legal difficulties they are likely to face should the immediate case give rise to a legal precedent. That is, resistance to gender identity fraud prosecutions needs to be situated within the context of broader legal and sexual political struggle. The difficulty here can perhaps be expressed in terms of a question: how can legal arguments that are effective in defending the client be advanced, without at the same time undermining efforts to defend other gender non-conforming people in the future?

This instrumental question needs to be supplemented by recognition of law's discursive effects. Thus criminal law courts do not merely convict or acquit defendants. They also reproduce a series of (mis)understandings about gender, sexuality, desire and the body. Thus future defendants are not only disadvantaged by legal arguments that contribute to establishing an unhelpful legal precedent. Their position is also problematised through judicial discourse which renders their perspectives and embodied experiences unintelligible. In addressing this difficulty, it should be recognised that law produces unintended as well as intended consequences. Some of the former might, in the present context, be described as queer effects, ones that might be pushed to their (il)logical conclusions. This notion of queer reasoning being internal to law is one long-recognised in terms of transgender law reform (Sharpe, 2002, pp. 7–8).

Thus, while seeking to shore up the 'heterosexual matrix', law introduces gender trouble. After all, through criminal prosecution, law brings into the public domain and dramatises that which might otherwise remain hidden. That is, it puts centre stage the fact that gender identity, and desire directed toward it, are complex. While it seeks to avoid this reality, and consolidate heterosexuality, through taking seriously complainant claims of ignorance regarding defendants' gender histories, it cannot quite contain what prosecution has introduced into discourse, namely, the fact that our desires exceed our identities. While sexual intimacy with gender non-conforming people might be experienced as 'harmful', and while complainants and law might emphasise the enormity of this harm, thereby highlighting the fragility of heterosexuality, it would seem nonetheless that we are undone by otherness (Butler, 2004, p. 19). While punishment seeks to cleanse the bodies of complainants, as well as the social body, otherness and other-oriented desires simply cannot be exorcised. These instrumental and discursive effects, produced through encounters between law and gender non-conforming people, are important ones which the book will consider in the context of resistance. In particular, this challenge will be taken up in Chapter 7 where *R v McNally*,[16] the lead decision both in relation to gender identity fraud and sexual fraud more generally, will be re-written or queered.

### *(vi) Law's bodily aesthetics*

Another theme the book will consider is law's bodily aesthetics. This is clearly an important theme given the type of fraud to be explored. In relation to gender identity fraud, a series of issues arise concerning the communion of bodies. It might be thought that the only legal issue in these cases is whether or not the defendant is male or female. However, while law's location of defendants within a binary gender system obviously assumes significance, we should not assume that legal recognition of gender identity claims precludes conviction. This is because the claim that a defendant deceived another regarding gender identity, may take several forms. Thus the claim may be that the defendant claimed to be a particular kind of man. Thus, while he is a man, and perhaps legally recognised as such, he may not be the kind of man he represented himself to be or, at least, not the kind of man the complainant believed him to be. For example, it might be said that he presented himself as a cisgender man and/or that he used a prosthetic device during sex in circumstances where the complainant believed it to be a fleshy penis. In these and in other cases, it might be said that a gap exists between reality and complainant belief, in circumstances where complainant belief is constituted through fraud. While the book will highlight difficulties with such arguments, difficulties that implicate questions of epistemology, ontology and power, it is important to recognise that such arguments also reveal something about law's bodily aesthetics. Whatever the defendant's truth may be, it would appear, in gender identity fraud cases, that law's aesthetic concerns exceed this truth. That is, and as we will see, the body, both in terms of its physical properties and anatomical extensions,[17] as well as its gender performances, remains tied to legal resolution.

### *(vii) Act/omission*

This distinction, one long-subject to criticism within criminal law jurisprudence (Ashworth, 1989; Elliot and Ormerod, 2008; Herring, 2015, Chapter 2) and

16 *McNally* above note 1.

17 Reference here is being made to the use of a prosthetic penis in many of the cases.

more generally (Finnis, 1993; Heyman, 1994; Keown, 1997; Ridolfi, 2000), has assumed significance in cases of gender identity fraud because a particular variant of it has, through doctrinal development, now become the means through which criminal liability for sexual fraud is to be determined. Thus, in gender identity fraud prosecutions, and indeed sexual fraud prosecutions more generally, conviction requires proof of active deception as opposed to 'mere' non-disclosure of information.[18] In considering this distinction, the book will highlight two interrelated issues. First, and as will be argued in Chapter 4, the distinction lacks a principled basis. Second, and as will see in Chapter 5, it lacks analytical robustness.

The deployment of this jurisprudential dyad recognises the fact that there are more ways than one to not tell the truth. Indeed, there are at least three ways in which this might occur: lying, actively misleading, and non-disclosure of information (Wilkinson, 2000). More importantly, the Court of Appeal's reliance on it assumes the distinction to be an appropriate way to resolve cases in a moral and/or practical manner. Yet, the distinction fails to find justification either in principles of liberty or causality (Sharpe, 2016, pp. 32–33). Nor, as we will see in Chapter 4, is it easily demonstrated that active deception is more morally culpable, represents a greater violation of sexual autonomy, or is more harmful to complainants, than non-disclosure of information. Irrespective of such jurisprudential, experiential and empirical questions, the current legal doctrine that distinguishes active deception (criminal) from non-disclosure of information (non-criminal), also lacks robustness. Certainly, and as we will see in Chapter 5, in cases of gender identity fraud, the distinction is vulnerable to analytical collapse. That is to say, it has proved difficult for gender non-conforming people to avoid having their sexual encounters with others described in ways other than active deception. Accordingly, particular attention will be paid to this distinction and its capacity for injustice will be highlighted.

This distinction will also be shown to produce the queer legal effect that recognition of gender identity hinges on the presence/absence of an active defendant. That is, law would appear to recognise complainant consent to sex, and therefore defendant gender identity, in circumstances where the defendant is constructed as 'passive'. In other words, and in view of the fact that gender identity is clearly treated as a material fact by the courts in the cases prosecuted, a finding that complainant consent is valid presupposes the 'truth' of facts, including the fact of gender identity. Accordingly, in addition to determining the presence/absence of consent, some form of legal recognition, or at least acknowledgment, of gender identity outside the terms of the Gender Recognition Act appears to turn, somewhat queerly, on whether or not the defendant acted in the world.

Of course, it might be objected that a legal conclusion of valid consent cannot necessarily be squared with the 'truth' of facts represented. Thus while the courts treat lying about wealth or social status in order to effect intimacy as a trivial

18 This distinction has been developed, most notably, in *McNally* above note 1.

matter,[19] this does not change the fact that the representation is false. However, in the case of transgender defendants the matter is more complex because a finding of valid consent can hardly be said to follow from an interpretation of gender identity as trivial. Indeed, and as findings of active deception reveal, the contested status of the gender identities of transgender and other gender non-conforming people proves fundamental. Ultimately, legal desire for consistency in thinking about gender identity meets its limit, at least ostensibly,[20] in the distinction between act and omission. Accordingly, legal doctrine opens up spaces for resistance, for the queering of law.

### *(viii) Consent*

The final three themes to be considered are a triangulation of concepts central not only to criminal law generally, but to sexual offences law in particular: *consent, harm* and *deception*. First, let us turn to consent. There is an enormous literature on the subject of consent in relation to sexual offences (for example, see Wertheimer, 1996; Franke, 2001; Munro, 2005; Cowan, 2007). For our purposes, it is important to distinguish between cases where deception is accompanied by some degree of coercion[21] or where consent is subject to some explicit condition, such as use of a condom,[22] and the kind of cases which this book is interested in, namely, those where the deception in question is said to reside in the defendant's representations or performance or in non-disclosure regarding his/her gender identity. In relation to consent generally, it is often argued that consent, in order to be good, must be informed. This argument is premised on the value and right to sexual autonomy (Herring, 2005; Herring, 2007). However, and putting to one side debate as to what kinds of information one ought to have a right to know, in the context of gender identity fraud we encounter a particular difficulty, one that overlaps with the theme of ideology. In this particular context, what we witness is not so much a demand for a legally sanctioned right to know, but a right to define. Whatever view one might take regarding other desire-led intimate scenarios in which consent is challenged, this subtext of colonisation of transgender and other gender non-conforming people through the criminal justice system ought to operate as a game

19 The courts have long taken the view that certain kinds of facts are too trivial to vitiate consent for the purposes of sexual offences. This legal position was most recently articulated by the Court of Appeal in *McNally* above note 1 per Leveson LJ at para 25. It can be traced to at least the nineteenth century (see *R v Clarence* [1888] 22 QBD 23). In *Clarence*, Wills J expressed the view that under certain circumstances it would be 'childish to say that [the complainant] did not consent' (at 27).

20 The sexual fraud legal doctrine that only acts expose one to criminal prosecution is problematised here. The point will be developed in Chapter 5, where it will be argued that the distinction between active deception and non-disclosure of information unravels in gender identity fraud cases.

21 Coercion can vary by degree. For two cases that illustrate different gradations, see *R v Olugboja* [1982] QB 320; *R v Jheeta* [2007] EWCA Crim 1699.

22 *Assange v Swedish Prosecution Authority* [2011] EWHC 2849 (Admin).

changer. As Judith Butler insists, we must distinguish between 'norms and conventions that permit people to breathe, to desire, to love and to live, and those norms and conventions that restrict or eviscerate the conditions of live itself' (Butler, 2004, p. 8).

### *(ix) Harm*

Turning to harm, criminal prosecution need not depend on demonstrating any physical, psychological or emotional harm. This is because it is possible to disaggregate harms from wrongs, and place emphasis on the latter in justifying criminalisation.[23] Thus, sex without consent (and remember our focus is on sex arising in circumstances of deception, not coercion) can be, and typically is, understood in terms of an encroachment on the right to sexual autonomy. However, most criminal law commentators, in justifying criminalisation, point to harm. Even Jonathan Herring, one of the foremost proponents of an 'informed consent' model of consent (Herring, 2005, Herring, 2007),[24] emphasises harms arising in the context of sex occasioned by deception (Herring, 2007, p. 228). In addressing these issues, I do not seek to deny harm or to minimise the experiences of complainants. However, the concept of harm requires interrogation. Thus the book will consider how harms are actually experienced, based on complainant evidence, as well as how they are imagined by law. It will also consider the question, and perhaps necessity, of a harm threshold as well as insisting on the need to adopt an appropriate harm calculus, one that recognises the defendant's interests in thinking through the question of harm in scenarios of deception.

In thinking through the harm question in the present context, the book will also emphasis how 'harms' are reimagined pleasures. That is, harm, which might be something experienced months, or even years, after a sexual encounter, involves the reinterpretation of the past, and indeed the pleasurable past. This issue of retrospectivity, as well as the attendant disavowal of complainant agency and desire produces a number of difficulties, including for feminism, which will be explored. One important issue to be considered is how complainant distress, repulsion and disgust are effects of an already existing set of power relations, ones reproduced through prosecution. That is to say, and as will be made clear, emotional responses to 'discovery' of gender history are conditioned by systemic homophobia, transphobia[25] and cissexism. In this regard, we are back in the territory of ideology and need to think through and beyond it.

23 While liberal scholars generally insist on the demonstration of harm or the risk of harm as a necessary pre-condition to the criminalisation of conduct, it is clear wrongs can occur in the absence of harm, as Gardner's 'pure rape' example illustrates (Gardner, 2007, p. 5). Gardner refers to scenarios where the victim (and everyone else) remains oblivious to the fact that she was raped while unconscious.

24 See also Dougherty, 2013.

25 'Transphobia is an emotional disgust toward individuals who do not conform to society's gender expectations … The "phobia" suffix is used to imply an irrational fear

### *(x) Deception*

Turning to the book's final theme, deception, it is important to recognise what is at stake in this concept in the present context. Of course, a legal focus on the presence or absence of deception speaks to a criminal law requirement to establish mens rea. However, in relation to claims of gender identity fraud, the question of deception also implicates questions of epistemology, ontology and power. Accordingly, in examining this issue, we need to tread carefully. In the first place, to claim deception might mean a number of different things. It might mean that the defendant failed to disclose information or it might mean that he or she actively deceived the complainant. In relation to the former, deception assumes a right to know information, one that trumps a right to privacy. If such a right ought to exist, should it extend to all information or only information considered material? If materiality should function as a threshold, should it be determined subjectively by complainants or should it be an objective question for courts? Of course, even if we were to recognise a right to know, which as we will see the English courts have, so far, chosen not to do, non-disclosure would not be proof of deception. For an intention to deceive cannot be read off the fact of non-disclosure. Thus, in the context of transgender defendants, even if we assume the existence of a desire to conceal information about gender history, and even an awareness of the importance of this information to the other sexual party, we should not necessarily conclude deception. In such circumstances, non-disclosure may be motivated not by a desire to deceive (and, of course, it may not even have occurred to the defendant that gender history might be material either to the complainant or in general normative terms), but by a desire for self-preservation both in physical and psychic terms.

Moreover, irrespective of whether we think of deception in terms of action or omission, a more fundamental problem exists if no relevant gap exists between complainant belief concerning the defendant's gender identity and his/her actual gender identity. Thus, if the complainant believes the defendant to be a man and he is a transgender man then we ought to say no relevant disjunction arises. This points to a question concerning what counts as 'material', and what public policy issues arise in relation to its resolution. More importantly however, it serves to highlight how what counts as material is inseparable from relations of power and the epistemologies and ontologies they produce. Thus, the reader might want to insist that the distinction between cisgender and transgender is material, and certainly to the complainant. However, such a claim either denies the authenticity of gender identity claims or, which amounts to the same thing, invokes hierarchies of men and women, whereby transgender people are located at the bottom. This

or hatred, one that is at least partly perpetuated by cultural ideology' (Hill and Willoughby, 2005, p. 91). Serano describes it in terms of the targeting of 'those whose gender expression and appearance differ from the norm' (Serano, 2007, p. 184). This can be contrasted with cissexism, which 'targets those whose assigned and identified sexes differ' (Serano, 2007, p. 184).

is a move that runs counter to important public policy aims concerned with self-determination, the reduction of transphobia and the achievement of equality. Part of the problem here lies in law's consolidation of one identity and its simultaneous refusal of another, a refusal which renders the deception claim intelligible. In other words, deception claims, at least in relation to questions of gender identity, rely on and reproduce something this book aims to challenge, namely, law's insistence on the coherence of cis-gender and correspondingly the incoherence of trans-gender.

## 1.3 Chapter outlines

The book is divided into eight chapters: an introduction, six substantive chapters and a conclusion. Chapter 2 will set the scene through providing an overview of the developing law of sexual fraud. In addition to mapping common law and legislative developments in this area, the chapter will identify social forces that help explain the growing legal appetite for prosecuting fraud in the context of sexual relations. This will involve consideration of feminist politics and, in particular, the wisdom of resort to the criminal law as a means of addressing perceived social injustices,[26] as well as wider political and historical developments that perhaps influence and shape prosecutorial decision-making practice. In the UK context, one important factor is perhaps what might be described as 'the Savile moment' (Furedi, 2013).[27] Indeed, in the context of gender identity fraud, the commencement of a wave of prosecutions correlates with this particular watershed and trauma in the contemporary social fabric. The chapter will also introduce the gender identity fraud cases which will be explored in subsequent chapters.

In chapters 3 and 4, the book will challenge prosecution of gender identity fraud through offering a series of principled objections. Chapter 3 will make four principled objections. First, it will be argued that prosecution for deception constitutes significant criminal law overreach. This is especially the case in circumstances of desire-led intimacy which lacks the feature of coercion. In developing this argument, the chapter will also consider the issue of 'fair labelling' as the sexual offences category may not be the most appropriate in which to locate gender identity fraud cases. Second, the framing of sexual autonomy as a non-negotiable right to know will be challenged. Not only does such an approach rob complainants of sexual agency. It also relies on an a priori claim as to the materiality of facts, in relation to which deception is said to have been perpetrated. In the context of gender identity fraud however, the 'facts', which may or may not be material, are typically disputed, and so sexual autonomy arguments are implicated

26 As Herbert Packer recognised long ago, '[t]he criminal sanction is at once prime guarantor and prime threatener of human freedom' (Packer, 1968, p. 366).

27 In an ITV documentary, *Exposure: The Other Side of Jimmy Savile*, broadcast on 3 October 2012, several women recounted sexual abuse by the British media personality. After the broadcast, many more women came forward to report abuse by Savile. This led the London Metropolitan Police to set up *Operation Yewtree*, to investigate claims of sexual abuse against Savile and other celebrities.

in questions of ontology, epistemology and power. In other words, assertions of autonomy are premised on constructions of 'truth' which bear no relation to defendant self-understandings of gender identity. Third, it will be argued that legal determinations as to the materiality of facts, and therefore the boundaries of non-consent within sexual offences law, produce legal inconsistency and are potentially discriminatory under Article 14 and under sections 7, 13 and 149 of the Equality Act 2010.[28] In particular, it will be highlighted how gender identity, at least in the UK context, is the only group identity to have attracted the attention of the state. That is, prosecutions have been confined to gender identity, as opposed, for example, to identities of race, sexuality or disability. Moreover, within the category of gender identity, it is only the gender identities of gender non-conforming people, rather than people at large, with which law appears to be concerned. In exploring these issues, the chapter will consider a number of possible justifications for state discrimination.

Finally, it will be argued that decisions to prosecute fail to consider, or weigh properly, other important rights and interests. In particular, and although other rights arise in contexts of sexual intimacy, the chapter will focus on the Article 8 right to privacy. In doing so, it will make a series of arguments. First, in considering the clash between the right to sexual autonomy and the right to privacy, it will be argued that privacy ought to prevail, at least in some circumstances, and that harm ought to operate as a key factor in any balancing act. Second, it will be argued that serious sex offence charges are, at least in the present context, unnecessary and disproportionate to the public interest aim of punishing sex offenders. Third, it will be argued that Article 8 is undermined by legal uncertainty surrounding the scope of illegality. This problem will be seen to be evident both at the level of legal doctrine and through reference to Crown Prosecution Service prosecutorial guidelines concerning transgender suspects. The chapter will then move beyond privacy analysis and consider how prosecution might be said to infringe upon a right to 'corporeal integrity' (Thomas, 1992), a suggested right that might be advanced through argument under Article 3.

Chapter 4 will consider four further principled objections to the prosecution of gender identity fraud. First, and following on from the previous chapter, it will be argued that calculations of harm fail to consider properly the position of transgender and other gender non-conforming defendants. This part of the chapter will think about appropriate limits to the harm concept which will, in the context of gender identity fraud, include consideration of its (ideological) source. It will also detail significant costs for transgender people associated with disclosing gender

28 Section 7 creates a protected head of 'gender reassignment', section 13 enables direct discrimination claims, and section 149 creates a public sector equality duty. While the protected category is limited to individuals undergoing surgery, or at least intending to do so, and while this provides a source of criticism, it nevertheless offers itself as a form of redress, at least in some instances. In relation to the public sector equality duty, it will be argued in Chapter 3 that Crown Prosecution Service legal guidance pertaining to prosecution of transgender suspects falls foul of this statutory obligation.

history. Second, it will be argued that deception is not a neutral category, but one which is ontologically and epistemologically constituted. In responding to this dilemma, it will be argued that (i) there is no deception regarding gender identity because the gender identity claims transgender people make are authentic, (ii) if there is deception, it relates to facts associated with gender history, not gender identity, and facts relating to gender history should not be considered legally material and (iii) even in cases where a gap arises between gender presentation and actual gender identity it does not necessarily mean that a gap existed at the time of legal liability. It will also highlight how, even in cases of deliberate deception, deception may not be motivated by a desire to deceive. Third, it will be argued that prosecution undermines important public policy interests concerning the realisation of equality and the amelioration of transphobia and cissexism. Finally, it will be argued that legal doctrine developed for the purposes of establishing criminal liability for sexual fraud, namely a distinction between active deception and non-disclosure of information, lacks a principled basis.

In Chapter 5, the focus will shift from legal principle to legal and social reality, from the merits of legal doctrine to the (im)possibility of its just application in the context of transgender and other gender non-conforming defendants. This chapter will be divided into three parts. First, it will consider the decision to prosecute. In addressing this question, the chapter will problematise what is implicit in the bringing of prosecutions, namely, the notion that complainants did not consent to sexual intimacy. This is not to claim that complainants lied about lacking knowledge of the defendants' gender histories. This may or may not be so, albeit believing at least some of the complainants rather fantastical accounts appears to have required, and to a quite extraordinary degree, 'a suspension of disbelief' (Coleridge, 1907, Chapter XIV, p. 6)[29] on the part of prosecutors, judges and juries. Rather, and while lack of knowledge does not, of itself, necessarily establish non-consent and/or deception as a matter of law (for some facts are not considered legally material), it is the idea that ignorance might more properly be considered a form of knowledge that will be explored.

In this respect, the book draws on the work of Eve Sedgwick (1988, 1993) and, in particular, her idea of the 'privilege of unknowing', whereby privileged onlookers, in a hetero and cisnormative society, learn not to know, or otherwise sense, difference. In thinking about complainant ignorance it is not intended to pathologise complainants, but to recognise how ignorance or unknowing, which is both a source of knowledge and its refusal, as well as a form of power, is a collective

29 The poet and aesthetic philosopher, Samuel Taylor Coleridge coined the phrase to suggest that if a writer could inject a 'human interest and a semblance of truth' (Coleridge, 1907, Chapter XIV, p. 6) into a fantastic tale, the reader would suspend judgment concerning the implausibility of the story. The 'semblance of truth' in the gender identity fraud cases lies in complainant claims of ignorance regarding the gender history of defendants. After all, no matter how otherwise implausible an account might be, young heterosexual cisgender women do not willingly choose to become sexually intimate with transgender or other gender non-conforming people.

phenomenon. Accordingly, a consideration of ignorance regarding issues of gender and sexuality, of desire and the body, raises issues that reach beyond the particular complainants in the gender identity fraud cases to have come before the courts. It points to collective and learned unknowings which operate to constitute power relations between those who have learned not to know and those whose lives are the object of these learned ignorances. Moreover, these ignorances, when challenged, including through encounters with transgender and/or genderqueer bodies, may produce repudiation, disavowal or wilful blindness in order to maintain the love object in tact and so as not to compromise sexual identity. These issues raise important questions for how we conceive of female agency and, relatedly, the concept of non-consent. The chapter will also problematise the bringing of prosecutions on the basis that they fail to meet evidential and public interest thresholds set by prosecuting authorities.

Second, the chapter will consider why defendants have generally pleaded guilty? It is curious that a guilty plea is such a routine feature of such cases, given fact implausibility. It will be argued that this somewhat odd pattern of pleading might be understood, at least in part, in the context of three interrelated factors: poor legal representation, criminal justice and media attrition, and the fundamental problem, faced by outsiders, of having one's truth resonate in courts of law. As the American sociologist, Howard Becker, noted long ago, we are always faced with the problem of a 'hierarchy of credibility' (Becker, 1967). It will be argued that the failure of justice in these cases resides in the fact that cisnormativity and heteronormativity exhaust the interpretative frames available and through which cases are processed and resolved. Thus, in a variety of ways, transgender and other gender non-conforming people are substantially disadvantaged in structural and cultural terms. These disadvantages make prosecution and conviction more likely.

Third, once important difficulties associated with the pre-trial process have been addressed, attention will turn to substantive legal doctrine as it has been applied to gender non-conforming people. In doing so, the chapter will focus on current English law which has established a particular act/omission distinction, namely a distinction between non-disclosure of information and active deception, as the jurisprudential means through which liability for sexual fraud is now to be determined.[30] In considering this distinction, it will be highlighted how, in the context of transgender and other gender non-conforming people, it is insufficiently clear-cut to avoid analytical collapse and therefore criminal law overreach? That is, gender non-conforming people are likely to find it very difficult to locate themselves on the omission, and therefore legal side, of the distinction. Consideration of this issue will entail a particular focus on the Court of Appeal's decision in *R v McNally*, a case where the distinction has received its clearest expression and enjoys its highest authority.

In Chapter 6, the book will move from considering questions of criminalisation and encounters between transgender and other gender non-conforming people

30 *McNally* above note 1.

and sexual offences law, in order to consider some important ethical questions concerning 'lying' and non-disclosure of information prior to sexual intimacy. While many liberal commentators appear sceptical regarding expansion of the fraud category within sexual offences law, a position that would appear to hold in relation to gender identity fraud (see, for example, Simester et al, 2010, p. 755; Ormerod, 2011, p. 734), it seems that this same scepticism often evaporates in the face of the ethical characterisation of the role transgender people play in sexually intimate scenarios. In other words, while many scholars view criminal prosecution as a step too far, a draconian affair, it would appear that the view that cisgender people have a right to know gender history, and that transgender people ought to disclose their gender backgrounds prior to intimacy, proves more resilient.

This claim is informed not only by what is implicit in criminal prosecution and by wider community sentiment (Moore, 2016), but by conversations I have had with numerous legal and non-legal academics over the last few years while researching these issues. What this outlook amounts to, and of course reproduces, is the view that transgender people who do not confess a 'truth' that is not their own are deceptive. In other words, while there is resistance to criminal prosecution for gender identity fraud and, to this extent, implicit, if not explicit, support for many of this book's objections to prosecution, ones to be detailed in chapters 3, 4 and 5, what remains is the central problematic one, which continues to exclude and dehumanise transgender people, namely, the widespread attitude that couples transgender people with notions of duplicity, subterfuge and dissimulation.

In many respects, challenging this view is as, if not more, important as challenging criminal prosecution, albeit under current English law, non-disclosure of information is, at least ostensibly, insufficient to ground prosecution. This is because it is the widespread view that transgender people are synonymous with deception that is most antithetical to the liveability of transgender lives. Accordingly, this chapter will challenge the characterisation of transgender people as unethical. In doing so, it will first adopt an external critique that will situate ethical thinking within the context of issues of epistemology, ontology and power. This approach will highlight how the centre-staging of an obligation to disclose gender history is both hubristic and demonstrative of a failure to approach moments of cis–trans sexual intimacy in an ethical manner. Second, the chapter will offer an internal critique, specifically an engagement with arguments derived from normative ethics. This part of the chapter will assume the authenticity of gender identity claims, but consider the argument that non-disclosure of other gendered facts might constitute unethical omission. It will argue however, that in normative ethical terms, this argument is unlikely to win the day. In developing my argument, a utilitarian focus on harm minimisation, and the determination of an appropriate harm calculus, will be preferred to Kantian imperatives (Carson, 2010, pp. 67–88). Finally, the chapter will look to the future and consider what it might mean to be 'ethically gendered' (Serano, 2013, p. 259), and the implications of being so for the way we think and feel about sexual encounters in a world characterised by gender variance.

Chapter 7 will revisit the Court of Appeal's decision in *R v McNally*. In opposition to the judgment of Leveson LJ, the chapter will present an alternative judgment that might have been written had judicial thinking been informed by queer principles. In doing so, the chapter will draw significantly on original and important feminist work done around legal judgment-writing (Hunter et al, 2010; Hunter, 2012; Rackley, 2012). As a prelude to providing a counter-judgment, the chapter will first attend to two preliminary matters. First, it will explain why the writing of a queer legal judgment by an academic has value. Second, it will detail some queer principles around which the judgment will be organised, while at the same time highlighting tensions between queer theory and engagement with law and judgment. It will be argued that like its feminist counterpart, queer judgment-writing has value because it 'engage[s] in a form of parodic – and hence subversive – performance' operating to 'powerfully denaturalise existing judicial and doctrinal norms, exposing them as contingent, and as themselves (the product of) performances' (Hunter et al, 2010, p. 8).

In other words, it will highlight how law is involved in 'a distinctive manner of imagining the real' (Geertz, 1983, p. 173) and, through counter-judgment, will attempt to enlarge law's (re)imaginative capacity. In doing so, the chapter will demonstrate how different legal conclusions might have been arrived at by the Court of Appeal. In order for the fictional counter-judgment to sit comfortably with the original judgment, that is, for it to be legally credible, it will be made subject to the constraints of judicial writing: legal precedent, custom and practice. In other words, it will not only be an act of ethical imagination, one that aims to centre-stage the experiences and perspectives of gender non-conforming people. It will also be a judgment that might actually have been written while remaining faithful to existing legal principles.

In relation to queer principles, the chapter and counter-judgment will seek to challenge dominant and binary understandings of the categories of sex, gender and sexuality, deconstruct ideas of normalcy and deviance, defend desire (Valdes, 1995, pp. 368–370), and place at the centre of analysis and critique, those located at the sexual and gender margins. The chapter will acknowledge tensions existing between queer theory and law. However, it will emphasise that while repudiating dominant norms is important, queer theory and activism should not succumb to antinormativity, which would commit us to a 'renunciation of prescriptive projects' (Zanghellini, 2009, p. 1). Moreover, while queer, influenced by poststructural thought as it is, conceives of the concepts of power, epistemology and ontology and their interrelationship, differently from liberalism, the chapter will emphasise how broader values of tolerance, pluralism and respect for agency (a queer and feminist version of liberal autonomy) belie some common and worthwhile ground. Finally, the chapter offers itself as a resource both for scholars working within the gender and sexuality and/or criminal law fields, especially those who pursue law reform, as well for judges who have to consider cases involving complex questions of identity pertaining to sex, gender and sexuality.

In the concluding chapter, the central arguments of the book will be summarised and the role of law emphasised, not only in perpetuating transphobia, homophobia and cissexism at sites of desire, but also in consolidating binary gender identity or either/or categories in a manner that fails to recognise the multiplicity of gender identities, and which precludes, or at least renders more difficult, gender identities to come.

Chapter 2

# Setting the scene

## 2.1 Introduction

In recent years, the UK has witnessed legal expansion of the categories of sexual fraud. This development might be seen as progressive, taking seriously the value of, and right to, sexual autonomy. However, the matter is more complicated. The legal reality has been, and continues to be, that men who lie to women about their social status, wealth or affections, or indeed, their past criminal record, including a criminal record for sexual offences, do not commit sexual fraud. This is because in all these circumstances, and many others, 'apparent' consent is considered to be legally valid. Conversely, many of the cases where sexual fraud is established involve young gender non-conforming defendants. As with the previous examples, the distinction between valid and invalid consent turns here on, among other things, normative assessments of the significance or triviality of the deception. It is precisely in this interpretative space, one that has never favoured gender and sexual outsiders,[1] that possibilities for injustice arise. Moreover, at least at this particular legal site, emphasis on sexual autonomy brings feminism into conflict with trans/queer interests and concerns. This is a theme that will be developed in subsequent chapters, where a series of objections to gender identity-based prosecution will be offered.

As a prelude to challenging gender identity fraud prosecutions, this chapter will provide a legal and social context to the expansion of the sexual fraud category generally and its specific application to gender and sexual minorities. This will require detailing legislative and common law developments. In the UK context, we will see that the Sexual Offences Act 2003, and the aims which motivated it

1 This problem with interpretation is evident in the English case of *R v Brown* [1994] 1 AC 212 where S/M sexual acts were translated into violence by the House of Lords (see Moran, 1995; Stychin, 1995a). It is also apparent in the constitution of the so-called defence to murder of 'homosexual advance' or 'homosexual panic', which has been used in the context of killings of gay men. Despite the fact that such a defence serves to mask a more plausible account, namely that the defendant robbed the victim, and that a bodily caress should never, in any event, justify lethal force, courts have readily accepted the 'excusatory' narratives put forward by defendants. For a critique of the defence see, for example, Comstock, 1992; Tomsen, 1998; Statham, 1999; Steinberg, 2005.

(Home Office, 2000), represent something of a watershed moment in the expansion of the category of sexual fraud. Thus, we will see that criminalisation on the basis of sexual fraud, though having a lengthy common law history, has until recently been a limited affair.

After charting this history, the chapter will detail what might be described as a 'prosecutorial turn'. In detailing this 'turn' it will first consider more general cases through which the domain of sexual fraud has been enlarged under English law, before proceeding to consider those cases that fall specifically within the ambit of gender identity fraud. In introducing these cases, the chapter will highlight important ways in which they can be distinguished from other cases that have served to extend the sexual fraud category. In this respect, it will be contended that appellate courts, while choosing not to do so, could have concluded that these cases lie outside established legal doctrine. Finally, the chapter will offer some tentative remarks concerning why sexual fraud prosecutions have increased significantly in the present and why this expansion of the law has extended to gender identity. In other words, and while more detailed empirical research is necessary here, it will seek to address what might be described in Foucauldian terms as the contemporary 'problematisation' (Foucault, 1998) of sexual fraud generally, and gender identity fraud specifically, through sexual offences law. In doing so, it will draw attention both to feminist activism and engagement with the state, and to a key cultural rupture in the British social fabric, one which might be described as the 'Savile moment' (Furedi, 2013).[2]

## 2.2 A brief history of sexual fraud

This section offers a brief history of the categories of sexual fraud. An historical account is necessary because it will assist the reader in understanding, and in disentangling, these categories. More importantly, it will serve to highlight their highly circumscribed nature before enactment of the Sexual Offences Act 2003 and judicial willingness to interpret the common law in a liberal manner. During the nineteenth century and prior to the case of *R v Clarence*,[3] there was legal uncertainty regarding the scope of sexual fraud (Laird, 2014, p 495).[4] However,

2 Jimmy Savile was a famous British media personality who sexually abused numerous women over several decades. In 2012, the London Metropolitan Police set up *Operation Yewtree* to investigate claims of abuse against Savile and other celebrities. Post-Savile there has been an increase in reportage of sexual offences and the Savile moment appears to have changed the climate in which prosecutorial decision-making takes place. This may be a factor relevant in the prosecution of young gender non-conforming people for gender identity fraud. Certainly, the recent wave of prosecutions considered in this book commences with Savile.

3 *R v Clarence* [1888] 22 QBD 23.

4 *R v Bennett* (1866) 4 F & F 1105; *R v Barrow* (1868) LR 1 CCR 156; *R v Dee* (1884) 14 LR Ir. 468.

with *Clarence*, the view, at least in relation to rape,[5] that fraud was restricted to two types of situation became settled. These two categories came to be known as *fraud in the factum* and *fraud in the inducement*. As the court made clear, only deception 'as to the nature of the [sexual] act itself, or as to the identity of the person who does the act' could negate consent because 'the act consented to is not the act done'.[6] Moreover, fraud as to identity referred to a quite specific identity. It was confined to inducing a married woman to have sexual intercourse though impersonating her husband.[7] That is, it was not rape to induce an unmarried woman. The reasoning of the court, in so delineating this particular offence, encompassed various factors touching upon the implications of a more expansive treatment of sexual fraud. However, chief among them was a concern that seduction or false promise might lead to a rape conviction.

While few cases exist in the twentieth century under these two common law categories, ones which criminal law teachers trot out to illustrate the point of legal application, what is most apparent about them is their somewhat implausible facts, especially when read through modern eyes and changing social mores. Thus sexual fraud categories appeared, in practical terms, to be confined to naive young women who believed missionary position sex would improve their singing technique[8] or that it was a medical procedure (*fraud in the factum*),[9] or to women who mistakenly believed the defendant to be their husband (*fraud in the inducement*).[10] While the more contemporary case of *R v Elbekkay*[11] demonstrates some persistence of naivety in the context of *fraud in the inducement*, what is clear is that until relatively recently, categories of sexual fraud were heavily confined and the kind of fact scenarios that occupy our criminal courts were unlikely to fall within their ambit. Indeed, we might say that, prior to the enactment of the Sexual Offences Act 2003, finding a suitable case to prosecute was something akin to a camel passing through the eye of a needle.[12]

Until the 2003 legislation, these categories exhausted the possibility of prosecuting sexual offences on the basis of fraud. Beyond these categories fraud was considered consistent with consent, a matter going only to surrounding circumstances or to an attribute of the defendant.[13] Thus, for example, in *R v Linekar*,[14] the court held that a sex worker, who had agreed to have sex with the defendant

5 It remained an offence to 'procure women and girls by fraud' (s. 3(2) Criminal Law Amendment Act 1885).

6 *Clarence* above note 3 at 44. While *Clarence* clarified the legal position pertaining to rape, the charges in the case were brought under ss. 47 and 20 of the Offences Against the Person Act 1861.

7 This was put on a statutory footing by s. 1(2) of the Sexual Offences Act 1956.

8 *R v Williams* [1923] 1 KB 340.

9 *R v Case* (1850) 4 Cox CC 220; *R v Flattery* [1877] 2 QBD 410.

10 *Advocate v Montgomery*, (Scot.) [1926] Justiciary Cas. 2.

11 *R v Elbekkay* [1995] Crim LR 163 (CA).

12 Matthew 19:24 *New Testament*.

13 *R v Richardson* [1998] 2 Cr App 200.

14 *R v Linekar* [1995] QB 250.

on the basis of an agreement to be paid a stated sum, had given legal consent. Her 'apparent' consent was viewed as valid consent because the fraud perpetrated did not go to the sexual act itself, but to a circumstance, namely, payment. However, through enactment of the Sexual Offences Act 2003, and subsequent interpretation of its consent provisions, there has been a significant expansion of the category of sexual fraud, one which, for our purposes, has had significant implications for sexually active gender non-conforming people.

## 2.3 The modern law of sexual fraud

The Sexual Offences Act 2003, informed by feminist advocacy and the *Setting the Boundaries Report* (Home Office, 2000, para 2.10.2), significantly revised the law of sexual offences in England and Wales. To the extent that these changes bear down on issues pertaining to sexual fraud, and gender identity fraud specifically, they are limited, at least in the main,[15] to the new consent provisions to be found in sections 74 and 76 of the Act.[16] The expansion, through s. 76, of situations in which consent will be considered absent and the willingness of the judiciary to adopt a liberal interpretation of s. 74, can be viewed as consistent with the aim of achieving some degree of substantive equality for women. While this is, in some obvious respects, welcome, expansion of the concept of non-consent has, as we shall see, had the opposite effect for gender non-conforming defendants.

By virtue of s. 76, the common law categories of *fraud in the factum* and *fraud in the inducement* have been placed on a statutory footing. They have also been expanded, though in limited ways. Thus *fraud in the factum* has been extended from covering fraud as to the 'nature' of the act, so as to also encompass fraud regarding the 'purpose' of the act.[17] In relation to *fraud in the inducement*, the category was, as already noted, confined to inducing a married woman to have sexual intercourse though impersonating her husband. By virtue of s. 76(2)(b), this fraud category now extends beyond the parameters of gender and marital status to include any person who induced the complainant into believing that s/he was a person known personally to the complainant.[18] It might be thought that s. 76(2)(b) is especially relevant in the context of gender identity fraud. However, none of the defendants in the cases so far prosecuted, if they 'impersonated' anybody, impersonated someone known personally to the complainant.

15 The shift from 'honest' to 'reasonable' belief as the new mens rea requirement for adult sexual offences also has relevance. While this change is generally to be welcomed, in the context of gender identity fraud cases, a standard of 'reasonableness' is likely to prove difficult to meet. This is because, in normative terms, cisgender people are viewed as unlikely to be willing to have sex with a transgender or other gender non-conforming person if aware of their gender history.

16 The evidential presumptions to be found in s. 75 of the Sexual Offences Act 2003 are irrelevant to the facts of the cases to be considered.

17 s. 76(2)(a) Sexual Offences Act 2003.

18 s. 76(2)(b) Sexual Offences Act 2003.

Of the two provisions, it is s. 76(2)(a) that is more likely to be relied on by prosecutors and have purchase with the judiciary. Certainly, this provision has received attention from the courts and from criminal law commentators, both generally and specifically in relation to gender identity fraud cases. Thus some commentators have suggested that s. 76(2)(a) should (Herring, 2005, pp. 522–523) or could (Williams, 2008, p 149; Laird, 2014, p 509) accommodate the facts of gender identity fraud cases. Jonathan Herring argues that a transgender person's failure to disclose gender history, in circumstances where the other sexual party's awareness of gender history would preclude intimacy, ought to fall within the provision (Herring, 2005, pp. 522–523), though it is unclear whether he so concludes because he considers deception to go to the 'nature' of the sex act (which is fundamentally different where a transgender body is involved) or because he favours a liberal interpretation of the word 'purpose' (the defendant's transgender status converts sex into a non-heterosexual kind). More cautiously, Laird argues that if a transgender man 'presented himself as chromosomally male and [the complainant] believes she is engaging in intercourse with someone who is chromosomally male, then it is not contrary to the legislative language to conceptualise this as a case involving deception as to the nature of the act' (Laird, 2014, p 509). These arguments will be considered and rejected in later chapters.

For present purposes, what needs to be emphasised is that courts have displayed a general reluctance to rely on s. 76(2)(a) in finding consent absent in sexual fraud cases. For example, in *Assange v Swedish Prosecution Authority* the High Court accepted that it could be said that 'sexual intercourse without a condom is different to sexual intercourse with a condom, given the presence of a physical barrier, a perceived difference in the degree of intimacy, the risks of disease and the prevention of pregnancy' and therefore that there had been a deception as to 'the nature or quality of the act'.[19] However, the court preferred to approach the issue through s. 74, taking the view that s. 76 should be given a stringent construction, because it provides for a 'conclusive presumption'.[20] Indeed, and as noted by Laird, it would appear that the applicability of s. 76 has been narrowed 'to near vanishing point' (Laird, 2014, p 500).[21]

Before proceeding to consider the legal expansion of sexual fraud through s. 74, it is worth noting how, in a number of important senses, the case put against transgender and other gender non-conforming defendants is essentially the same whatever provision is relied on. That is, while the route through which non-consent is legally determined matters in terms of how cases are defended, and in terms of prospects for acquittal,[22] the core substantive issues remain the same. After all, a

19 *Assange v Swedish Prosecution Authority* [2011] EWHC 2849 (Admin) at para 87.
20 *Ibid.*
21 The case of *R v Devonald* [2008] EWCA Crim 527 is an exception to this general tendency of the courts.
22 Where the presumptions in s. 76(2) (a) and (b) of the Sexual Offences Act 2003 apply, consent and reasonable belief are presumed to be absent. Crucially, these presumptions are conclusive or irrebuttable. This makes defending cases considerably more difficult

finding that consent is lacking under the general consent provision amounts to a conclusion either that the defendant has perpetrated *fraud in the factum* or something akin to *fraud in the inducement.* More pertinently, behind this act/identity distinction lies the fact that in reality complainants, prosecutors and judges are all ultimately concerned with the defendant's gender identity. While successful prosecution necessarily requires legal articulation in terms of wrongful sex acts, such claims can usually only be sustained by an *a priori* claim that the defendant was not the man or woman s/he claimed to be. In other words, however the courts approach the question of consent, in the context of gender non-conforming defendants, we are always in the territory of identity. In this sense, we cannot escape questions of ontology, epistemology and power.

## 2.4 The general consent provision

Turning to the general consent provision through which sexual fraud has been expanded, and specifically in relation to gender identity, s. 74 requires: 'agreement by choice where a person has the freedom and capacity to make that choice'.[23] There has been academic disagreement regarding the proper relationship of this more general provision and the older law governing sexual fraud. For some scholars, the old law, now to be found in updated form in s. 76 of the Sexual Offences Act 2003, exhausts the category of sexual fraud (see, for example, Miles, 2008; Rogers, 2013). On this account, the general provision concerning consent has no application to fraud. However, most criminal law commentators have not viewed s. 74 as being restricted in this way. Moreover, this latter view appears to have prevailed as the courts have expanded the category of sexual fraud precisely through s. 74. Accordingly, while this chapter, and the book generally, will refer to s. 76 and its potential application, the focus will lie with the general consent provision. Before turning to consider gender identity fraud cases that have been prosecuted in English and Scottish courts, we will first consider the more general expansion of sexual fraud under s. 74 which precedes these cases. This is not only important in terms of establishing a line of precedent, but also because many of these cases can be distinguished from gender identity fraud cases and in ways that call prosecution of the latter into question. This way of dividing up cases is also, broadly speaking, chronological.

The trend toward expanding the concept of non-consent for the purposes of sexual fraud can in England and Wales be dated to the case of *R v EB*[24] and has, so far, culminated in the Court of Appeal's decision in *R v McNally.*[25] However, in considering this series of cases, we need to distinguish them from *McNally* and

and is a key reason why courts have interpreted s. 76 restrictively, preferring to expand the category of sexual fraud through the general consent provision in s. 74.

23 s. 74 Sexual Offences Act 2003.

24 *R v EB* [2006] EWCA Crim 2945 (CA).

25 *R v McNally* [2013] EWCA Crim 1051.

other cases involving young gender non-conforming people. This is because the latter cases stand apart conceptually for at least three reasons: (i) they lack the element of coercion, (ii) they lack an explicit condition insisted on by the complainant, and (iii) identity in a non-trivial sense lies at their core. In view of these important differences, legal constructions of non-consent, in cases involving gender non-conforming defendants, might be understood as instances of the way in which 'law disciplines bodies differentially as between different genders and different sexual orientations' (Duncan, 1995, p 326). Let us begin with coercion. In *R v Jheeta*[26] and *R v Bingham*[27] the facts cannot be viewed as purely deceptive. On the contrary, these two cases each contain, and in a significant way, the element of coercion. In *Jheeta*, consent was found to be lacking because sexual intercourse followed the complainant's receipt of texts from the defendant, purporting to come from the police, and which advised her to continue sexual relations lest a fine be incurred due to stress caused to the defendant. Thus, in addition to deception, the bogus police texts, there was also coercion, the threat of sanction. In *Bingham*, the defendant, having created false identities on a social media website, blackmailed a female victim into engaging in sexual activity through the threatened use of sexually explicit photographs shared between the parties. Again, coercion vies with deception in terms of accurate characterisation of the facts.

Second, other sexual fraud cases where consent was considered vitiated under s. 74 involved situations where a clear condition articulated by the complainant in advance of sexual intercourse was ignored by the defendant. Thus, in the *Assange* case,[28] consent was found to be absent in circumstances where the defendant had sexual intercourse without a condom, or continued sexual intercourse after removing, damaging or tearing a condom, after it had been made clear to him that consent was conditional on condom use. Similarly, in *R (on the application of F) v DPP*,[29] a case which involved judicial review of a Crown Prosecution Service (CPS) decision not to prosecute, a wife had sexual intercourse with her husband on the understanding that he would not ejaculate inside her vagina. Her consent was found to be vitiated when, in flagrant disregard of her wishes, he ignored this condition.

Third, apart from the cases to be considered involving gender non-conforming defendants, the few other cases which raise an issue of gender identity only do so in a trivial sense. Thus, for example, in *R v Devonald*,[30] a father pretended to be a 20-year-old woman on the internet in order to seduce a young man to masturbate in front of a webcam as revenge for what he believed to have been the man's mistreatment of his daughter. While conviction in this case relied on s. 76, and in

26 *R v Jhetta* [2007] EWCA Crim 1699.
27 *R v Bingham* [2013] EWCA Crim 823.
28 *Assange* above note 19.
29 *R (on the application of F) v DPP* [2013] EWHC 945 (Admin).
30 *Devonald* above note 21.

this sense the case appears to be something of an anomaly in terms of the developing jurisprudence of the courts, the nature of the claim about gender identity is clearly trivial and obviously false. This can be juxtaposed to the non-trivial and much more complicated gender identity claims made by transgender and other gender non-conforming defendants.

Distinguishing gender identity fraud cases from other sexual fraud cases successfully prosecuted is important for a number of reasons. First, it is clear that important differences exist between cases, ones which bear down on criminalisation debates. That is, if cases like *Bingham* and *Assange*[31] are rightly prosecuted, it does not follow that this is so in relation to cases like *McNally*. To reiterate, cases like *McNally* lack the element of coercion and explicit conditions established by the complainant. Moreover, any suggestion that a condition was or ought to be implied would raise difficulties for the prosecution because to give legal effect to an implied condition would be tantamount to criminalising mere non-disclosure of personal information.[32] As we will see below, this possibility has been precluded, at least ostensibly, by the developing jurisprudence of the courts. Accordingly, prosecution here ought to be viewed as more problematic. And this is especially so when we add to these factors the fact that identity claims are not false, or at least not necessarily so, or at least not so at the relevant temporal moment, that is, the moment of legal liability. These observations might be utilised both in debates over the proper reach of the criminal law, an issue to be explored in Chapter 3, and as a basis for the judiciary to distinguish sexual fraud cases involving gender non-conforming people from sexual fraud cases more generally. Indeed, this point will be made in Chapter 7, where it will form part of an academic counter-judgment to *McNally*, albeit its conclusions will not rely on distinguishing cases.

Having sought to outline some important differences between sexual fraud cases involving gender non-conforming people and other sexual fraud cases, we now turn to identify some important features of legal doctrine pertaining to consent as it has developed under s. 74. At common law, the idea that sexual fraud vitiated consent in some general sense never found favour with the bench. Rather, consent was only considered invalid where the complainant was deceived

31 The prosecution of Julian Assange has proved contentious because of the surrounding political context concerning WikiLeaks. However, objections of legal principle have also been raised concerning the High Court's finding, during extradition proceedings, that complainants did not consent, as a matter of law, on the basis of their versions of the facts. Thus Andrew Simester et al have expressed scepticism regarding this judicial finding. They argue that if Assange's conduct vitiated consent under s. 74, then it must also follow logically, though perhaps counter-intuitively, that 'a man's consent would be vitiated if he made it clear that he would not have sexual intercourse with a woman unless she was practising contraception, and the woman, wishing to get pregnant, told him that she was when she was not' (Simester et al, 2013, p. 475).

32 It would also potentially conflict with legal obligations under European and international law. Thus, criminalisation of non-disclosure of information may conflict with privacy rights protected under Article 8 of the European Convention on Human Rights and Article 17 of the International Covenant on Civil and Political Rights.

concerning facts considered legally material. Other facts, sometimes considered trivial, did not serve to vitiate consent. This appeared to accord with 'commonsense', a judicial outlook that continues to prevail in the legal present. Thus the view of Wills J. in *R v Clarence* that under certain circumstances it would be 'childish to say that [the complainant] did not consent',[33] has received expression by contemporary judges. Thus, in *R (on the application of F) v DPP*,[34] Judge CJ emphasised that such questions 'must be approached in a broad commonsense way', while in *McNally*, Leveson LJ noted that deceptions as to wealth 'will obviously not be sufficient to vitiate consent'.[35] Of course, the question of 'materiality' is a normative one, falling to be interpreted within a legal and social world. I do not necessarily agree with what judges consider to be legally material and what they do not.

The important point to note however, is that sexual autonomy is, and it would appear, always was, subject to limits. As Austin Sarat et al note, '[l]aw has a strangely complicated relationship to lies, deception, and truth. Sometimes it takes a hard line on behalf of truth ... but more often ... looks the other way as lies are told. It tolerates deception, and regards truth as an inconvenient barrier to the attainment of some other value' (Sarat et al, 2015, p 2). In the context of sexual fraud, that other value is the liberty of the subject. In view of law's limits, it is worth stressing that many facts, including some facts about gender, are not legally relevant or material to the question of consent. This is something which, given the legal and media attention they often receive in gender identity fraud cases, might easily be overlooked.

In addition to this question of fact materiality there is another important component of legal doctrine, one that has developed over the last decade. Together they prove determinative of the presence or absence of consent. This new component takes the form of an act/omission distinction, specifically a distinction between non-disclosure of information (where consent is considered valid) and some form of 'active deception' (where it is not). The incorporation of this distinction into the actus reus element of non-consent is curious and unhelpful in that conflates the actus reus and mens rea requirements of sexual offences involving fraud (Laird, 2014, p 505). In any event, it is the emergence of this distinction, as an integral part of legal doctrine bearing down on the question of

33 *Clarence* above note 3.

34 *R (on the application of F) v DPP* above note 29 at para 26.

35 *McNally* above note 25 at para 25. This approach to fact materiality is one generally evident within other common law jurisdictions. However, Israeli courts have adopted a much broader approach to determining fact materiality and prosecutions for sexual offences have been successful in circumstances where defendants have lied about their age (*State of Israel v Mehadakar*, 522/07 Nazareth District Court (2007)) or falsely made an offer of financial reward or other social goods in exchange for sex (Crim 2411/06 *Saliman v State of Israel* [Aug. 17, 2008] Nevo Legal Database). For discussion of these cases, see Gross, 2015, pp. 5–6; Bergelson, 2016, p. 157. See also E. Volokh, 'Israeli Rape by Fraud Cases' *The Volokh Conspiracy* 7/10/10 available at http://volokh.com/2010/10/07/israeli-rape-by-fraud-cases/ (last accessed: 3/2/17).

consent, to which we now turn. It can perhaps be traced to the case of *R v EB*.[36] In this case, counsel for the prosecution suggested that a failure to disclose HIV positive status prior to sexual intercourse served to vitiate consent. The suggestion was roundly rejected by the Court of Appeal. While consent would be vitiated in such circumstances in relation to charges brought under the Offences Against the Person Act 1861, Latham LJ insisted that:

> Where one party to sexual activity has a sexually transmissible disease which is not disclosed to the other party any consent that may have been given to that activity by the other party is not thereby vitiated. The act remains a consensual act.[37]

In other words, non-disclosure of HIV positive status was considered 'not relevant to the issue of consent under s. 74 in relation to the sexual activity'.[38] However, and as Richard Card notes, this left open 'the possibility that if the defendant lies, when asked about his HIV positive status by the complainant, this may be viewed as a relevant consideration' (Card, 2012, p 340). Indeed, Latham LJ, in referring to an article by professors Temkin and Ashworth, acknowledges this possibility, limiting his finding of valid consent to the case of non-disclosure of information.[39] In the later extradition case of *Assange v Swedish Prosecution Authority*, the Divisional Court emphasised that *R v EB* 'goes no further than deciding that a failure to disclose HIV infection is not *of itself* a relevant consideration under s. 74'.[40] Moreover, and in providing further clarity on the matter, the court made clear that if a jury accepted the complainants' evidence that Assange had sexual intercourse without a condom, or continued sexual intercourse after removing, damaging or tearing a condom, after it had been made clear to him that consent was conditional on condom use, this would constitute active deception inconsistent with s.74.

In the more recent decision of *R (on the application of F) v DPP*, the Court of Appeal again emphasised the active nature of the defendant's deception, namely, ejaculating into his wife's vagina after it had been made clear to him that her consent was conditional on non-ejaculation.[41] In mapping the boundaries of the act/omission distinction, the court was, as Doig and Wortley note, 'at pains to underline that it was not concerned with situations where a man ejaculates prematurely or "accidentally" before withdrawal' (Doig and Wortley, 2013, p 288). It noted that, while in practice distinguishing accident from deliberation is likely to prove impossible in most cases, the defendant had 'announced his intention in advance to commit the act' (Doig and Wortley, 2013, p 289) because he had wanted to demonstrate sexual control over his wife. Thus, while the case endorses an act/omission distinction, it also straddles the deception/coercion divide. This

36 *EB* above note 24.
37 *Ibid*, para 17.
38 *Ibid*, para 21.
39 *Ibid*, para 19.
40 *Assange* above note 19, para 90 (my emphasis).
41 *R (on the application of F) v DPP* above note 29.

developing jurisprudence has culminated in the case of *McNally*. This is a case that will be detailed below and which will be critiqued in later chapters. For present purposes, it is sufficient to note that Justine McNally was found, through statements and deeds, to have 'actively deceived' the complainant into believing that she was a man.[42]

## 2.5 Mens rea and sexual fraud

If consent is considered vitiated under s. 74, it is still necessary for the prosecution to establish the required mens rea. Thus, not only must it be established that there is active deception, curiously both for the purposes of proving non-consent and mens rea. It must also be established that the defendant lacked a reasonable belief in consent.[43] In other words, even where the courts find deception and consider it to be of an 'active' kind, this does not resolve the question of what the defendant believed or, more importantly, the reasonableness of his belief. Thus, for example, while a defendant may make a representation which the court subsequently finds to be both false and material, and while the complainant may rely on it in her decision to become sexually intimate, this does not mean that the defendant considered it false, or that he thought the complainant would rely on it. Crucially, his belief in consent may be reasonable. Thus, and by way of example, a defendant may claim to be physically well-endowed. While this is unlikely to be considered a material fact, for reasons already discussed, he may believe that he is well-endowed and/or that the complainant's decision to have sex with him was not influenced by his claim. Indeed, even where the fact to which deception relates is one invested with greater legal and cultural significance, the same difficulties may arise. Thus, if a defendant lied about his HIV positive status, he may have done so for reasons of privacy and the avoidance of stigma, rather than in order to deceive the complainant, and he may believe that her decision to have sex with him was uninfluenced by his lie. Thus it may be that the parties had protected sex or that the defendant had knowledge of the complainant's participation in sex, including unprotected sex, with HIV positive men in the past.

Ultimately, the main difficulty for the defence in cases like these lies with the concept and test of 'reasonableness'. Thus, in our HIV example, it may prove difficult to convince a jury that the defendant had a reasonable belief in consent. Though 'reasonableness' is to be determined 'having regard to all the circumstances',[44] it would perhaps require a very particular set of facts for a jury to conclude that the defendant's belief in consent was reasonable given the potential seriousness of contracting the HIV virus.[45] In the case of transgender and other

42 *McNally* above note 25 at para 26.
43 s. 1(1)(c) Sexual Offences Act 2003.
44 s. 1(2) Sexual Offences Act 2003.
45 Though the risk may be extremely low if the defendant is on antiretroviral drugs and uses a condom. A study by Cohen et al, found the risk to be reduced by 96% (Cohen

gender non-conforming defendants, the yardstick of reasonableness is as, if not more, likely to thwart defence counsel. This is because 'reasonableness' is a normative, not an objective concept. In this particular context, the reasonableness of a transgender man's belief will be constructed from a cisnormative perspective. From this perspective, and despite the actuality of consensual unions of this kind,[46] it is inconceivable that a cisgender woman would knowingly become intimate with a transgender man and therefore inconceivable that a transgender man could reasonably, or indeed honestly, believe in the presence of consent. In other words, reasonable belief becomes almost indistinguishable from cis-sexist conceit. That is, transgender defendants can only be understood as self-loathing individuals who can never legitimately or convincingly claim to be the object of another's desire. This difficulty will be explored in subsequent chapters. Attention now turns to detailing the gender identity fraud cases that have come before the courts.

## 2.6 Gender identity fraud

From the outset it should be emphasised that all of the gender identity fraud prosecutions have involved defendants who, irrespective of their present gender identity, were designated female at birth, and complainants who identify as cisgender women and as having a heterosexual orientation. A number of important issues arise here, ones which will be explored in subsequent chapters. First, the gender identities of the defendants are complicated and sometimes mobile in ways that raise serious questions regarding any discussion of mens rea.[47] Second, while complainants consistently assert their heterosexuality, such assertions are contested by defendant versions of the facts. Third, no transgender woman has so far been prosecuted for gender identity fraud. While an adequate explanation of this fact requires proper empirical investigation, it may be accounted for, at least in part, by extra-judicial solutions resorted to by 'affronted' men. Certainly, violence against transgender women, both in sexual and other contexts, is well documented and pervasive.[48]

et al, 2011) and follow up studies have confirmed very low infection rates (see, for example, Baeten, 2012).

46 A recent US YouGov poll found that 21% of female respondents considered themselves 'somewhat or very open' to dating/being in a relationship with a transgender man, either 'casually or seriously' and 17% considered themselves open to 'sexual relations with a transgender man' ('21% of Americans Believe That Being Transgender is a Mental Illness', *YouGov US*, 9/2/17 available at https://today.yougov.com/news/2017/05/17/21-americans-believe-identifying-transgender-menta/) (last accessed: 20/5/17). In relation to non-binary people, the figures for this same female cohort were 19% and 15% respectively.

47 While some defendants are clearly transgender, precise gender identification (transgender, genderqueer, lesbian) is not always clear from legal and media reporting of cases, a fact which serves only to complicate the relevant legal issues and their legal resolution.

48 In the UK context, Whittle et al found that 'in every sphere of life' transgender people 'are subject to high levels of abuse and violence' (Whittle et al, 2007). See also Morton, 2008.

Thus, the limited scenario that has consistently presented before the courts is one of a man (or in the eyes of the law, a lesbian pretending to be man) who has deceived a young woman. This template for understanding the evolution of sexual fraud jurisprudence generally, and gender identity fraud jurisprudence specifically, is one that draws on and reproduces a series of culturally embedded ideas about gender, ones that have operated to the disadvantage of gender non-conforming defendants in the cases prosecuted, and ones which undermine the sexual agency of women. First, it distributes men and women across an active/passive divide. Second, and relatedly, it invokes a victim/perpetrator dyad as an unproblematic mode of analysis. Of course, this latter distinction often comes to the fore when thinking about sexual offence allegations across gender lines. The intention here is not to trivialise power imbalances that exist between men and woman. On the contrary, the aim is to tease out more complicated relations of power, ones masked by unnuanced characterisations of actors as victims or perpetrators (Carmody and Carrington, 2000; Carmody, 2004).

This is especially important in the present context because of the marginal status of the defendants, and because the legally designated gender of the defendants as well as their gender socialisation experiences place them outside any notion of privileged masculinity. Despite these realities, complainants are routinely constructed as naive and vulnerable, while defendants emerge as deviant and predatory. In subsequent chapters, this framing of things will be challenged and the vulnerability of (especially young) transgender and other gender non-conforming people, across structural, cultural and psychic vectors, emphasised. In Chapters 3–5, it will be argued that cisnormativity and heteronormativity serve to preclude a more accurate, and in Chapter 6 a more ethical, understanding of what is at stake in these particular instances of sexual intimacy. In this chapter however, let us begin by detailing the cases to have been prosecuted so far.

### *(i) R v Jennifer Saunders*

The first case to be prosecuted in the UK, or indeed any jurisdiction as far as I am aware, on the basis of gender identity fraud is the case of *R v Saunders*.[49] In this case, Jennifer Saunders, then aged 16, was convicted at Doncaster Crown Court of two counts of indecent assault[50] after becoming sexually intimate with two

In the US context see GenderPAC, 1997; Waters et al, 2016. Waters et al note the disproportionately high number of black transgender women sexually assaulted and murdered annually. According to their study, of the 24 recorded homicides of LGBTQ and HIV-affected people for 2015, 16 (67%) were of transgender or gender non-conforming people, and 13 (54%) were of transgender women of colour (p 9).

49 *R v Saunders* 12/10/91 (Unrept, Doncaster Crown Court, Judge Crabtree). For a discussion of the case, see Smith, 1995.

50 This offence was repealed by the Sexual Offences Act 2003 and has been replaced by Sexual Assault (s. 3), which is committed where the defendant intentionally touches the victim without her consent.

cisgender women, then aged 16 and 17 respectively. His Honour Judge Crabtree sentenced Saunders to six years imprisonment.[51] The case is something of an anomaly, having no precedent and preceding the Sexual Offences Act 2003. It would be nearly a quarter of a century before similar prosecutions would be brought in the UK. The case is important however, because it provides a template that has been consistently replicated in terms of defendant/complainant profile and legal/media representation of the facts, and because of comments made by the sentencing judge which, though today are perhaps unutterable, reveal important ideological factors that continue to underscore such prosecutions.

The facts of *Saunders* are, like most gender identity fraud cases, disputed. What is not disputed is that Saunders presented as male and became sexually intimate with two young cisgender women. The allegation of fraud was based on the claim that Saunders was not male and in presenting as 'Jimmy' had deliberately led the complainants to believe the contrary, which had served to undermine their sexual autonomy. There was evidence to suggest that at least one of the complainants was aware of Saunders' gender history and that complaint was motivated by parental discovery of the same and a desire to disavow lesbianism. These matters, as well as the complexity of the relationship ignorance bears to knowledge more generally, will be explored in Chapters 3 and 5, where they will emerge as important issues. For now, I want to emphasise three things that will be seen to be replicated in most, if not all, subsequent cases. First, the complainants were young cisgender women while the defendant was a young gender non-conforming person; the complainants insisted that they did not know the defendant's gender history and, had they done so, would not have become sexually intimate with the defendant; and the defendant disputed the complainants' claim concerning knowledge. Second, the victim/perpetrator dichotomy is presented in absolute terms with the sexual parties represented as occupying different moral universes. This is not only an effect of legal discourse, but also of wider media discourses. Third, 'harm', a concept to be interrogated in Chapter 4, proves to be a retrospective affair and, as legally imagined, inextricably tied up with the 'undoing' of heterosexuality. Thus, in sentencing Saunders, His Honour Judge Crabtree asserted that the defendant's conduct was far more serious than heterosexual rape. As he put it, the defendant had:

> called into question [the complainants'] whole sexual identity ... and I suspect both those girls would rather have been actually raped by some young man than have happened to them what you did.[52]

This judicial articulation, while lacking in sensitivity and out of step with contemporary sensibilities, is significant. The content of the statement and the

51 The Court of Appeal later reduced the sentence to two years probation. By the time she was released Saunders had spent nine months in prison (*R v Saunders* (1992) (EWCA Crim.) unpublished (see Gross, 2009, p. 173)).

52 Smith above note 49 at 165–166.

anxieties which animate it are absolutely central to an adequate understanding of why gender identity fraud prosecutions are commenced.[53] The statement implicates a number of judicial and societal concerns that will be explored in subsequent chapters, ones which require an analysis and critique of assumptions regarding the notion of harm, the stability of identity, and the coherence of desire.

### *(ii) R v Gemma Barker*

After *Saunders*, the next gender identity fraud case to come before the courts, and the first in a new wave of prosecutions, was *Barker*.[54] The case of Gemma Barker is in many ways a re-run of *Saunders* except that the parties met online, which is a feature of more recent cases and reflects the impact of technology on contemporary dating practices, especially those involving young people. Barker, who was 19 at the time, presented as male and the two female complainants, who were 16 and 15 respectively, claimed to believe she was male. She was convicted at Guildford Crown Court of two counts of sexual assault[55] and sentenced by His Honour Judge Moss to 30 months imprisonment on the basis of deception as to gender identity. She was also placed on the Sex Offenders Register,[56] a feature of conviction that will be seen to mark all subsequent gender identity fraud convictions. It is important to emphasis that she was not convicted in relation to any penetrative sexual act. Rather, her convictions were based on the finding that she kissed and cuddled the complainants, having deceived them. Accordingly, *Barker*,

53 Indeed, in the *Newland* case (*R v Newland* 15/9/15 (Unrept, Chester Crown Court, Judge Dutton)), the complainant made precisely this claim (see S. Linning, 'I'd rather have been raped by a man, says woman sexually assaulted by female friend who used bandages and a sex toy to pretend she was male' *The Daily Mail Online* 8/9/15 available at www.dailymail.co.uk/news/article-3226030/Woman-posed-man-befriend-naive-25-year-old-Facebook-used-bandages-bind-chest-sex-toy-dupe-thinking-male.html (last accessed: 3/2/17)).

54 *R v Barker* 5/3/12 (Unrept, Guildford Crown Court, Judge Moss). For media reporting of the case, see M. Blake, '"I Felt Repulsed and Dirty and Wanted to Kill Myself": Schoolgirl Victims of Teenage Girl Who Dressed as Boy to Date them Speak of their Anguish as She is Jailed', *The Daily Mail Online*, 6/3/13 available at www.dailymail.co.uk/news/article-2110430/Gemma-Barker-jailed-Vctims-girl-dressed-boy-date-speak-anguish.html (last accessed: 3/2/17); E. Stretch, 'My Boyfriend was Really a Girl: Teenage Victim of Sex Con Tells of Her Horror', *The Mirror*, 6/3/13 available at www.mirror.co.uk/news/real-life-stories/agony-of-teen-victims-of-gemma-barker-752654 (last accessed: 3/2/17); R. Sabey et al, 'Boy-Girl Groper Gemma Barker Ruined my Life', *The Sun*, 7/3/13 available at www.thesun.co.uk/sol/homepage/news/4176927/Boy-girl-groper-ruined-my-life.html (last accessed: 3/2/17).

55 s. 3 Sexual Offences Act 2003. Barker's sexual acts consisted in kissing and cuddling the complainants.

56 A defendant convicted of a sexual offence and sentenced to 30 months imprisonment or more will be put on the Sex Offenders Register for Life. For lesser custodial sentences, the period varies. If less than 30, but more than 6 months, a period of 10 years will apply. If less than 6 months, the period is set at 7 years (Sex Offenders Act 1997, as amended by the Sexual Offences Act 2003).

in particular, serves to emphasise the need to derail the sexual autonomy juggernaut. Of all the cases so far prosecuted, it might, at least in this sense, be viewed as the best example of criminal law overreach. By the same token, the fact that such minimal contact became the basis both for prosecution and for a conclusion of harm serves to emphasis what is at stake in these kinds of cases, namely, the fragility of heterosexuality.

It is also important to note that Barker, like Saunders, contested complainant claims of ignorance and that these claims bordered on the fantastical. While this issue is not confined to the *Barker* case, as we will see, legal overcoming of the implausibility of the prosecution case is especially notable and surprising in *Barker*. Thus, in the case, one complainant, who knew Barker as Gemma from school, claimed not to appreciate her 'boyfriend' was Barker despite having a relationship with Barker in different 'guises', first as Luke Jones and subsequently, after breaking up with Jones, as Connor McCormack. This is an issue we will return to in Chapter 5. One of the complainants was 15, and therefore below the statutory age of consent. This fact might be thought to be significant. However, no criminal charges relating to sex with a minor were brought against Barker, or indeed against any of the defendants in the gender identity fraud prosecutions. Moreover, in the absence of overt coercion or other aggravating factors, prosecutorial guidelines tend against the bringing of such charges where the parties are young and close in age.[57]

### *(iii) R v Justine McNally*

In 2013, two further cases followed on the heels of *Barker*. First, the English case of Justine McNally,[58] and then the Scottish case of Chris Wilson. In *McNally*, the parties met online. At this point, McNally was 13 and the female complainant 12. Over three years later, during which time they continued their cyber relationship, the parties met in person and on several occasions. At this stage, McNally was 17 and the complainant 16. On two of these occasions McNally digitally and orally

57 *Crown Prosecution Service Legal Guidance: Rape and Sexual Offences: Chapter 2* available at www.cps.gov.uk/legal/p_to_r/rape_and_sexual_offences/soa_2003_and_soa_1956/#a21 (last accessed: 3/2/17). The cases of *Barker* and *Wilson* (see below) involved complainants who were 15 at the time of the alleged offences. In relation to *Wilson* however, a 'reasonable belief' that one of the complainants was at least 16 at the time of the offence appears to have existed. It should be noted that the guidelines do identify deception as an aggravating factor. However, in the *Barker* case it seems doubtful that there was any operative deception. In any event, in a case where a defendant is a transgender man (the matter is somewhat ambiguous in *Barker*) we ought to conclude that there is no deception regarding gender identity.

58 *McNally* above note 25. Using the name Justine and female pronouns in describing McNally reflects my understanding of her present gender identification. However, at the time of the alleged offences she claimed to identify as male. This is an important issue to be considered in Chapters 4 and 5.

penetrated the complainant.[59] She was subsequently charged with six counts of assault by penetration,[60] convicted and sentenced by His Honour Judge Patrick to three years imprisonment.[61] As in *Barker*, the complainant's consent to sex was found to have been vitiated due to deception regarding gender identity. That is, McNally had presented as male, while the court found her to be female. In fact, at the time of trial and subsequent appeal, McNally asserted a female gender identity. The reader might think that these facts render the conviction unproblematic. However, as we will see in Chapters 4 and 5, legal characterisation of McNally as deceptive, both through judicial interpretation of a series of statements that she made and because of a 'change of heart' regarding her gender identity, remains deeply problematic and in multiple ways. In particular, Chapter 5 will scrutinise the complainant's claim of ignorance, as well as the notion that ignorance bears only a negative relation to knowledge, and it will consider the possibility that the assertion of a male gender identity, prior to and at the time of the sex acts, and therefore at the time of legal liability, may have been a genuine articulation.

### *(iv) R v Chris Wilson*

In the same year, Chris Wilson was convicted by the Scottish High Court of two counts of 'obtaining sexual intimacy by fraud'.[62] While a custodial sentence was anticipated, Lord Bannatyne sentenced Wilson to three years probation and 240 hours of community service.[63] He was also placed on the Scottish Sex Offenders Register.[64] The background story to his convictions can be described as follows:

59 Oral penetration refers here to penetration of the vagina via the tongue. Digital penetration refers to the penetration of the vagina by the finger(s).

60 s. 2 Sexual Offences Act 2003. The offence of Sexual Assault by Penetration requires non-consensual and intentional penetration of the vagina or anus by any part of the body or any object.

61 On appeal, the sentence was reduced to 9 months detention in a young offender institution suspended for 2 years with a supervision order (*McNally* above note 25 at para 2). At the time of release McNally had served almost 3 months in prison (para 52).

62 'Obtaining sexual intimacy by fraud' is an odd choice of words for the indictment. There is no such offence contained within the Scottish Sexual Offences Act 2009. The most appropriate charges appear to be s. 2 (sexual assault by penetration) in relation to vaginal penetration by an object and s. 3 (sexual assault) in relation to kissing.

63 *R v Wilson* 7/3/13 (Unrept, Edinburgh High Court, Lord Bannatyne). A copy of the sentencing judgment is on file with the author. For media reporting of the case, see J. Morgan, 'Man "Guilty" of Fraud for not Telling Girlfriend he was Trans', *Gay Star News* 7/3/13 available at www.gaystarnews.com/article/man-'guilty'-fraud-not-telling-girlfriend-he-was-trans070313/ (last accessed: 3/2/17); C. Pinfold, 'Scotland: Case of Trans Man facing Jail for Sex "by Fraud" raises Concerns of Scottish Transgender Alliance', *Pink News* 12/3/13 available at www.pinknews.co.uk/2013/03/12/scotland-case-of-trans-man-facing-jail-for-sex-by-fraud-raises-concerns-of-scottish-transgender-alliance/ (last accessed: 3/2/17); 'Sex Fraud Woman Put on Probation', *BBC News* 9/4/13 available at www.bbc.co.uk/news/uk-scotland-north-east-orkney-shetland-22078298 (last accessed: 3/2/17).

64 He was placed on the register for three years commensurate with his probation period.

Wilson met two cisgender girls on separate occasions. In relation to the first girl, who was either 15 or 16 at the time (there is uncertainty on this point), sexual contact was limited to kissing. Wilson was aged 20 at the time of kissing girl 1. Two years later he commenced a relationship with the second girl. She was aged 15 at the time, but told Wilson that she was 16. This relationship culminated in penetrative sexual intercourse by means of a prosthetic device. While Wilson was designated female at birth, he identified and presented as male prior to, at the time of, and subsequent to the incidents and he stated his intention to undergo gender reassignment surgery.[65] The use of a prosthetic device in this case, as well as in all subsequent cases, is an issue of some importance. It might be viewed as providing a justification for conviction independent of questions of gender identity. This is an issue to be taken up in Chapter 5.

### *(v) R v Gayle Newland*

In 2015, two further prosecutions were brought. First, in the case of Gayle Newland, the defendant, who like the complainant was then aged 25, was convicted of three counts of assault by penetration at Chester Crown Court.[66] The defendant, who identifies as lesbian, was found to have initially met the complainant through Facebook where she used the name, Kye Fortune, though the defendant denied that this was how the parties first met (see Chapter 5, section 5.2).[67] The

65 Morgan above note 63.

66 *R v Newland* 15/9/15 (Unrept, Chester Crown Court, Judge Dutton). Two of the counts related to prosthetic, and the third to oral, penetration of the complainant's vagina. For media reporting of the case, see 'Woman Who Pretended to be Man to Trick Friend into Sex Jailed for Eight Years', *The Guardian* 12/11/15 available at www.theguardian.com/uk-news/2015/nov/12/gayle-newland-sentenced-eight-years-prison-duping-friend-having-sex (last accessed: 3/2/17); M. Scott, 'The Gayle Newland Sentence Sets a Dangerous Precedent for Transgender Rights', *The Telegraph* 13/11/15 available at www.telegraph.co.uk/news/uknews/crime/11993361/The-Gayle-Newland-sentence-sets-a-dangerous-precedent-for-transgender-rights.html (last accessed: 3/2/17).

67 The defendant created the Facebook account for Kye Fortune when she was 13 years old, and as a way to express herself: 'It was a way to talk to girls pretending to be a boy. It was easier for me. ... I am gay, I don't know how to behave or to react to this situation, I am not confident as myself. I couldn't just speak to girls, I didn't know how to do it or what to be' (Summing Up of His Honour Judge Dutton, 14/15 September 2015 at Chester Crown Court, p. 68. Document provided by Nigel Power QC, defence and appellant counsel for Newland, 7 Harrington Street Chambers, Liverpool). However, she insisted that the complainant always knew she was Gayle and that the use of the Kye Fortune persona in their relationship took the form of sexual/gender role play and a desire on both their parts to conceal their lesbian sexuality. Thus, and according to Newland's account, both were closeted and the Kye Fortune persona provided the complainant with a ready-made boyfriend to guarantee her heterosexuality outside the relationship. That is, Fortune had an online presence, including multiple photographic images and a backstory that could be referred to in interactions with third parties.

defendant did not appear as male in person. However, the court found that the complainant believed her to be so, despite having sex with her on multiple occasions, because the defendant had presented as male online and crucially, had insisted that the complainant wear a blindfold on all occasions when the parties did meet in person. The court found the defendant to have deceived the complainant regarding her gender identity and, in a moment that shocked the nation,[68] His Honour Judge Dutton sentenced her to eight years' imprisonment and placed her on the Sex Offenders Register for life. On 12 October 2016, after serving 11 months in prison, the Court of Appeal (Halley LJ, King and Dove JJ) quashed Newland's conviction on the basis that they considered it unsafe in view of the trial judge's direction to the jury in summing up the case.[69] At her retrial at Manchester Crown Court in June 2017, she was again convicted on all three counts.[70]

The conviction of Newland might seem less problematic than other gender identity fraud cases, and especially those where defendants are clearly transgender, like *Wilson*.[71] However, the *Newland* case is deeply troubling in other respects,

68 A. Sharpe, 'There's More Than Meets the Eye in the Case of Gayle Newland' *The New Statesman* 18/9/15 available at www.newstatesman.com/politics/feminism/2015/09/theres-more-meets-eye-case-gayle-newland (last accessed: 3/2/17).

69 See 'Gayle Newland: Woman Accused of Posing as Man Wins Appeal', *BBC News* 12/10/16 available at www.bbc.co.uk/news/uk-england-merseyside-37632913 (last accessed: 3/2/17); S. C. Nelson, 'Prosthetic Penis Case: Gayle Newland Conviction Overturned', Huffington Post 12/10/16 available at www.huffingtonpost.co.uk/entry/prosthetic-penis-case-gayle-newland-conviction-overturned_uk_57fe32dce4b08e08b93d6149 (last accessed: 3/2/17).

70 *R v Newland* 29/6/17 (Unrept, Manchester Crown Court, Judge Stockdale). On the 20 July 2017, Newland was sentenced to six years in prison in relation to the sexual offending and to an additional six months, to run consecutively, in relation to separate financial fraud offences unrelated to the case (J. Humphries 'Gayle Newland to be Sentenced for Posing as Man to Dupe Friend into Sex with Fake Penis' *The Liverpool Echo* 20/7/17 available at www.liverpoolecho.co.uk/news/liverpool-news/gayle-newland-sentenced-posing-man-13358713 (last accessed: 20/7/17)).

71 While Newland asserted a lesbian identity, there was some evidence to suggest that she may be transgender. Thus, Newland allegedly discussed with the complainant, the film, *17 Again* (Summing Up of His Honour Judge Dutton, above note 67, p. 32). While this is not a film about a transgender person, it does deal with bodily transportation and dissonance in the form of a middle-age man being transmogrified into his earlier self. This might be viewed as a metaphor for gender dysphoria, a condition where there exists a disjunction between gender identity and anatomical form (Fisk, 1973). Further, and more significantly, Newland allegedly said to the complainant: 'I asked to be better than this and this is what happened, they put me in this body, this is what happened' (p 32). Further, in his sentencing remarks (12/11/15), His Honour Judge Dutton referred to the importance of Newland's 'blurred gender lines' (p 3). Sentencing document provided by Nigel Power QC, defence and appellant counsel for Newland, 7 Harrington Street Chambers, Liverpool. The possibility that Newland might be transgender was rendered more explicit after her conviction by a second jury in 2017. While self-identifying as lesbian before and during both trials, a pre-sentencing psychiatric report, referred to by Newland's barrister by way of mitigation, noted that Newland

and especially in terms of its disputed facts. Thus the defence argued that the complainant is a lesbian who was fully aware of Newland's gender identity and that both parties were 'playing a role game, a complex sexual role game'.[72] These issues will be explored further in Chapter 5 where a critique of the case will be offered. In particular, the chapter will consider the complainant's perception of the defendant's gender identity in terms that refuse an innocence/knowledge binary.

### *(vi) R v Kyran Lee (Mason)*

In the same year, Kyran Lee (Mason), then aged 25 (the complainant was 27), was prosecuted and convicted at Lincoln Crown Court of one count of assault by penetration by means of a prosthetic device, on the basis that he had deceived the complainant regarding his gender identity. He received a two year suspended prison sentence and was placed on the Sex Offenders Register for ten years.[73] The parties met through Facebook, where the defendant used the name Joey G-Star Crislow, and a relationship developed online and through text messages and phone calls. After a year, they met in person and became sexually intimate. More pertinently, His Honour Judge Heath accepted that the defendant did not penetrate the complainant for sexual gratification, but rather reluctantly and in order to avoid relationship breakdown, factors which proved significant in the handing down of a non-custodial sentence.[74] However, while he did not consider the defendant's 'deception' to be 'a ruse to practice lesbian behaviour',[75] he clearly considered him to be a lesbian. Yet, like Wilson, the defendant was clearly a transgender man. And, like *Wilson*, this did not serve to preclude conviction, an

suffered from a number of mental health conditions, including gender dysphoria (Humphries above note 70).

72 Summing Up of His Honour Judge Dutton, above note 67, p. 4.

73 *R v Lee (Mason)* 16/12/15 (Unrept, Lincoln Crown Court, Judge Heath). For media reporting of the case, see 'Woman Who Used Fake Penis to have Sex with a Woman Avoids Jail', *The Guardian* 15/12/15 available at www.theguardian.com/uk-news/2015/dec/15/woman-who-used-fake-penis-to-have-sex-with-a-woman-avoids-jail (last accessed: 3/2/17). Kyran Lee was charged with two counts of assault by penetration in relation to another female complainant relating to a relationship in 2008. However, he was acquitted of those charges by a jury, who believed his claim that sex had not taken place (see L. Smith, 'Woman Pretended to be a Man by Wearing Body Suit and Sex Toy to Trick Single Mum into Sex', *The Mirror* 7/11/15 available at www.mirror.co.uk/news/uk-news/woman-pretended-man-wearing-body-6719202 (last accessed: 3/2/17)).

74 Smith above note 73.

75 R. Pattinson, '"The Pain was Excruciating, I Couldn't Eat or Sleep": Woman Duped by Lesbian with Fake Penis Reveals Her Horror', *The Sun*, 15/12/15 available at www.thesun.co.uk/archives/news/872703/the-pain-was-excruciating-i-couldnt-eat-or-sleep-woman-duped-by-lesbian-with-fake-penis-reveals-her-horror/ (last accessed: 3/2/17).

issue to be explored in Chapter 4, where we will address more fully attendant questions of ontology, epistemology and power.

### *(vii) R v Jason Staines*

The most recent case to have come before the courts, at least at the time of writing, is the case of Jason Staines. In this case, a Bristol Crown Court convicted the defendant,[76] then aged 23, of two counts of assault by penetration by means of a prosthetic device in relation to female complainants 1 and 2, who were both 17, and one count of sexual assault and one count relating to indecent images of a child,[77] in relation to complainant 3, a 12- or 13-year-old girl (there was some uncertainty on this point, though the age difference is not without legal significance).[78] His Honour Judge Cotter handed down a sentence of 39 months, a sentence upheld on appeal,[79] and Staines was placed on the Sex Offenders Register for life. In relation to the 12/13-year-old complainant, the sexual activity was apparently confined to kissing. In relation to the other complainants, penetration was effected by means of a prosthetic device. The defendant, who met all three complainants online, used the name Jason Spiller.[80] Like Lee (Mason) and Wilson, Staines, whose lawyer stated that he had gender dysphoria, identifies as a

76 *R v Staines* 24/3/16 (Unrept, Bristol Crown Court, Judge Cotter). For media reporting of the case, see 'Woman Abused Three Young Girls by Pretending to be Man with Prosthetic Penis', *The Telegraph* 23/3/16 available at www.telegraph.co.uk/news/uknews/crime/12202567/Woman-abused-three-young-girls-by-pretending-to-be-man-with-prosthetic-penis.html (last accessed: 3/2/17); S. Osborne, 'Woman Posed as Man to have Sex with Teenage Girls', *The Independent* 23/3/16 available at www.independent.co.uk/news/uk/crime/woman-posed-as-man-to-have-sex-teenage-girls-jennifer-staines-bristol-a6948491.html (last accessed: 3/2/17).

77 It is unclear from the reporting which offence he was convicted of, or what exactly he did in relation to photographic images. The charge was most likely, *Possessing an Indecent Photograph of a Child* contrary to s. 160 of the Criminal Justice Act 1988.

78 Sexual assault of a child under 13 is a more serious offence and attracts a greater maximum penalty. Thus, in relation to a child aged 13–15, the maximum penalty is 10 years (s. 9 Sexual Offences Act 2003). Where the child is under 13, the maximum penalty increases to 14 years (s. 7 Sexual Offences Act 2003). While not condoning Staines' actions, it is noted that his conduct in relation to the 12/13-year-old appears to have been confined to kissing.

79 The Court of Appeal considered Staines' appeal against sentence on 12 October 2016. Giving reasons for the ruling, King J stated: 'Our conclusions are these, given the number of victims, the extent of the harm caused to them, the extent of the appellant's overall offending which lasted years, we can see no basis for any argument that this sentence was manifestly excessive' (J. Dunn, 'Woman Who Tricked Girls Between 12 and 17 Years Old into Having Sex With Her Loses Appeal Over Sentence' *Mail Online* 12/10/16 available at www.dailymail.co.uk/news/article-3834475/Woman-pretended-man-sex-victim-wins-appeal.html (last accessed: 1/3/17)).

80 L. Churchill, 'Woman Posed as Man to have Sex with Teenage Girls', *Bristol Post* 24/3/16 available at www.bristolpost.co.uk/exclusive-woman-posed-man-sex-teenage-girls/story-28979462-detail/story.html (last accessed: 3/2/17).

transgender man.[81] Accordingly, while Staines' conviction cannot be objected to in relation to complainant 3, legal findings of non-consent and deception are especially problematic in relation to his sexually intimate encounters with the other complainants.

It should also be noted, that in all of these cases, with the exception of *Newland*, the defendants pleaded guilty. This might be thought only to emphasise the correctness of criminal justice outcomes. However, as we will see in Chapter 5, the question of plea cannot be uncoupled from forms of injustice that travel along structural and cultural axes. In other words, like the substantive law of sexual fraud, rules pertaining to criminal procedure also play themselves out within a cisnormative and heteronormative field of power. In subsequent chapters, we will address these issues of ideology and power. Before doing so however, this chapter will conclude by offering some analysis regarding factors that may help explain the recent expansion of sexual fraud generally, and specifically in relation to those at the gender and sexual margins.

## 2.7 A socio-political context

The expansion of sexual fraud is not, in any significant sense, an effect of changing public attitudes. Indeed, the public typically demonstrate scepticism regarding criminalisation of sexual fraud.[82] Rather, this development of the law is connected to the embedding of the value of sexual autonomy within criminal law jurisprudence, a shift associated with the impact of feminist advocacy and lobbying.[83] Of course, it is recognised that as women we face a range of injustices within the criminal

81 D. Bunting, 'Jennifer Staines – Woman Jailed for Posing as a Man to "Get Sex"', *UK Criminal Law BLOG* 23/3/16 available at http://ukcriminallawblog.com/jennifer-staines-woman-jailed-for-posing-as-a-man-to-get-sex/ (last accessed: 3/2/17).

82 In one US study (Bryden, 2000), 519 male and female respondents across a range of age cohorts were asked to indicate whether criminal penalties were appropriate in relation to 18 specific examples of deception prior to sex. A majority of respondents answered affirmatively in relation to only five, one of which also involved coercion. The other four examples concerned intimate medical examination, impersonation of the victim's husband, lying about having a venereal disease, and failing to disclose a venereal disease (pp 471–472). Interestingly, in the English context, the first two constituted offences at common law long before the enactment of the Sexual Offences Act 2003. In relation to deception concerning 'infidelity, wealth, marital status, use of a birth control device (by a woman), intention to marry, [and] intention to pay a prostitute' the respondents 'rejected criminal liability by a wide margin' (p 472).

83 Indeed, in the recent Transgender Inquiry, conducted by the Women and Equalities Committee (2015), some feminist groups opposed reform of sexual fraud law to remove transgender people from its ambit. See, for example, the written submission by the *Campaign to End Rape* (CER) 21/8/15 available at www.parliament.uk/business/committees/committees-a-z/commons-select/women-and-equalities-committee/inquiries/parliament-2015/transgender-equality/publications/ (last accessed: 3/2/17).

justice system, ones that have their sources in substantive, procedural[84] and evidential legal rules,[85] as well as in cultural norms,[86] and feminist advocacy has rightly sought to address them. However, 'carceral' or 'governance' feminism (Estrich, 1986; Chamallas, 1988; MacKinnon, 1989; Falk, 1998; Gotell, 2015),[87] is considered problematic and in many ways counter-productive because, as noted by Bernstein (2007, 2012) and Halley (2006), it tends to be overly punitive[88] and non-redemptive, and because it runs the danger of 'codify[ing] within the law the very powerlessness it aims to redress' (Brown, 1995, p 21). As Wendy Brown has noted, there is a danger that some feminists are prepared to sacrifice freedom for political protection, adding that '[m]ore recent history suggests that legally and politically codifying justice as matters of protection, prosecution, and regulation tends to turn us away from "practicing' freedom"' (Brown, 1995, p 21, fn 38).[89]

84 For example, the corroboration rule requiring a judge to warn a jury of the dangers of convicting a defendant on the sole testimony of a female rape complainant. This rule, which has operated historically to infantilise women, was abolished by s. 32 of the Criminal Justice and Public Order Act 1994. However, discretion to give the warning remains.

85 For example, prior to the enactment of s. 41 of the Youth Justice and Criminal Evidence Act 1999, cross-examination regarding a complainant's sexual history was common. The legislation introduced a general ban on admission of such evidence. However, it can still be admitted under a series of exceptions stipulated in the provision, ones which might be viewed as punishing 'promiscuity' and 'deviant sexuality' (s. 41(3)(b) and (c)).

86 Reference is made here to cultural attitudes towards women (see, for example, studies by Finch and Munro, 2005; Ellison and Munro, 2006; Ellison and Munro, 2009; Ellison and Munro, 2010; Ellison and Munro, 2013). Various polls also indicate pervasive sexist attitudes towards women. Thus, for example, a 2005 Amnesty International Report found that many respondents believed a woman to be fully or partially responsible for rape if she 'behaved in a flirtatious manner' (34%), 'was drunk' (30%), wore 'sexy or revealing clothing' (26%), or had had 'many sexual partners' (22%) Amnesty International Report on Attitudes to Sexual Assault in the UK 2005, available at www.amnesty.org.uk/press-releases/uk-new-poll-finds-third-people-believe-women-who-flirt-partially-responsible-being (last accessed: 3/2/17).

87 For a critique of this feminist approach see Brown, 1995, pp. ix–xiii, 21–29, 43–47, 52–95; Halley et al, 2006, 340–342. Resort to the criminal law to address perceived human rights abuses is especially problematic for feminism because reliance on criminal law requires the mobilisation of the carceral state and therefore teases out tensions that exist with basic tenets of feminism (see Martin, 1998; Gruber, 2009).

88 A recent example of this kind of punitiveness can be found in the case of premier league footballer, Chad Evans, who was convicted and sentenced for rape in 2012. After serving his sentence, many feminists demanded extra-legal sanctions, namely that he be prevented from resuming his career as a professional footballer (see, for example, S. Moore, 'No Football Club Should Touch Ched Evans, Even if he Does Apologise' *The Guardian* 5/1/15 available at www.theguardian.com/commentisfree/2015/jan/05/football-club-ched-evans-apologise-rehabilitation (last accessed: 3/2/17)).

89 It should be recognised that these problems are also evident within some forms of LGBTQI political activism. Like their feminist counterparts, such queer investments in punishment have been subjected to sustained critique (for example, see Spade, 2011; Lamble, 2013).

It is not suggested here that there exists a direct causal relationship between carceral or governance feminism and the prosecution of transgender and other gender non-conforming people. Rather, it is contended that such prosecutions are more likely in a world in which cisgender women's sexual autonomy is utterly juridified. In any event, the setting in train of an absolutist understanding of a right to sexual autonomy, as well as the invocation of the punitive state regarding desire-led intimacy, especially between young people, is a significant cause for concern within transgender and genderqueer communities. In Chapter 3, it will be argued that the right to sexual autonomy, though important, must be limited, lest it continue to produce the instrumental and discursive fallout at the sexual and gender margins that this book documents.

It is also important to note societal concern regarding the vulnerability of children and young adults generally, especially in relation to sexual practices. While Aries dates the category of childhood, though not the sentiment expressed toward children, to the turn of the eighteenth century (Aries, 1965), other scholars have emphasised how thereafter, childhood became increasingly associated with innocence and vulnerability (Zelizer, 1994; Robinson, 2013, Chapter 3), a coupling which, after the emergence of the social sciences, became caught up in power/knowledge spirals which sought to regulate and normalise children (Foucault, 1977; Foucault, 1981). Indeed, 'childhood' and 'youth' are categories which seem to have increasing elasticity (Blos, 1979; Arnett, 1998), stretching beyond earlier understandings of maturity and extending infantilisation in a society characterised by 'risk' and aspirations to control the future (Giddens and Pierson, 1998, p 209).

These developments have a range of historical and cultural influences which do not concern us here. Rather, what I want to emphasise is the fact that what has been described as the 'sacralisation of childhood' (Zelizer, 1994, Chapter 1) has intensified in recent decades. More pertinently, it continues to serve 'as one of the main conduits for the channelling of moral sentiment' (Furedi, 2013, p 44. See also Meyer, 2007). As Alan Hunt has put it, innocent children 'have become important triggers of moral politics' and trespass on their innocence is likely to unleash 'sensitive feelings of indignation, unfairness and anguish' (Hunt, 2011). In the context of sexuality, these concerns have concentrated, in particular, on the loathsome figure of the paedophile and on inter-generational sex more generally. However, other gender and sexual outsiders may be caught up in the criminal justice system and in other economies of judgment should they be considered to have trespassed on innocence.

These discourses of childhood are important, for our purposes, because of the nature of the cases to be considered and because of the capacity of the innocence–childhood nexus, which appears to operate increasingly as a kind of Nietzschean 'sign-chain' (Nietzsche, 1969, p 77) to influence outcomes within criminal justice settings. Certainly, there appears to be a link between the trope of (especially female) childhood innocence and its apparent loss which attends gender identity fraud cases. Moreover, this emphasis on complainant innocence and vulnerability persists despite the fact that most complainants had reached the age of consent, were generally of a similar age to the defendants, and were engaged in desire-led intimacy. Importantly, the cases are not ones of inter-generationality, a fact that might easily be lost sight of in view of legal and media emphasis on teenage 'girls' and the 'women' who 'groomed'[90] and 'preyed' on them (Moore, 2016). The fact that the defendants are all young gender non-conforming people is also important, both in emphasising how social and legal concern over vulnerability is delimited, and in intensifying anxiety around the possibility that sexually active cisgender heterosexual sex might go 'awry'. Thus, what might be considered a contemporary 'moral panic' (Cohen, 1972. See also Jenkins, 1992), if not a witch-hunt, is perhaps, at least in part, explicable in terms of a constellation of intersecting factors: childhood, innocence, vulnerability, sex, gender variance and queer sexuality. Accordingly, gender identity fraud prosecutions might be understood in terms of what Phillip Jenkins has described as the 'politics of substitution' (Jenkins, 1992), that is, as the expression and amplification of moral concern over sex, effected through a focus on childhood and the deviant forces that threaten it.[91]

It is necessary also to draw attention to the *Savile* case and Operation Yewtree.[92] It would seem, at least anecdotally, that these sexual abuse scandals have sensitised the CPS to sexual offence allegations. Of course, such allegations must be taken seriously. However, a concern arises, at least in the context of the gender identity fraud cases, that CPS rules regarding prosecutorial thresholds are not being met. It is also important to note that the recent series of cases beginning with *Barker* coincides with the *Savile* moment. While it is not being argued that there is a causal relation, the two things clearly correlate and, to that extent, raise concern and require further investigation. These issues will be explored in subsequent chapters and, in particular, CPS claims to have prosecuted in the public interest and/or on the basis of credible evidence will be considered and challenged in Chapter 5.

## 2.8 Conclusion

This chapter has provided an overview of the development of the category of fraud within sexual offences law. It highlighted how, in the English context, the category of fraud has expanded significantly since the Sexual Offences Act 2003 and the further embedding of a right to sexual autonomy through liberal interpretation of s. 74. Having detailed this general development, the chapter focused specifically on prosecutions for gender identity fraud. To this end, it detailed a spate of cases

90 See, for example, Blake above note 54.

91 Indeed, such concerns can even lead to moral panics being generated around VIP ritualistic satanic abuse of children as Operation Midland clearly demonstrated (R. Waterhouse, 'The Historic Sex Abuse Investigation needs a Dose of Common Sense' *The Spectator*, 5/5/17 available at https://blogs.spectator.co.uk/2017/05/the-historic-sex-abuse-investigation-needs-a-dose-of-common-sense/ (last accessed: 10/7/17)).

92 *Operation Yewtree* above note 2.

that have come before the courts since 2012. Moreover, it sought to distinguish these cases in a variety of ways from other successfully prosecuted sexual fraud cases, though appellate courts have, so far, chosen not to do so. This legal background sets the scene for a critique of gender identity fraud prosecutions that will be provided in subsequent chapters. In developing this critique, we will return to some of this history and to (agreed and contested) case facts. This will, among other things, involve challenge to legal constructions of fact materiality, complainant knowledge, harm, active deception, and the reasonableness of belief.

# Part II

# Principles

Chapter 3

# Principled objections I

## 3.1 Introduction

This chapter will offer four principled objections to prosecutions for gender identity fraud. First, it will be argued that prosecution for deception constitutes significant criminal law overreach. This is especially the case in circumstances of desire-led intimacy which lacks the feature of coercion. In developing this argument, the chapter will consider the issue of 'fair labelling' as the sexual offences category may not be the most appropriate to locate such cases. Second, the framing of 'sexual autonomy' as a non-negotiable right will be contested. The chapter will consider how such an approach removes complainants from the realm of sexual agency. It will also emphasise how sexual autonomy arguments rely on a priori claims as to the materiality of facts, in relation to which deception is said to have been perpetrated. In the context of gender identity fraud however, the 'facts', which may or may not be material, are typically disputed, and so sexual autonomy arguments are implicated in, as well as serving to conceal, questions of ontology, epistemology and power. In other words, assertions of autonomy are often premised on constructions of 'truth' which bear no relation to defendants' self-understandings of gender identity.

Third, it will be argued that legal determinations as to the materiality of facts, and therefore as to the demarcation of one of the boundaries of consent/non-consent, produce legal inconsistency and are potentially discriminatory. In particular, the chapter will highlight how gender identity, at least in the UK context,[1] is the only group identity to have attracted the attention of the state. That is, prosecutions have been confined to gender identity, as opposed to, for example, identities of race, sexuality or disability. Moreover, within the category of gender identity, it is only the gender identities of gender non-conforming people, rather than people at large, with which law appears to be concerned. This latter point, in particular,

1 The Israeli courts have convicted Arab men who lied about their ethnic background or failed to disclose it prior to sexual intimacy with Jewish women, although only *Kashur* was convicted of a sexual offence (CrimA 5734/10 *Sabbar Kashur v State of Israel* [2012] Takdin (Isr.), Nevo Legal Database). For a discussion of *Kashur* and the other cases see Gross, 2009; Gross, 2015.

serves to foreground the question of discrimination. In exploring this question, the chapter will consider a number of possible justifications for state discrimination.

Finally, it will be argued that decisions to prosecute fail to consider, or weigh properly, other important rights and interests. In particular, the chapter will focus on the Article 8 right to privacy, although other rights arise in contexts of sexual intimacy. In doing so, it will make a series of arguments. First, in considering the clash between the right to sexual autonomy and the right to privacy, it will be argued that privacy ought to prevail, at least in some circumstances, and that harm ought to operate as a key factor in any balancing act. Second, it will be argued that serious sexual offence charges are, at least in the present context, unnecessary and disproportionate to the public interest aim of punishing sex offenders. Third, it will be argued that Article 8 is undermined by legal uncertainty surrounding the scope of illegality. This problem will be seen to be evident both at the level of legal doctrine and through reference to Crown Prosecution Service (CPS) prosecutorial guidelines concerning transgender suspects. The chapter will then move beyond privacy analysis and consider how prosecution might be said to infringe upon a right to 'corporeal integrity' (Thomas, 1992), a suggested right that might be advanced through argument under Article 3.

## 3.2 Criminal law overreach

Let us begin with the liberal observation that use of criminal law should not be triggered easily, but rather should be the approach of last resort (Jareborg, 1995; Husak, 2008; Baker, 2011). As Ashworth has put it, analysis should begin from a starting point which assumes 'a right not to be punished' (Ashworth, 2013, p 22). In relation to sexual fraud, proposals to further extend the law have been described as 'preposterous' (Simester et al, 2010, p 755), 'so far off the beaten path' (Bohlander, 2007, p 426) and 'frightening in [their] ramifications' (Ormerod, 2011, p 734). This latter view, offered by David Ormerod, the current Law Commissioner for criminal law in England and Wales, is one I share and especially so in relation to prosecutions for gender identity fraud. Most conversations about the limits of criminal law begin with 'the harm principle' (Feinberg, 1984, 1985, 1986, 1988). While harms can be disaggregated from wrongs, and criminalisation defended on the basis of the latter alone, most criminal law commentators insist on the demonstration of some kind of significant harm as a precursor to criminalisation. This Millian approach has received its clearest contemporary expression from Joel Feinberg. Moreover, and while not dictating criminalisation as a solution to perceived social problems, Feinberg suggests that it ought to be preceded by a conclusion 'that it would be effective in preventing harm' to others and 'that there is probably no other means that is equally effective at no greater cost to other values' (Feinberg, 1984, p 26). Thus the harm minimisation approach also requires consideration of and the weighing of other available effective options. In the following chapter, we will explore in detail the question of harm in contexts of gender identity fraud where it will be argued that a harm case has not been established. For present purposes however, it should be recognised that, in the context of sexual intimacy, there are clearly alternatives to criminal prosecution.

After all, in these contexts, intimacy is desire-led. There is no coercion involved. Rather, parties choose to become intimate with each other, albeit they lack perfect information. We might ask: why, prior to intimacy, should gender non-conforming people be required to disclose personal information? Surely, a preferable alternative to such an approach would be to place the burden not on those who exercise privacy, who choose reticence over disclosure in the face of a prying world, but on those for whom particular information is considered important or material. This is, perhaps, especially the case where reasons for not wanting to have sex are in some sense phobic. For example, if a white woman does not want to have sex with black men she is free to exercise her autonomy accordingly, although it might be better here to speak of agency, given that concept's ability to capture the socially constructed nature of desire/repulsion. If however, she chooses to have sex with a man who stands before her, assuming him to be white when in fact he is mixed-race, he ought to bear no obligation to disclose his racial/ethnic history. Such an obligation should certainly not arise because some people approach the world as though it were populated by racially 'pure' categories of people. In other words, criminal law is not an appropriate vehicle for channelling a sense of outrage occasioned through a racist worldview.[2] If a complainant disprefers certain groups within the sexual pool of men, she ought to be proactive, taking steps to investigate and verify.[3]

Of course, I acknowledge that this might not always be a simple matter, but consider it more reasonable that phobic people limit their sexual partners than other people be expected to disclose personal information that ought not to be considered material in public policy terms. The mixed-race scenario just outlined is one of non-disclosure of information, which, as we will see, is not criminalised under English law. However, and while more 'active' forms of deception might illicit different reader responses regarding both criminalisation and ethical characterisation, in the context of gender identity fraud the distinction between non-disclosure and active deception is a dubious one, which as we will see in Chapter 5, can break down in quite spectacular ways. That is, despite a legal fetish for action, transgender and other gender non-conforming people appear in practice to have been convicted for 'mere' omission. This is because, in this particular context, a claim of lying cannot always easily be separated from epistemological privilege through which ontology is constituted.

Finally, in thinking about the limits of criminal law in the context of gender identity fraud, attention is drawn to 'fair labelling', which requires 'that widely felt distinctions between kinds of offences and degrees of wrongdoing are respected

2 For a discussion of why sexual preferences based on race are racist see Stember, 1978. In 2015, an Australian study found people with sexual preferences based on race correlated strongly with general racist attitudes (Callander et al, 2015).

3 Such an approach has been endorsed more generally. See, for example, Slater, 2011.

and signalled by the law, and that offences are subdivided and labelled so as to represent the nature and magnitude of the law-breaking' (Ashworth and Horder, 2013, p 77).[4] Thus, even if non-disclosure of gender history and/or active deception were to be viewed as wrong, harmful and justifying criminalisation, sexual offences law might still be considered the wrong category in which to locate the behaviour/omission. In my view, fair labelling, through which law communicates to society not only that behaviour is wrong, but also why it is wrong, would require locating gender identity fraud outside of the sexual offences category altogether or, at least, framing it as a lesser sexual offence. This is because it is not fair or accurate to locate and communicate the 'wrongness' of this kind of desire-led intimacy within the very serious and stigmatising category of sexual offences.[5] The danger of diluting the seriousness of sexual offences in the public mind through further criminal law expansion into the territory of deception, as distinct from coercion, should also be recognised to be a significant consideration both in broader criminalisation debates and in relation to judicial interpretation of consent provisions (Temkin, 1982; Henderson, 1988; Bronnitt, 1991; Dripps, 1992; West, 1996; Horder, 1999).

In saying this, I do not take the view that criminalisation of fraud is nothing more than 'legal moralism' (Gross, 2007), though I do think some arguments advanced in support of criminalisation come close, as Hyman Gross has suggested, to placing 'the sex act on an elevated moral plane' (Gross, 2007, p 225). Certainly, the absolutist approach to sexual autonomy advocated by Jonathan Herring and Michelle Madden-Dempsey (Herring, 2005; Herring, 2007; Herring and Madden-Dempsey, 2007; Madden-Dempsey, 2010) appears to involve the trumping of all other rights and interests. Nevertheless, it is acknowledged that deception may cause harm. The difficulty here lies in describing the nature and degree of harm (assuming we are not dealing with 'mere offense'; Feinberg, 1985), and in being satisfied that it meets a threshold justifying criminal intervention. An analysis of harm also requires that we attend to the needs of the defendant, and therefore the costs of disclosing personal information. In the context of gender identity fraud cases, it will be argued that these costs, though often neglected, are considerable. The question of harm will be considered in detail in the following chapter.

## 3.3 The limits of sexual autonomy

This section of the chapter will challenge uncritical resort to a right to sexual autonomy as justification for gender identity fraud prosecutions. In a later section, I will consider and oppose the claim made by some jurists, that it trumps, or ought to trump, other rights claims. Here however, it will be argued that the trend

4 See also Chalmers and Leverick, 2008; Williams, 1983. There is, of course, a danger here, one expressed by Lindsay Farmer, that fair labelling may lead to 'an inflationary logic in the criminal law' (Farmer, 2016, p. 114).

5 See Amit Pundik, who makes a strong case for distinguishing sex occasioned by coercion from sex occasioned by deception in terms of fair labelling (Pundik, 2015).

within criminal law jurisprudence toward embedding sexual autonomy as an absolute right, one fostered by 'carceral' or 'governance' feminism (Estrich, 1986; Chamallas, 1988; MacKinnon, 1989; Falk, 1998; Gotell, 2015),[6] is problematic because it serves to rob complainants of autonomy or, as I prefer to frame things, agency. An emphasis on liberal autonomy runs the risk of eliding complex configurations of structural, cultural and psychological constraints that shape action. Of course, liberal scholars working with the idea of autonomy recognise constraints (Sherwin, 1996). Nobody thinks autonomy to be pure. Nevertheless, the idea of agency is preferred because it places greater emphasis on constraints, and crucially, on ways in which constraints play a role in constituting desire (Abrams, 1999; McNay, 2000).

Indeed, sexual autonomy, in contrast, can be viewed as oxymoronic. As Rubenfeld notes, while 'autonomy jealously guards [physical boundaries], fearful of every puncture or penetration ... sexuality ... desires nothing other than this boundary's violation, both physically and psychologically' (Rubenfeld, 2013, p 1421). Accordingly, from the perspective of desire, sexual autonomy can be viewed as both undesirable and ultimately unattainable. These observations are especially pertinent in the present context given that we are dealing with desire-led intimacy. Moreover, because I am working within the paradigm of social constructionism, and see it as the necessary ground of freedom,[7] the concept of agency better describes our relationship to the world and our capacity to negotiate it. As Judith Butler notes, '[t]hat my agency is riven with paradox is the condition of its possibility' (Butler, 2004, p 3).

To be clear, the expression of consent, that is, apparent consent, is seen as an assertion of agency. Importantly, when one consents, one acts as a subject in the world and with this comes the possibility to 'disrupt dominant sexual discourses' (Abrams, 1999, p 839). That is, and as Tuerkheimer notes, 'agency leans toward a positive understanding of sex – sex not only as pleasure, but as resistance to subordination' (Tuerkheimer, 2013, p 339). Thus, to deny consent because perfect information is lacking can be viewed as contrary to the aims of feminism. If perfect information were required, valid consent, and therefore agency, would be impossible. As Tuerkheimer insists, 'it cannot be said that defrauded consent ... is no consent at all' (Tuerkheimer, 2013, p 342).[8] Of course, Turkheimer does not argue that such consent will always be consistent with legal consent. I agree. As she notes, 'what constitutes being informed is a matter of degree' (Tuerkheimer, 2013, p 343) However, it is perhaps less a matter of *degree*, and more a matter of the *kind* of information that is lacking. Certainly, courts view consent as valid in all

6 For a critique of this feminist approach see Brown, 1995; Halley et al, 2006; Bernstein, 2007, 2012; Gruber, 2009.

7 The concept of *freedom* is used here in the Foucauldian sense, that is, as referring to the possibility of being otherwise, a possibility precluded by any notion of essentialised identity (Foucault, 1988, p. 154).

8 In making this point, Deborah Tuerkheimer is responding to and contesting a claim made by Jed Rubenfeld in his recent polemic on rape law (Rubenfeld, 2013).

kinds of circumstances where, due to deception, there exists an informational deficit. Vitiation of consent occurs only where a legal determination is made that the information in question is important or material.

Accordingly, the important question which arises is, how is fact materiality to be legally determined? To begin with, it is not, as a matter of law, determined subjectively, though an absolutist position on sexual autonomy, one favoured by Jonathan Herring (Herring, 2005), would require such an approach. In other words, facts are not legally material merely because complainants attribute importance to them. In my view, such an approach would trivialise the abuse of women by counting as rape, sexual intercourse that follows, for example, a false declaration of love (Horder, 1999, p 108). While Herring insists, that for some people, a declaration of love makes 'all the difference in the world' (Herring, 2005, p 521), I consider the adoption of a subjective approach to be too far-reaching in its consequences, and at odds with any notion of female agency that I would want to advance.

In any event, as a matter of law, the materiality of facts is determined objectively, though as a matter of reality, normatively, given the lack of clear reasons provided by courts for fact differentiation. Of course, whether facts are determined subjectively, 'objectively' or normatively does not necessarily mean a difference in outcome. While the courts view deception regarding wealth or social status to be trivial and would almost certainly agree with Jennifer Temkin that consent ought not to be viewed as vitiated in circumstances where a man 'falsely assures a woman that he will love, marry, promote or house her if she has intercourse with him' (Temkin, 1982, p 405), they tend not to view as trivial, 'deceptions' perpetrated by those at the gender and sexual margins. In other words, whatever approach is adopted to fact determination, gender identity or history is likely to be found material.

At least two difficulties arise here. First, an issue arises concerning the 'truth' of gender identity and who gets to determine that truth. Here it will be argued, at least in relation to transgender defendants, that the truth was always already in the open and therefore a relevant material fact, upon which a court might hang its hat, is lacking. Second, arguments about the truth of gender identity, or indeed the importance of gender history, serve to mask the broader context in which agentic choices take place. Let us turn then to my first objection to a sexual autonomy argument. The argument I resist rests on the claim that gender identity is a material fact in prosecuted cases and that deception concerning it vitiates consent and ought to do so. In my view, gender identity ought not to be treated as a material fact. To treat it as such is to cast doubt on the authenticity of the gender identities of transgender people.

Transgender people are not engaged in some form of pretence or masquerade. Their gender identities should not be understood as trivial but rather as speaking to a sense of (dis)embodiment, psychic reality and experiential truth. Indeed, the gender identities of transgender people tend to manifest early in life and the phenomenon of transgenderism is recognised by the medical community[9] and the state provides both public funding for treatment and provision for legal gender recognition.[10] Further, and while it is not my contention that the legitimacy of prosecution should turn on whether gender identity claims have been legally recognised, the fact of legal recognition appears to introduce a further objection to prosecution. It does so because possession of a Gender Recognition Certificate signifies legal recognition of 'acquired' gender 'for all legal purposes'.[11]

Ultimately, claims of encroachment on a right to sexual autonomy only make sense in the present context, if they make sense at all, in circumstances where a gap exists between complainant belief about the defendant's gender identity and his actual gender identity. Where no gap exists, all that is left is to give effect to agentic choice. Of course, it might be objected that although a defendant is a man, and his male status has perhaps received the imprimatur of law, he is nevertheless not the kind of man the complainant considered him to be, and that *kind* matters in determining the question of materiality. Such an objection however, should be resisted. To accept it would imply, and give legal life to, the idea that there is a hierarchy of men before the law. We should accept neither an argument that negates gender identity, through allowing a complainant's interpretation of a defendant's gender identity to trump his own, nor one that seeks to otherwise diminish him.

Sexual autonomy is an important right, but it must have limits. One clear limit surely, must be where the claim of a right to know amounts to 'a right to define' people against their will. In other words, the right claimed is not one directed toward knowledge, but its refusal. In my view, apparent consent should be viewed as legally valid because the important fact, namely authentic gender identity,[12] is

9 It should also be recognised, though my argument does not depend on it, that there is scientific support for the view that the gender identity claims of transgender people, or at least a subset of transgender people, have a biological basis. Thus scientific studies conducted post mortem on transgender women suggest they possess a female brain structure (Gooren et al, 1995; Kruijver et al, 2000; Govier et al, 2010). Such studies support the hypothesis that gender identity develops as a result of an interaction of the developing brain and sex hormones. The tiny region of the brain that has been scrutinised is the central subdivision of the bed nucleus of the stria terminalis, known as BSTc. It is part of the hypothalamus which helps to keep the different systems of the body working in harmony and which is viewed as essential for sexual behaviour. This area of the brain is ordinarily larger in men than in women, while in transgender people, studies suggest that size corresponds with gender identity. This has led Gooren et al, to conclude that transgender people 'are right in their belief that their sex was wrongly judged at the moment of birth' (Gooren et al, 1995, p. 70).

10 Gender Recognition Act 2004.

11 *Ibid*, s. 9. None of the transgender defendants in the cases under consideration had received a Gender Recognition Certificate at the time of the offences, a fact perhaps due to their tender age.

12 In placing emphasis on 'authentic' gender identity, I am not suggesting an essentialist understanding of identity. Rather, while all identities are, in various senses, socially constructed, they have a reality in lived experience. This is no less true for transgender people than it is for cisgender people. This is important to emphasise because we live in

already in the open and there ought not to be a right to know other personal facts about the body and its history. To claim otherwise is, of necessity, to imbue other facts with a weight they ought not to bear, at least not if we wish to take self-determination of gender identity seriously. It is also important here to recognise a point often neglected in discussions of sexual autonomy concerning cisgender/transgender sexual relations, namely, transgender people also have a right to sexual autonomy. Moreover, this right is not unconnected to a right to informational privacy. After all, reticence about, or revelation of, facts about the body, its history and/or surgical alteration are directly linked to experiences of sexuality and pleasure.

In any event, irrespective of a transgender person's legal and/or ontological status, and indeed, irrespective of whether a person is actually transgender or otherwise gender non-conforming, a focus on fact materiality serves to mask the broader context in which complainant agency is exercised. In particular, insistence that particular facts are material serves, much like the deployment of autonomy arguments, to elide the complexity of desire. The first, more general observation to make is that deception only makes sense in terms of an already established set of genders/sexes from which there can be no movement. In other words, deception claims presuppose gender stability in relation to subjects and objects of desire. Yet, neither gender nor desire are static, even for people who are not transgender or gender non-conforming. However, while prosecutions reproduce the idea of binary and stable gender, I want to focus here on the dynamics of desire and, in particular, to highlight the inauthenticity of the repudiation of attraction.

The female complainants in the gender identity fraud cases consistently assert their heterosexuality. On their account, an exclusive desire directed toward men somehow went awry. The difficulty here lies in assuming that masculinity is necessarily connected to particular body parts, especially genitalia. The reality, of course, is that we lack knowledge of a person's genitals when desire arises. Rather, desire can relate and respond to all kinds of stimuli: physical (a person's height, weight, eye colour, skin tone); sensory (a person's smell, voice, touch); personality traits (whether a person is gregariousness, charming, cultured, confident or coy); as well as many other characteristics (a person's fashionability, sense of humour, intelligence and so forth).[13] In other words, desire is the effect of a constellation of factors, none of which are necessarily gendered. To the extent that it is gendered behaviour that attracts us, this does not simplify matters. Thus, in the cases that have been prosecuted, defendants designated female at birth have presented

a society where the 'realness' of the gender identities of transgender people is never fully acknowledged, as both criminal prosecution and disclosure discourse demonstrate.

13 Thus in the Gayle Newland case (*R v Newland* 15/9/15 (Unrept, Chester Crown Court, Judge Dutton)), the complainant noted, and seemed to value the fact, that the 'man' she claimed to be in a relationship with (Newland) was 'a very sensitive man' (Summing Up of His Honour Judge Dutton, 14/15 September 2015 at Chester Crown Court, p. 53). Document provided by Nigel Power QC, defence and appellant counsel for Newland, 7 Harrington Street Chambers, Liverpool.

as men and have performed masculinity. It seems trite to deny obvious attraction to the masculinity on offer.

It seems clear that the complainants, even if ignorant of the defendants' gender histories, were attracted to transgender men and/or genderqueer people. As Natalie Reed notes, in considering the situation of intimacy between cisgender men and transgender women, '[i]t's not trans women you aren't attracted to (you clearly are), it's women you know are trans. Therefore it's the *idea* of transsexuality that creeps you out. It's a conceptual issue, and based on socio-cultural messages, not on anything related to your actual sexuality.'[14] Indeed, and following the logic of this observation, she notes that a cisgender man would respond in exactly the same way if a cisgender woman told him falsely, and post-coitus, that she was transgender.[15] In these respects, assertions of sexual autonomy and the disavowal of desire which grounds them, prove disingenuous. Accordingly, it might be better, and more accurate, to say that complainants are 'disappointed' upon 'discovery' rather than 'tricked'. Indeed, in the seventeenth century, and as noted by Adam Phillips, the word 'deceive' bore both meanings: 'to trick' and 'to disappoint' (Phillips, 2013, p 4). What we are perhaps witnessing, in the context of gender identity fraud prosecutions, is the translation of disappointment into deceit and therefore blame. If so, it is something we, as a society, ought to strenuously resist.

However, I want to make a stronger claim or, at least, raise another important question. It may be that attraction to transgender and/or other gender non-conforming defendants in gender identity fraud cases is not so much an attraction conditioned by ignorance (a desire 'in spite of'), but an attraction mobilised precisely by gender difference (a desire 'because of'). In other words, it may be, as Judith Butler has suggested, that gender ambiguity or dissonance can sometimes be central to, or constitutive of desire (Butler, 1990, p 123).[16] It may be that 'uncertainty about identity, blurring of lines, and loss of control over all of the information are part of the world of desire' (Gross, 2009, p 203), and that the relationship between disgust and desire is one of ambivalence (Raj, 2016, p 87). As Katherine Franke has put it: '[d]esire is not subject to cleaning up, to being purged of its nasty, messy, perilous dimensions, [it is] full of contradictions and the complexities of simultaneous longing and denial. It is precisely the proximity to danger, the lure of prohibition, the seamy side of shame that creates the heat

14 N Reed, 'The "Ethical Imperative" Of Disclosure, Or: How to Believe Your Victim Owes You an Opportunity for Abuse' *FreeThoughtBlogs.com* 20/3/12 available at http://freethoughtblogs.com/nataliereed/2012/03/20/the-ethical-imperative-of-disclosure-or-how-to-believe-your-victim-owes-you-an-opportunity-for-abuse/ (last accessed: 3/2/17).

15 *Ibid.*

16 It is precisely ambiguity of this kind that may have drawn Brandon Teena's cisgender girlfriend (Halberstam, 2005, Chapter 2). Brandon's subsequent rape and murder at the hands of two cisgender men is depicted in the harrowing film, *Boys Don't Cry*, directed by Kimberly Peirce (Fox Searchlight Pictures, 1999).

that draws us toward our desires, and that makes desire and pleasure so resistant to rational explanation' (Franke, 2001, p 212). In this sense, prosecution emerges as restrictive of sexuality, as corralling desire, and as a disavowal of the fact that '[d]isgust follows desire' (Raj, 2016, p 87). Moreover, these observations appear to fit well with the facts of the cases under consideration.

All involved defendants designated female at birth, none of whom, at least not at the stage of prosecution and conviction, had commenced hormonal treatment. Accordingly, while a masculine gender performance might, in the present context, be taken as evidence of deception, we might ask instead: what does it mean for a woman to desire a man who has a body generally considered female, that is female to the touch, and who has a voice falling within the female range? In other words, how can we avoid recognising the fact that complainant desire/pleasure was connected to experiences of bodies/masculinities that lie beyond dominant ideas of being male. In saying this, I do not mean to cast doubt on the masculinity of defendants, on defendant gender authenticity. Rather, the point being made is that even on complainants' own accounts, desire appears to be linked to some degree of gender ambiguity.

This creates problems for claims based on sexual autonomy which insist on a gap between assumed gender and actual gender. In other words, if there is a gap, an ontological question we shall return to, it is, at the very least, narrower than acknowledged by complainants, prosecutors and judges. More importantly, for present purposes, a diminished gap points to the possibility that complainant trauma may be less about an experience contrary to sexuality, than one associated with its consummation, an acting out of desire that calls into question an understanding of sexual identity as fixed. As Butler notes, 'despite one's best efforts, one [can be] undone, in the face of the other, by the touch, by the scent, by the feel, by the prospect of touch, by the memory of the feel' (Butler, 2004, p 19). Accordingly, in the context of gender identity fraud, arguments based on sexual autonomy can be viewed as amounting to an abdication of agency, of responsibility for complainant desire. Read in these lights, prosecutions might be viewed as having less to do with 'protect[ing] sexual autonomy against fraudulent solicitation of sex' and more to do with 'protect[ing] gender norms and compulsory heterosexuality' (Gross, 2009, 165. See also Rich, 1980), and therefore as being about shaping 'which bodies one "can" legitimately approach as would-be lovers and which one cannot' (Ahmed, 2004, p 145). Ultimately, they are about legal and social denial of the blindness of desire.

## 3.4 Legal inconsistency and discrimination

Prosecution for sexual offences on the basis of gender identity fraud is also objectionable because of legal inconsistency and related discriminatory effects. In relation to most of the cases that form the corpus of an emerging sexual fraud jurisprudence, the deception involved can be described as involving a state of affairs or surrounding circumstances (a promise to wear a condom, a promise not to ejaculate, etc).[17] However, unlike these examples of what might be described as 'conditional consent', the gender identity fraud cases centre stage and problematise defendant identity. The shift to include identity is of particular concern because it creates a tension between defendant self-determination and state regulation. Indeed, even in circumstances where we might agree that a serious deception as to identity has been perpetrated, a problem remains. This is because identity-based prosecutions have, so far, been confined to a single slice of subjectivity, namely gender and, perhaps of greater concern, to a subset of people within the gender category, namely gender non-conforming people. As Sharon Cowan notes, perhaps with a degree of under-statement, prosecution has had a 'disproportionate impact on those who are already marginalised within a binary, heteronormative sex/ gender system' (Cowan, 2018, forthcoming).[18] Let us turn then to considering how the courts have arrived at this position and the difficulties that it presents.

In determining whether consent is vitiated, the courts now consider two questions. First: did the defendant perpetrate an active deception or did he 'merely' fail to disclose information? Only the former currently serves to vitiate consent.[19] Second: if there is some kind of active deception, does it relate to a material fact? The act/ omission distinction is a problematic one, not only in terms of identifying an underlying principle that convincingly explains the distribution of liability it effects, an issue to be explored in Chapter 4, but also because, and especially in relation to transgender defendants, it approaches analytical collapse, a theme to be considered in Chapter 5. For present purposes, we will focus on the important, though troublesome, question of fact materiality. The courts have made clear that not all deceptions will negate consent as a matter of law. Their reasoning is that some deceptions pertain to facts that are too trivial to meet the threshold of materiality.[20] In determining materiality, the courts have preferred a normative approach, rather than concluding that facts considered important to the complainant are material.

Thus, courts have made clear that false statements concerning social status and/ or wealth or willingness to pay for sex,[21] do not vitiate consent. Other forms of deception producing no legal consequences are likely to include deception concerning drug addiction and/or prior criminal convictions. Indeed, it would appear that no legal consequences arise even in circumstances where male under-cover police officers infiltrate protest groups and form sexual relationships with female group members, not even where those relationships persist over many years and

17 *Assange v Swedish Prosecution Authority* [2011] EWHC 2849 (Admin); *R (on the application of F) v DPP* [2013] EWHC 945 (Admin).
18 A copy of a draft, kindly supplied by Professor Cowan, is on file with the author.
19 *R v McNally* [2013] EWCA Crim 1051.
20 Most recently, Leveson LJ endorsed this judicial approach in *McNally* above note 19 at para 25. The point was also emphasised in *R (on the application of F) v DPP* above note 17, where Judge CJ emphasised that such questions 'must be approached in a broad commonsense way' (at para 26).
21 *R v Linekar* [1995] QB 250.

produce children.[22] Certainly, the CPS have refused to prosecute such cases.[23] While I do not support criminal prosecution in any of these contexts, at least not for sexual offences, the unethical nature of such acts is acknowledged. However, I do not consider deceptions perpetrated by transgender or other gender non-conforming defendants to be necessarily unethical, a point that will be developed in Chapter 6. This latter observation only adds weight to objection to the criminalisation of gender identity fraud.

The key thing being emphasised here however, is legal inconsistency in determining fact materiality. Of course, it might be objected that deception relating to a history of criminal convictions or drug addiction, is less fundamental than is the case with deception as to gender identity. This is because, so the argument goes, gender identity is especially important in sexual contexts. Yet, sexual partners may consider a whole panoply of facts to be material in the context of sexual encounters and, at least in some instances, for example, where a potential sexual partner has a history of child sexual abuse, such concerns may have normative support. I remain sceptical about singling out gender identity.

Further, this legal focus on gender identity raises the issue of discrimination. Certainly, prosecutions in the UK have, so far, not been brought in relation to deceptions concerning other kinds of identity, such as those of race,[24] disability or sexuality. Indeed, prosecution in relation to each of these examples, perhaps especially race, seems legally and politically inconceivable, a point we will return to in Chapter 4, where state opposition to racism, at least in sexual contexts, will be contrasted with state perpetuation of transphobia. Thus prosecutions for gender identity fraud point not only to legal inconsistency, but also to the additional, though related, problem of discrimination. After all, prosecuting sexual frauds committed in relation to gender, rather than race, disability or sexuality, a series of other categories protected under anti-discrimination law, requires some justification. Accordingly, we now turn to this question of the relationship prosecution bears to discrimination, and to consider justifications that might be offered for differential treatment.

Justification of differential treatment as between gender and other identity categories must presumably rest on the assumption that facts about gender identity are more fundamental to know than facts about other identities, and therefore

22 R Camber, 'Undercover Police Officers who Slept with Women they were Spying on to Escape Prosecution' The Daily Mail 22/8/14 available at www.dailymail.co.uk/news/article-2731553/Undercover-police-officers-slept-women-spying-escape-prosecution.html (last accessed: 3/2/17).

23 'Undercover Police Officers will not Face Sex Charges' *BBC News* 21/8/14 available at www.bbc.co.uk/news/uk-28877001 (last accessed: 3/2/17); P McGuffin, 'State Rapes: Undercover Police Escape Charges' *The Morning Star* 22/8/14 available at www.morningstaronline.co.uk/a-5941-State-rape-undercover-police-escape-charges#.WFll8HecZz8 (last accessed: 3/2/17).

24 Prosecutions have been brought on the basis of racial/ethnic fraud in Israel. See above note 1.

bear down more directly on questions of sexual autonomy and consent. Yet, it is far from clear that this is the case. On the contrary, a person's race, diability and/or sexuality, like many non-identity based facts, might be of enormous importance, at least for some sexual partners. Indeed, they may be 'deal breakers'. Nevertheless, let us consider two possible justifications which might justify a different kind of legal response in the case of gender identity fraud. We will do so in order to dismiss them and to problematise some of the implicit assumptions upon which they are premised.

First, in relation to transgender people, it might be argued that there has been a change of gender and that change is material to the question of consent. Second, it might be argued that transgender can be distinguished from race, disability and sexuality on the basis of its greater invisibility. The first claim is overstated. This is because gender identity is not so malleable. On the contrary, change or transition is not about a transformation in gender identity. Rather, while there may be a change of gender role, anatomy and/or legal status, gender identity does not change. For most transgender people, a sense of gender identity which is out of step with birth designated gender, is something we have been aware of since early childhood. Further, an argument emphasising change as a distinguishing consideration fails to recognise that race, diability and sexuality are not stable categories.

All three categories can be viewed as socially constructed rather than referring to definite or fixed groups of individuals living in the real world. These categories, like gender, are best described as contingent. Thus, and by way of example, disability is a legal category that can change either by way of expansion or contraction over time depending on the drawing of legal boundaries. Accordingly, it is possible for this status to be legally acquired or lost without any physical change occurring. Moreover, legal definitions of disability do not necessarily accord with clinical or self-understandings (Albrecht and Levy, 1981, p 14). In relation to race, the category has no proper scientific basis. Rather, it is an idea that has its origins in a racist and colonial past.[25] As for sexuality, the categories of homosexuality and heterosexuality are nineteenth-century sexological constructs (Foucault, 1981; Greenberg, 1988; Weeks, 1991). Their relationship to the sexual life-world can, as queer theory contends, be viewed as reductive (Butler, 1990; Sedgwick 1990).

Of course, race, disability and sexuality might be said to have relatively stable normative meanings. The important point however, is that these meanings are no more stable than those applicable to gender. The possibility of change exists across all these categories. Indeed, gender is not perhaps the category where change is most likely. Of course, the reader might object that, while gender change is no

25 The 'scientific' study of race commenced in the mid-eighteenth century with Carl von Linneaus' taxonomic study of human beings in *Systema Naturae* published in 1735. In the text he presented five 'racial' groups: (i) the Americanus, (ii) the Asiaticus, (iii) the Africanus, (iv) the Europeanus, and (v) the Monstrosus (see Anderson, 1997; Blunt, 2001; A. Polaszek, 2010). The view that racial categories are socially constructed and lack a biological basis has been reinforced by the advent of, and advances made in the study of, DNA (Marks, 1995).

more likely than change in other respects, reliance on gender stability is more significant to a sexual partner than the stability of race, disability or sexuality. This may be so, though it remains a properly empirical question. What needs to be reemphasised in the transgender context is lack of ontological change.

The second claim, the claim of invisibility, assumes that at least some transgender people are read as cisgender.[26] Moreover, gender identity fraud prosecutions, by definition, assume such readings and target those transgender and other gender non-conforming people likely to be read in this way. Accordingly, it can be said that those who are prosecuted for gender identity fraud are invisible in social terms. However, it is important to be clear about what precisely it is that is invisible. What is typically not invisible is present gender role, gender identity and anatomical form. In any event, it needs to be recognised that the other categories under consideration, namely race, disability and sexuality, do not lend themselves to total transparency. Thus many disabilities are not written on the surface of the body. They are not therefore necessarily visible to sexual partners. For example, many disabled people are read as able-bodied. In relation to the category of race, persons of mixed race may appear to be black or white. By the same token, many gay men are read as straight in various social contexts. Homosexuality, and perhaps more pertinently in the context of sexual fraud, bisexuality, is not typically written on the body. The important point to note here is that invisibility is not in any way unique to the lives of transgender or other gender non-conforming people. Ultimately, there appears to be no 'valid reason for privileging gender above all else' (Valverde, 1987, p 56) in determining fact materiality and therefore the presence/absence of consent. Moreover, like Mariana Valverde, I do not assume 'that gender difference is essentially erotic while other differences are not' (Valverde, 1987, p 56).

26 Use of the word 'passing' is avoided in this book because it is controversial both as an idea and as a practice. As an idea, the term 'passing' suggests appearing to be what one is not, yet for most transgender people presentation is not about performance or masquerade but reflects a strongly and deeply felt sense of self (Prosser, 1998, Chapter 2; Serano, 2007). It might be better and more accurate to say that, when cisgender people consider transgender people not to 'pass', what has really transpired are misreadings/misgenderings of transgender people. Of course, all gender can be viewed as performance/performative in the Butlerian sense (Butler, 1993). The difficulty lies in viewing transgender performance as especially artificial, in contrast to some supposedly 'natural' performance of masculinity and femininity by others. The word 'passing' also poses the problem of eliding cisgender people's relationship to what the term describes. That is, it reproduces the notion that cisgender people lie beyond social construction, inhabiting some pre-discursive natural realm. Moreover, as Julia Serano notes: 'the word "pass" is used to shift the blame away from the majority group's prejudice and toward the minority person's presumed motives and actions' (Serano, 2007, p. 177). As a practice, 'passing' is problematic because, for many transgender people, it is difficult, if not impossible, to achieve. Therefore, the medico-legal and societal emphasis on 'passing' may be inconsistent with the psychological well-being of many transgender people. Moreover, the practice of 'passing' serves to bolster the existing binary division of gender and tends toward the disappearance of transgender as a distinct and viable gender position in its own right (Bornstein, 1994).

More fundamentally, and perhaps more crucially in terms of possibilities for legal redress, the problem of discrimination is not only an inter-group problem. Rather, it operates at an *intra* level. That is, it is not only that gender, as distinct from race, disability or sexuality, exhausts legal desire for historical knowledge that calls for attention. It is also the fact that law is not concerned with gender at large, but only with a small subset of the gender pool, namely, gender non-conforming people. In other words, cisgender people are generally assumed not to have gender histories and are certainly not required to disclose gendered facts relating to the past. Thus, for example, they are not required to disclose the fact that in childhood they were considered tomboys or sissies and perhaps enjoyed these gender roles (Rottnek, 1999; Abate, 2009), and perhaps still do. Law's disinterest in cisgender people's gender identities, in the present context, is an effect of the 'gender entitlement' (Serano, 2007, pp. 165–168) they enjoy, and which law confers upon them. It is a privilege which has its root in the legal and cultural fantasy of natural gender, one rarely, if ever, extended to transgender people. It is because law assumes only transgender people experience gender change or fluidity, that it fixates on this particular kind of gender experience. Thus it would seem that gender identity fraud prosecutions may constitute direct discrimination under the Equality Act 2010[27] and under Article 14[28] in conjunction with Article 8[29] of the European Convention on Human Rights. That is, the singling out of gender identity for the special attention of the criminal law may be discriminatory because it treats transgender people 'less favourably' than cisgender people.

27 s. 13 Equality Act 2010. The Act specifically protects against discrimination based on 'gender reassignment' (s. 7), which is defined in the same terms as espoused by the European Court of Justice in its interpretation of the scope of the term 'sex' under Article 14 of the European Convention on Human Rights in *P v S and Cornwall County Council* Case C-13/94 [1996] ECR 1-2143 and confirmed in *Sarah Margaret Richards v Secretary of State for Work and Pensions* Case C-423/04 [2006] ECR 1-3585: 'persons intending to undergo, undergoing or having undergone gender reassignment'. Unfortunately, because emphasis has been placed on surgery, or at least an intention to undergo surgery, many transgender people are presently excluded from the protection of the law, though the cases of Chris Wilson (*R v Wilson* 7/3/13 (Unrept, Edinburgh High Court, Lord Bannatyne)) and Kyran Lee (Mason) (*R v Lee (Mason)* 16/12/15 (Unrept, Lincoln Crown Court, Judge Heath)), in particular, would appear to be covered. It is not clear why surgery should have any bearing on a person's right to be protected against discrimination. According to Yogyakarta principle number 3: 'No one shall be forced to undergo medical procedures, including sex reassignment surgery, sterilisation or hormonal therapy, as a requirement for legal recognition of their gender identity' (*The Yogyakarta Principles: The Application of International Human Rights Law in Relation to Sexual Orientation and Gender Identity* (2007) available at www.yogyakartaprinciples.org/principles_en.htm (last accessed: 3/2/17)).

28 Article 14: The enjoyment of rights and freedoms set forth in the Convention 'shall be secured without discrimination on any ground such as sex, race, colour, language, religion, political or other opinion, national or social origin, association with a national minority, property, birth or other status.'

29 Article 8: 'Right to respect for private and family life, home and correspondence.' Possible violation of the right to privacy will be considered below.

Moreover, the bringing of prosecutions appears to conflict with the Equality Act's public sector duty[30] which requires the CPS, as a public authority, to have due regard, in the exercise of its functions, to the need to eliminate discrimination, harassment and victimisation; advance equality of opportunity; and foster good relations between persons who share a relevant protected characteristic and persons who do not. This is because current CPS legal guidance regarding prosecutorial decision-making in the context of transgender suspects,[31] does not appear to have been subject to public consultation,[32] and if it is has, it demonstrates lack of adequate regard to equality needs established under the public sector equality duty. Certainly, it fails to pay proper attention to the actual and/or anticipatory impact of gender identity fraud prosecutions on transgender people.[33] As McCombe LJ has noted, the DPP 'must assess the risk and extent of any adverse impact and the ways in which such risk may be eliminated before the adoption of a proposed policy'[34] and 'the duty must be exercised in substance, with rigour, and with an open mind'.[35]

## 3.5 Conflicting rights claims

In this section, four distinct arguments will be offered. First, it will be argued that the right to privacy ought to trump the right to sexual autonomy, at least in some circumstances. To this end, consideration will be given to Article 8 of the European Convention on Human Rights. Second, it will be argued that irrespective of striking the correct balance between rights to privacy and sexual autonomy, the bringing of serious sexual offence charges, in gender identity fraud cases, is unnecessary and disproportionate to the public interest aim of punishing sex offenders and is therefore incompatible with Article 8. Third, it will be argued that Article 8 is engaged because of considerable legal uncertainty surrounding the scope of illegality, a fact preventing transgender people from being able to plan their affairs

30 s. 149 Equality Act 2010.

31 Crown Prosecution Service Policy and Guidance on *Rape and Sexual Offences: Chapter 3: Consent*, available at www.cps.gov.uk/legal/p_to_r/rape_and_sexual_offences/consent/ (last accessed: 3/2/17).

32 *R v North and East Devon Health Authority, ex parte Coughlan* [2001] QB 213.

33 This is particularly alarming given that gender identity fraud prosecutions dehumanise transgender people, premised as they are on a fundamental denial of self-determination of gender identity, and dehumanisation of this kind can only be expected to contribute negatively to well-documented and high levels of violence and discrimination against transgender people (Whittle et al, 2007; Morton, 2008. See also 'LGBT Facts and Figures' *Stonewall* 8/3/16 available at www.stonewall.org.uk/media/lgbt-facts-and-figures (last accessed: 3/2/17); P Yeung, 'Transphobic Hate Crimes in Sickening 170% Rise as Low Prosecution Rates Create Lack of Trust in Police' *The Independent* 28/7/16 available at www.independent.co.uk/news/uk/home-news/transphobic-hate-crime-statistics-violence-transgender-uk-police-a7159026.html (last accessed: 3/2/17)).

34 *Bracking and others v Secretary of State for Works and Pension* [2013] EWCA Civ 1345 at para 25.

35 *Ibid*, quoting Aikens LJ in *R (Brown) v Secretary of State for Work and Pensions* [2008] EWHC 3158 (Admin).

in accordance with law. Fourth, it will be argued that beyond an abstract and disembodied right to privacy, we should recognise what Kendall Thomas has described as 'a basal right of corporeal integrity' (Thomas, 1992, p 1460). In some ways, a tension exists between asserting this right and a right to privacy, especially as Thomas' argument presents itself as a critique of liberal privacy rights. However, while I find Thomas' Foucauldian influenced argument persuasive, and while I recognise more general critiques of liberal privacy within feminism (for example, Pateman, 1983; Okin, 1989; Gavison, 1992; Chinkin, 1999)[36] and queer theory (Morgan, 1994), I think it also important to defend and carve out at least some space for an inner life. Moreover, while tensions exist, they are not necessarily antithetical to a queer legal approach which, after all, eschews legal consistency. In any event, liberal privacy, despite its considerable baggage, offers itself as a ready-made right to which defence lawyers can appeal, and is one more likely to resonate with the judiciary.

### *(i) A right to privacy*

One leading criminal law scholar has posed the following question: 'would a trans-person be required to reveal their bodily history to their partners in case they would not consent to sexual relations if they knew' and, if so, 'would it be an improper invasion of the rights of privacy of a trans-person to require disclosure?' (Herring, 2005, pp. 522–523). While recognising that disclosure would constitute an invasion of private life, Jonathan Herring expressed the view that a right to privacy 'must be subservient to the right to sexual integrity of their partner' (Herring, 2005, p 523). Others, while somewhat more cautious in their approach, have supported this view (Williams, 2008, p 149). This section of the chapter will challenge this view that the right to privacy is or ought to be trumped by the right to sexual autonomy.[37] Before proceeding to my argument however, it is first necessary to attend to a preliminary matter, lest the reader think I am here tilting at windmills. Given the legal distinction developed by the courts between non-disclosure of information and active deception it might be thought that the privacy of gender non-conforming people is guaranteed under the law. That is, while Herring and others might support criminalisation irrespective of this act/omission distinction, it might be thought current law provides space for a private life.

However, this view, while correct at the level of legal form, is complicated by the fact that the distinction lacks analytical robustness and tends to break down in the context of prosecution of gender non-conforming people, a theme to be

36 In particular, the private realm has long functioned as a site of gendered violence and it is recognised that state intervention into this realm is, in many contexts, warranted.

37 While maintaining a distinction between privacy and sexual autonomy is both practically and analytically useful, it should be recognised that the latter can be encompassed within the former. Indeed, in the US context and between 1965 and 1977, the Supreme Court, as Richard Posner notes, 'created a constitutional right of sexual or reproductive autonomy which it called privacy' (Posner, 1992, p. 324).

explored in depth in Chapter 5. For present purposes, it is far from clear that convicted defendants, if deceptive, were actively so. That is, there is a distinct possibility that at least some convictions were sustained on the basis of non-disclosure of gender history alone both before and after the landmark case of *McNally*. Certainly, in *R v Wilson* conviction appears to have rested squarely on omission as Lord Bannatyne made clear, in his sentencing judgment, that 'deception lay in not disclosing ... biological sex'.[38] Accordingly, the argument that sexual autonomy ought to trump privacy can be seen as referring both to a present legal reality as well as a law reform objective even in relation to the 'mere' non-disclosure of information. In any event, it is argued that the right to sexual autonomy should not necessarily trump other rights,[39] though the focus here will be on the right to privacy protected under Article 8. Before proceeding to consider this right however, it is important to reiterate a point made earlier, namely, sexual autonomy is not a right enjoyed only by cisgender complainants. Decisions made by transgender people about which biographical details to disclose to sexual partners, and the timing of those disclosures, cannot easily be separated from a right to sexual autonomy. In particular, it cannot be said that control over personal information concerning administration of cross-sex hormones, the undertaking of surgeries, and earlier coerced gender performances are divorced from this right.

A legal requirement to disclose gender history, one that appears to operate *de facto* if not *de jure*, requires disclosure of highly personal and private information. Yet, as Thomas Nagel notes, 'the boundary between what we reveal and what we do not, and some control over the boundary, are among the most important attributes of our humanity' (Nagel, 1998, p 4). In developing his argument, one he grounds in 'cultural liberalism' (Nagel, 1998, p 23), Nagel favours 'respecting individual autonomy through social conventions, rather than legal rules' (Nagel, 1998, p 5) and insists that 'reticence and limits on disclosure and acknowledgment are part of every type of human relation, *including the most intimate*' (Nagel, 1998, p 5, my emphasis. See also Fried, 1984, p 290; Bok, 1998, p 13).

Accordingly, a legal requirement to disclose gender history might be viewed as constituting a breach of Article 8. According to Article 8, 'everyone has the right to respect for his private and family life, his home and his correspondence'. The content of the phrase 'private and family life' has been interpreted widely.[40] In *R*

38 *Wilson* 7/3/15 above note 27. A copy of Lord Bannatyne's sentencing judgment is on file with the author.

39 These include the right to human dignity which emphasises the 'intrinsic worth' of persons and the 'respect and concern' that should be afforded them (Article 1, EU Charter of Fundamental Rights; Article 1, Universal Declaration of Human Rights).

40 See, for example, *X and Y v the Netherlands* [1985] 8 EHRR 235, para 22; *Mikulic v Croatia* [2002] 1 FCR 720, para 53; *Pretty v UK* [2002] 35 EHRR 1, para 66; *R (Wood) v Commissioner of Police of the Metropolis* [2009] EWCA Civ 414. In more philosophical terms there are two conceptions of privacy: spatial and informational (Laurie, 2002, p. 6). Spatial privacy captures the idea of sovereignty over the physical and psychological self. Informational privacy refers to the control of personal information about oneself. It is this latter notion of privacy with which we are concerned for

*(Wood) v Commissioner of Police of the Metropolis*, Laws LJ suggested that the core value protected by the right is 'the personal autonomy of every individual'.[41] The 'physical and psychological integrity'[42] and the 'physical and social identity'[43] of individuals have also been noted to fall squarely within the protection of the right, as has 'the personal and psychological space within which each individual develops his or her own sense of self and relationships with other people'.[44] In particular, and for present purposes, Laws LJ highlighted that an individual's personal autonomy should make him 'master of all those facts about his own identity'.[45] In a similar vein, and in an earlier House of Lords decision, Lord Hoffmann noted that 'the law now focuses upon the protection of human autonomy and dignity' and that this includes 'the right to control the dissemination of information about one's private life'.[46] A legal requirement to disclose gender history might therefore be viewed as contravening Article 8(1). Certainly, in the context of non-disclosure of gender history prior to sexual intercourse, the Law Commission have taken the view that to see this as sexual fraud would be incompatible with the state's Article 8 obligations (Law Commission, 2000, para 5.32).[47]

However, there are limits to the right to privacy. Thus Laws LJ noted three qualifications. First, if Article 8 is to be engaged, 'the alleged threat or assault to the individual's personal autonomy must ... attain "a certain level of seriousness."'[48] It can hardly be suggested that compulsory disclosure of highly personal information pertaining to gender history lacks seriousness. Second, enjoyment of the Article 8 right assumes that on the facts the claimant has 'a reasonable expectation of privacy'.[49] Again it seems clear that transgender and other gender non-conforming people have a reasonable expectation of privacy regarding their gender history. The central issue that arises here however, is whether the interest of the

the purposes of this chapter. However, while they can be analysed separately, privacy jurisprudence has tended to develop in such a way as to encapsulate both.

41 *R (Wood)* above note 40 at para 20.

42 *Pretty v UK* above note 40 at para 50 per Von Hannover J; para 66 per Marper J.

43 *Ibid* para 66 per Marper J.

44 *R (on the application of Countryside Alliance) v Attorney-General* [2007] UKHL 52 at para 116. See also Buxton, 2009.

45 *R (Wood)* above note 40 at para 21.

46 *Campbell v MGN Ltd* [2004] 2 AC 457 at para 51.

47 It should be acknowledged that the Law Commission confined its comments to those transgender people who, unlike the defendants in the cases under consideration, have undertaken gender reassignment surgery (para 5.33). However, the Gender Recognition Act 2004 provides for legal recognition of gender identity irrespective of surgical intervention. Accordingly, for the purposes of English law, gender status is not contingent on surgery. This being so, gender claims cannot be viewed as false or fraudulent on the basis of the defendant's surgical status. The same point holds in relation to possession of a Gender Recognition Certificate. This legal document does not effect any kind of change in a person's gender identity. Rather, it simply gives legal effect to pre-existing gender identity.

48 *R (Wood)* above note 40 at para 22.

49 *Ibid.*

state and/or the other sexual party in knowing historical facts concerning gender outweighs a transgender or other gender non-conforming person's right to privacy. It is precisely this concern to balance interests that Laws LJ posits as his third qualification.[50] Specifically, Article 8(2) provides states with an escape clause if they can show that breach of the right to privacy is justified on the basis of 'national security, public safety or the economic well-being of the country, for the prevention of disorder or crime, for the protection of health or morals, or for the protection of the rights and freedoms of others'.

If the state is to rely on Article 8(2) as justification for criminal prosecution for gender identity fraud, it is 'the protection of the rights and freedoms of others' that would be the most appropriate part of Article 8(2) to assert in order to establish proportionality. In relation to the rights of others, the court in *Goodwin v UK* made clear that a fair balance has 'to be struck between the general interest of the community and the interests of the individual'.[51] It is contended that to conclude that the interests of others, the community and/or the state outweigh the interests of transgender or other gender non-conforming people in this context would, in order to be convincing, require a demonstration that sexual intimacy with transgender or other gender non-conforming people is, in some significant sense, harmful. In other words, it is precisely an assumption of harm that would create the right Article 8(2) is designed to protect. Moreover, without the possibility of consequential harm it is difficult to see how a right to know the gender history of a sexual partner could arise or, at least, be legitimately defended. An argument that, even without harm, encroachment on the right to sexual autonomy is sufficient to justify prosecution is one we will consider in Chapter 4, where it will be rejected. At least in the context of gender identity fraud, it ought to be 'harms' rather than 'wrongs' that govern judicial development of legal doctrine. In Chapter 4, the issue and concept of harm will be considered in depth and it will be argued that if gender identity fraud causes harm significant enough to register in legal and moral terms, this harm must be balanced against those harms associated with disclosing gender history. It will be argued that this balancing exercise typically favours privacy.

### *(ii) Privacy and proportionality*

Irrespective of determining where an appropriate balance lies between the right to privacy and the right to sexual autonomy, it might be argued that the prosecutorial decision to prosecute young gender non-conforming people for sexual offences based on non-disclosure of information, or indeed active deception, clashes with Article 8 for another reason. It might be argued that the very serious charge of assault by penetration,[52] a charge brought in nearly all of the gender identity fraud

50 *Ibid.*
51 *Goodwin v UK* (2002) 35 EHRR 18 para 72.
52 s. 2 Sexual Offences Act 2003.

cases, was unnecessary and disproportionate to the public interest aim of punishing sex offenders. Certainly, in the sexual offence case of *R v G*,[53] Lords Hope and Carswell held that the decision to charge G, a 15-year-old boy, with the rape of a child under 13, to be disproportionate and contrary to Article 8(2) in circumstances where he had pleaded guilty 'on the basis that the girl had willingly agreed to have sexual intercourse, and had told him that she was 15' (Malkani, 2011, p 946). While G was ultimately unsuccessful with his appeal, the important points to note here are that the majority of their Lordships found prosecutorial policy and decision-making to fall within the scope of Article 8, and four Law Lords were evenly divided on the question of whether the decision to prosecute G for rape of a child under 13 was, in the circumstances, lawful and justifiable under Article 8(2).[54]

The reason why Lords Hope and Carswell found the prosecution to be disproportionate was because they took the view that a charge under s. 5 was unnecessary and a disproportionate interference with G's rights given the availability and appropriateness of the less serious charge of s. 13.[55] Their view appears to have been founded on considerations of stigma associated with a rape conviction and the available life sentence.[56] For their part, Lord Mance and Baroness Hale concluded that prosecution under s. 5 'was proportionate to the legitimate aim of protecting vulnerable underage girls' (Malkani, 2011, p 949). In 2011, the European Court of Human Rights ruled G's application to Strasbourg inadmissible.[57] The court, while recognising that prosecutorial decision-making may potentially violate Article 8, 'noted that Member states enjoy a wide margin of appreciation in matters concerning the prevention of rape' (Malkani, 2011, p 955).

Nevertheless, the argument might retain force in relation to gender identity fraud prosecutions, especially given that in these cases we are dealing with adult sexual offences. As Malkani notes, 'it is arguable that art. 8 is applicable when the decision is made to prosecute a particularly vulnerable person, or when the decision is made to prosecute a person for a crime that has a certain degree of stigma attached to it' (Malkani, 2011, p 955). Of course, concern over stigma cannot be pushed too far. Stigma is an appropriate consequence of conviction for serious sexual offences. However, in the context of cases where intimacy is desire-led, between adults, non-coercive, and especially where defendants are gender non-conforming people, factors of vulnerability and stigma ought to assume weight in prosecutorial decision-making and its consideration in light of Article 8. Such defendants are members of highly vulnerable and marginalised groups within society (Whittle et al, 2007; Morton, 2008). Moreover, when, for example, a transgender man is convicted of a serious sexual offence on the basis of gender

53 *R v G* [2008] UKHL 37.

54 Lord Hoffmann considered Article 8 to be inapplicable to prosecutorial policy and decided the case on this ground.

55 *R v G* above note 53 at para 39. s. 13 pertains to child sex offences committed by children or young persons and has a maximum penalty of five years.

56 *Ibid*, at para 17.

57 *G v United Kingdom* (37334/08) [2011] ECHR 1308.

identity fraud, stigmatisation is not confined to offence commission, but rather takes an ontological form. If prosecution and conviction are appropriate (an argument this book rejects), it should at least relate to lesser sexual offences, and preferably non-sexual offences. This returns us to the issue of fair labelling which we considered earlier in this chapter in the section on criminal law overreach.

### *(iii) Privacy and legal certainty*

Article 8 is also potentially engaged due to lack of legal certainty over the scope of illegality in the gender identity fraud context. One function of the criminal law, one consistent with the rule of law, is to warn people that if they behave in a manner which it prohibits they are liable to prosecution and punishment. If interference with Article 8 rights is to be lawful, it must occur pursuant to laws or rules that are accessible and are formulated in such a way and with sufficient precision that an individual is able 'to foresee, to a degree that is reasonable in the circumstances, the consequences which a given action may entail'.[58] As Lord Hope has noted, '[a] law which confers a discretion is not in itself inconsistent with this requirement, provided the scope of the discretion and the manner of its exercise are indicated with sufficient clarity to give the individual protection against interference which is arbitrary.'[59]

In the context of gender identity fraud prosecutions, it can be argued that the legal requirements of accessibility and foreseeability are not met because the judicial distinction between non-disclosure of information and active deception proves porous in the context of gender non-conforming defendants, and because current CPS guidance on transgender suspects is insufficiently clear regarding the factors individual prosecutors should take into account in making decisions and how these factors are to be weighed.[60] In this section of the chapter, I will focus on the latter issue. The former will be considered in depth in Chapter 5. In *R (Purdy) v DPP*, the House of Lords made clear that the DPP must identify facts and circumstances which are to be taken into account when making decisions in assisted suicide cases, and in such a way that a person considering providing assistance is able to foresee, to a degree that is reasonable and adequate in the circumstances, the consequences of doing so.[61]

58 *Sunday Times v United Kingdom* (1979) 2 EHRR 245 at para 49.

59 *R (Purdy) v DPP* [2010] 1 AC 345 at para 41. See also *Goodwin* above note 51 at para 31; *Hasan and Chaush v Bulgaria* (2000) 34 EHRR 1339 at para 84.

60 It should be noted that, in certain respects, the CPS was not assisted by the Court of Appeal's decision in *McNally* (above note 19) in formulating guidelines. This is because, while noting that 'deception as to gender can vitiate consent', the court made clear that this 'depend[ed] on the circumstances', yet failed to provide any elaboration regarding the kinds of circumstances that might vitiate consent as a matter of law (para 27).

61 *R v Purdy* above note 59, at para 55.

In relation to gender identity fraud prosecutions, current CPS guidance[62] is insufficiently clear and accessible for several reasons. First, and despite being a response to *McNally*, the guidance fails to articulate the Court of Appeal's distinction between non-disclosure of information (non-criminal) and active deception (criminal). In this respect, transgender people may feel they are required to disclose information concerning their gender history prior to intimacy with sexual partners. While the law, at least ostensibly,[63] does not require disclosure, this failing may nevertheless contribute to feelings of vulnerability and unsafety, and might be considered a form of institutionalised 'outing'. Second, the guidance fails to weigh the various factors to be considered. Third, the evidential factor concerning what steps a transgender person has taken 'to live as his/her chosen identity', is highly discretionary and gives no indication of the sorts of steps the CPS has in mind, or their relative importance.

Fourth, the public interest factor directing attention to 'whether the offending occurred as a result of the suspect's uncertainty or ambivalence about his/her gender identity', is problematic for at least two reasons. It is unclear what *uncertainty* or *ambivalence* are thought to indicate, and there is perhaps a real danger that evidence of either will be taken to establish 'doubt' about gender identity rather than the fact of personal struggle in the face of a disbelieving society. Further, the guidelines fail to demonstrate any appreciation of the fact that such states are typical, rather than exceptional, for young transgender people negotiating their way in a ciscentric society. Fifth, the guidance fails to state that if a person is transgender this should be dispositive of the public interest question given that the mens rea cannot be satisfied. Finally, and relatedly, the guidance states that prosecutors 'will need to know the suspect's position in relation to the Gender Recognition Act'. This creates significant uncertainty. It implies that a person lacking a Gender Recognition Certificate, perhaps because they are not yet in a position to apply for one, is more, rather than less, likely to be prosecuted. It is far from clear why this should follow and it can only serve as a source of anxiety for sexually active transgender people who, for whatever reason,[64] have not had their gender identities legally recognised. So far, we have considered a series of arguments based on the right to privacy protected by Article 8. In the following section, we turn our attention to consider another right that might be viewed as

62 Above note 31.

63 The idea that legal doctrine, as developed by the courts, insulates *omission* from sexual fraud prosecution will be challenged in Chapter 5, where it will be argued that convictions for gender identity fraud have proved possible irrespective of this act/omission dyad.

64 Reasons why a transgender person may not have a Gender Recognition Certificate include the following: they are too young to apply; they have not, as yet, satisfied the medico-legal conditions which, for example, include a period living in 'gender role'; they refuse to submit to pathologisation, which remains an integral part of the process; or, for whatever reason, do not feel it necessary to have their gender identity receive the endorsement of the state. None of these things indicate gender inauthenticity.

having been violated by gender identity fraud prosecutions, one that be located under Article 3.

### *(iv) Beyond privacy: a right to corporeal integrity*

This section of the chapter recognises the limits of liberal privacy and, following Thomas (1992), suggests that we might also invoke a right to bodily integrity in the face of state violations. In terms of legal provisions, this might mean pursuing an action under Article 3 of the European Convention on Human Rights.[65] Let us begin with the analysis provided by Thomas. In the context of the infamous US Supreme Court decision in *Bowers v Hardwick*,[66] he highlights the limits of relying on a right to privacy which conceives of the subject as a moral self. In the case at hand, this led to legal argument over whether Michael Hardwick had the right to engage in sodomy. The privacy argument failed both because the Supreme Court rejected the existence of any such right, but also because it entailed undue analysis of the morality or otherwise of Hardwick's private life. Instead, Thomas argues for recognition of a right to corporeal integrity as a kind of a priori right (Thomas, 1992, p 1435). While he does so within a Foucauldian frame of analysis, such a right might also be recognised in Hobbesian terms. After all, the state's first obligation must be to protect its citizens (Hobbes, 2008).

In the context of *Bowers*, Thomas stresses how the public/private distinction collapses in the face of the actions of institutional state actors (Thomas, 1992, p 1435). Thus, Bowers' arrest was preceded by police violence and harassment in the public domain as well as in his home. More significantly, for our purposes, Thomas understood the State of Georgia sodomy statute as representing a theory of the state. As he put it, with reference to the plurality of such legislation in the US at the time, 'homosexual sodomy statutes express the official "theory" of homophobia' (Thomas, 1992, p 1485).[67] Moreover, and in developing his claim that the public/private distinction is overrun by such statutes, he argues 'that violence against gays and lesbians perpetrated by other citizens represents the

65 Article 3: Prohibition of Torture: 'No one shall be subjected to torture or inhuman or degrading treatment or punishment.' While Article 3 might be thought to be confined to torture and more extreme instances of inhuman and degrading treatment, it is clear that the Convention right has been interpreted more widely. Thus, in the context of deportations, it has been interpreted to cover a series of social and economic hardships and/or risks (*D v United Kingdom* (1997) 24 EHRR 423; *R (Adam, Limbuela and Tesema) v Home Secretary* [2005] UKHL 66), as well as the state's failure to protect children from parental abuse where the state through its agencies ought to have been aware of the abuse (*X, Y and Z v United Kingdom* (2001) 34 ECHR 97). Moreover, and of particular relevance to the right asserted here, Article 3 has been recognised to cover not only state persecution of citizens, but also the private acts of individuals (*Ahmed v Austria* (1997) 24 EHRR 278).

66 *Bowers v Hardwick* 478 US 186 (1986).

67 All US state sodomy laws, still on the statute books in 2003, were struck down by the Supreme Court in *Lawrence v Texas* 539 U.S. 558 (2003).

states' *constructive delegation* of governmental power to these citizens', adding that while homophobic violence typically occurs within private relations, it nevertheless has 'public origins [and public] consequences' (Thomas, 1992, p 1482). In other words, '[t]he apparently private character of homophobic violence should not blind us to the reality of the state power that enables and underwrites it' (Thomas, 1992, p 1482).

Turning to gender identity fraud prosecutions, let us press the analogy and approach. While sexual fraud prosecutions are not confined to gender non-conforming people, they increasingly bear the brunt of such prosecutions. Moreover, in terms of gender identity fraud, gender non-conforming people prove to be the almost exclusive object of legal concern,[68] an issue we explored above under the rubric of discrimination. Accordingly, gender identity fraud prosecutions might be conceptualised as giving expression to a transphobic theory of the state. Moreover, in addition to a fundamental denial of self-determination, of humanness, this state theory reproduces the notion that transgender and other gender non-conforming people are synonymous with deception, a discursive move that not only devalues us, but one which legitimises the well-documented and pervasive violence and discrimination transgender and other gender non-conforming people experience (Whittle et al, 2007; Morton, 2008). In invoking a right to corporeal integrity, as part of a politics of resistance, the aim is both to encourage consideration of the use of Article 3 as a law reform strategy, and to feed into wider public debates which tend to focus on transgender and other gender non-conforming people as moral selves rather than people whose bodies are subjected to state sanctioned violence. What needs to be grasped is that prosecution is both an act of legal violence and an act which begets violence.

## 3.6 Conclusion

This chapter presented four principled objections to prosecution for gender identity fraud. First, it was argued that prosecution constitutes significant criminal law overreach, especially given that we are dealing with desire-led intimacy between adults which lacks the feature of coercion. Second, the framing of sexual autonomy as a non-negotiable right was challenged. To frame it as such not only removes complainants from the realm of sexual agency. It also assumes the materiality of facts, which in the context of transgender and other gender non-conforming people are contested. In other words, it was emphasised how sexual autonomy arguments are implicated in questions of ontology, epistemology and power. Third, it was argued that legal determinations of fact materiality, and therefore the boundary between consent and non-consent, produce legal inconsistency and are potentially discriminatory under the Equality Act and Article 14 of the European Convention on Human Rights. Specifically, the chapter highlighted how gender identity, at least in the UK context, is the only group identity to have attracted

68 The case of *Devonald* provides a rare exception (*R v Devonald* [2008] EWCA Crim 527).

state attention, and that state interest in gender identity has been confined to the gender identities of gender non-conforming people.

Finally, it was argued that decisions to prosecute fail to consider, or weigh properly, other important rights and interests. In developing this argument, the chapter focused on the Article 8 right to privacy. This involved consideration of a series of arguments regarding violation. In particular, and in considering the clash between the right to sexual autonomy and the right to privacy, it was highlighted how harm operates, or ought to operate, as a key factor in any balancing act. The chapter then considered a right to corporeal integrity, one which serves to complicate thinking about the public/private distinction. While privacy rights should not be abandoned, we need to recognise the relationship between state prosecution and the creation of a world in which disclosing gender history is not experienced as a viable option. That is, and as a matter of both theory and strategy, we must focus on the way that the very allegation of gender identity fraud reflects and reproduces the 'unintelligibility', as well as precluding the liveability, of transgender and other gender non-conforming lives. In the following chapter we will consider four further objections to the prosecution of gender identity fraud.

Chapter 4

# Principled objections II

## 4.1 Introduction

This chapter will consider four further principled objections to the prosecution of gender identity fraud. First, and following on from the previous chapter, it will consider the concept of harm, and the need to set appropriate limits to the degree and kind of harm necessary to warrant criminalisation. To that end, it will be argued that calculations of harm fail to consider properly the position of transgender and other gender non-conforming defendants. In particular, it will be contended that disclosing gender history entails significant costs for transgender people. The chapter will also highlight how the kind of harm gender identity fraud complainants detail, has an ideological source, and it will think through the implications of criminalising conduct that only produces harm when understood and experienced through ideology, that is, through a retrospective and ideological reimagining of pleasure.

Second, it will be argued that deception, at least in the present context, is not a neutral category, but rather an effect of power, one which serves to constitute epistemological and ontological limits regarding sex/gender. In responding to this dilemma, it will be argued that claims of deception as to gender identity are false; were false at the time when criminal liability falls to be attributed; and/or, if true, that deception is not necessarily motivated by a desire to deceive. This section of the chapter will also address the fact that gender identity fraud cases have typically involved prosthetic penetration. This might be thought to render questions of gender identity superfluous and to provide clear evidence of deception. However, and in response, a series of counter-arguments will be offered.

Third, the chapter will argue that legal doctrine developed for the purposes of establishing, but also limiting, criminal liability for sexual fraud, namely a particular kind of act/omission distinction, lacks a principled basis. That is, the distinction articulated by the courts between non-disclosure of information and active deception will be shown to be unsupported by considerations of distribution of moral culpability, relative encroachment on sexual autonomy or degree of harm. Finally, it will be argued that prosecution undermines important public policy interests. This is an important theme, one that serves to emphasise that the sexual autonomy of complainants is not the only interest at stake in gender identity fraud prosecutions. Specifically, this section of the chapter will emphasise the liberal state's commitment to, and failure to realise in this particular context, its equality and diversity obligations, which include the amelioration of transphobia.

## 4.2. Calculating harm

The question of harm is important to consider for several reasons. It is important because where rights conflict, harm assumes, or at least ought to assume, importance in any resolution. Moreover, irrespective of identifying a conflicting right to assert against sexual autonomy, such as a right to privacy, there ought to be a demonstration of a link between encroachment on sexual autonomy and harm arising. After all, harm sets a threshold to criminalisation according to basic liberal principles, a position widely adopted by criminal law commentators. As Wertheimer contends, rights violations 'are largely, if not entirely, parasitic on [experiential harm]' (Wertheimer, 2003, p 100). As he argues, we regard acts 'as rights violations or violations of autonomy precisely because such acts typically give rise to experiential harm' (Wertheimer, 2003, p 100). It is also important to interrogate harm in the context of gender identity fraud because we are not dealing with physical harm. In saying this, I am not suggesting that harm should be restricted to physical harm. Clearly, harm can be psychological, as criminal courts have recognised.[1] Nevertheless, the characterisation of harm is important here, as is its source. As complainant testimony reveals, harm tends to be articulated in somewhat nebulous terms. Further, in the context of gender identity fraud scenarios, we should recognise that harm, if it is sufficient to meet a criminalisation threshold, is not confined to complainants. Accordingly, the wider criminalisation debate ought to balance harms, that is, consider their distribution within sexual scenarios involving transgender and other gender non-conforming people. These interrelated points will now be elaborated.

In my view, in order to conclude that gender identity fraud prosecutions are justified, it should be demonstrated, by those who favour prosecution, that potential or actual harm suffered by cisgender people is (a) significant and (b) outweighs the harm to transgender or other gender non-conforming people associated with disclosing gender history. Without the possibility of significant consequential harm it is difficult to see why an informational right to know gender history should operate as a trump card. According to the testimony of complainants in the cases that have come before the courts, harm suffered appears to consist in feelings of distress, disgust and/or revulsion. Thus in *R v McNally*,[2] and according to prosecuting counsel, the complainant felt 'physically sick'[3] upon discovery, while in the retrial of *R v Newland*,[4] the complainant claimed to feel 'filthy,

1 *R v Chan-Fook* [1994] 1 WLR 689; *R v Ireland* [1998] AC 147.
2 *R v McNally* [2013] EWCA 1051.
3 *Ibid*, para 10.
4 *R v Newland* 29/6/17 (Unrept, Manchester Crown Court, Judge Stockdale).

disgusting'.[5] A question arises here as to whether we are actually in the territory of harm, as opposed to 'mere offence' (Feinberg, 1985). If not, then a further objection to criminalisation has been identified.

The embodied and visceral response of complainants to 'discovery' of gender history, and the implicit claim that such a response communicates a harm suffered, requires attention. In the first place, it might be thought that if harm is precipitated by disgust, and disgust belongs to the realm of primordial and instinctual drives, then any harm arising lies outside or beyond complainant agency and responsibility. Yet, as William Miller notes, disgust is an emotion and what defines it as such is the fact that it is 'a feeling about something and in response to something not just a raw unattached feeling' (Miller, 1997, p 8). As Sarah Ahmed explains, emotions are cultural practices, not psychological states, they presuppose 'investments in social norms' (Ahmed, 2004, p 196). Disgust is a feeling grounded in the view that one's object of desire threatens to engulf and contaminate the self (Douglas, 1966). Thus, it might be argued that what complainants experience is 'belief-mediated distress' (Thomson, 1990, p 253), such as might be experienced as a result of hate speech or obscenity, and it ought therefore not to count in terms of establishing harm for the purposes of criminal law. This is, perhaps, especially so where the belief in question might be considered irrational. As Judith Thomson argues, 'irrational beliefs ought not to constrain a defendant's behaviour' (Thomson, 1990, pp 253–254). In describing disgust or distress, consequent upon discovery of a sexual partner's gender history, as 'irrational', emphasis is being placed on the homo/transphobic nature of complainant reactions. No doubt, a claim of irrationality is contestable given that such responses are expected, if not mandated, by cisnormative society. Nevertheless, I want to emphasise the ideological nature of beliefs about gender and sexuality, the fact that harms suffered are inextricably tied up with those beliefs, and the way in which law reproduces, rather than contests, those beliefs.

In any event, if we are in the territory of harm, and if harm minimisation is our goal, it remains necessary to balance such harms against harms associated with disclosing gender history. Disclosing gender history is not an act undertaken without risks. Coming out as transgender exposes a person to considerable and well-documented physical risks.[6] We need only think of the tragic case of Brandon Teena, so graphically illustrated in the film, *Boys Don't Cry*. This concern assumes particular significance in relation to transgender and other gender non-conforming youth and therefore in relation to all defendants prosecuted so far. Moreover, we should recognise that 'mere' disclosure to a sexual partner would not serve to

5 See S. Hattenstone, '"I was Pretending to be a Boy for a Variety of Reasons": The Strange Case of Gayle Newland', *The Guardian* 15/7/17 available at www.theguardian.com/uk-news/2017/jul/15/gayle-newland-retrial?CMP=share_btn_tw (last accessed: 15/7/17).

6 In the UK context, Whittle et al found that 'in every sphere of life' transgender people 'are subject to high levels of abuse and violence' (Whittle et al, 2007, p 23). See also Morton, 2008. In the US context, see GenderPAC, 1997; Waters et al, 2016.

insulate transgender people from criminal prosecution. This is because, in the event that a cisgender complainant denies disclosure, a transgender defendant is unlikely to be believed in a court of law. This is because of the cisnormative conceit that a cisgender person would not, at least not knowingly, become sexually intimate with a transgender person, that is, would not engage in 'deviant' sex. Accordingly, in order to avoid an encounter with criminal law, transgender defendants may need to disclose to a wider group of people surrounding the complainant, and therefore expose themselves to further dangers. This might be described as a kind of 'hostage' problem. In effect, what law incites is a form of institutionalised 'outing'.

In pursuing this theme of relative exposure to harm, and while the media and the criminal justice system routinely portray transgender people as unruly, predatory and dangerous, it is in fact our bodies, not those of cisgender people, that are most likely to be violently marked, often lethally so (Stotzer, 2009; TPOCC, 2015). In other words, social anxiety about the dangers transgender people are considered to pose appears to be directly and inversely related to their extreme vulnerability in a cisnormative society. These points are important ones to identify because, although they do not meet or refute a criminal case brought by the state, they serve to highlight the failure of the state to live out its equality and diversity commitments, as well as turning on its head, legal and media deployment of a victim/perpetrator dyad, one which foregrounds predatory defendants and vulnerable complainants. In addition to the not inconsiderable physical risks associated with disclosing gender history, we also need to recognise its psychological and emotional impact. For many transgender people, having to disclose their chromosomal status, present and/or past genital and/or gonadal condition as well as a history of coerced gender performance is a source of pain and trauma. Finally, it is worth reiterating that a balancing of harms requires recognition of the fact that complainant distress, disgust and revulsion are emotional responses conditioned by systemic transphobia and/or homophobia, and for this reason also should not be viewed as sufficient in meeting a threshold of harm justifying criminal intervention, and especially not to target vulnerable minority groups. In this respect, criminal prosecution implicates law in perpetuating intolerance and inequality, the very things, at least rhetorically, it seeks to counter.

However, in thinking of harm as an embodied reaction to 'inadvertent' communion with the 'homosexual', I want to extend the argument. The revulsion felt by complainants should not, or not necessarily, be understood in terms of horror produced by the presence/visibility of a transgender or genderqueer body. As Bornstein explains, 'the real awful truth [in 'discovery' scenarios] may reveal itself like this: "Wait. I'm still attracted to this person!"' (Bornstein, 2006, p 237). To the extent that Bornstein properly characterises such moments, complainant claims to feel sick 'can be seen not so much as a sign of revulsion as an admission of attraction, and the consequent upheaval of … gender identity and sexual orientation' (Bornstein, 2006, p 237), as an experience of 'terror over losing proper gender' (Butler, 1993, p 238). In such circumstances, characterisation of the experience as harmful is particularly problematic. That is, where a complainant acted on desire, derived pleasure from intimacy, and where desire, though disavowed, persisted beyond the moment of 'discovery', it seems misplaced to describe the experience as harmful. Legal attempts to characterise it as such not only perpetuate transphobia and/or homophobia, but mask agentic choice. This is both unfair to defendants and antithetical to progressive forms of feminism.

## 4.3 Deception: epistemology, ontology and power

In objecting to the criminalisation of gender identity fraud, attention now turns to the question of deception itself. In many respects, this concept and its legal construction go to the very heart of the criminal justice problem that I want to address. Indeed, more than that, deception, and the way law and society conceive of it, lies at the epicentre of most of the problems transgender people face on a daily basis. That is, transgender, despite its so-called 'tipping point' (Time Magazine, 2014), continues to be understood as a synonym for duplicity, subterfuge and dissimulation, and it is precisely this legal and cultural view which both guarantees future criminal prosecutions and precludes full social inclusion, that is, recognition of transgender and other gender non-conforming people as fully human (Butler, 1993, p 8). Accordingly, there is a great deal at stake in the way we choose to understand the term *deception*.

In approaching this question of deception and how its resolution takes shape in law, let us begin by reiterating what the prosecution are legally required to establish in relation to a defendant charged with gender identity fraud. First, they must prove deliberate deception in relation to a material fact. Second, they must show that the deliberate deception took an active form. Third, they must show that the defendant lacked a reasonable belief in consent. This section will deal with the first matter, proof of deliberate deception. The issue of whether deception is active or passive will be considered in section 4.4 of this chapter and in Chapter 5. In section 4.4, it will be argued that the distinction lacks a principled basis for attributing liability. In Chapter 5, it will be highlighted how the distinction proves unsustainable in its application to transgender and other gender non-conforming people. In Chapter 2, it was stressed that 'reasonableness' is a normative, not an objective concept. Accordingly, this produces the fundamental difficulty that the reasonableness of a transgender man's belief in consent will be constructed from a cisnormative perspective. From this perspective, and despite the actuality of consensual cis–trans unions, it is inconceivable that a cisgender woman would knowingly become intimate with a transgender man and therefore inconceivable that a transgender man could reasonably, or indeed honestly, believe in the presence of consent. It is worth noting here that, while the belief of a transgender person that desire-led intimacy was consensual is located outside or at the margins of reasonableness, the rather fantastical accounts offered, by at least some cisgender complainants, appear to meet the reasonableness standard with little judicial quandary.

However, and putting to one side for now contestable claims that a transgender person's belief in consent is unreasonable and that his/her behaviour should be characterised as active, successful prosecution still requires proof of deliberate deception as to a 'material' fact. It is this issue of whether there is deliberate deception as to a material fact that will comprise the main focus of this section. Three broad arguments as to why such a conclusion should be resisted will be offered. First, it will be argued there is no deception regarding gender identity because the gender identity claims transgender people make are authentic. Second, if there is deception, it will be argued that it relates to facts concerning gender history, not gender identity, and, more importantly, that such facts should not be considered legally material. Third, even in cases where a gap arises between gender presentation and actual gender identity, it will be argued that this does not necessarily mean that a gap existed at the time when legal liability falls to be attributed. As we will see, this issue, which obviously raises questions of mens rea, also points to gender fluidity, something which prosecutions seek to erase. Finally, if there is deception as to a material fact, it will be argued that we should not assume its purpose is to deceive. Let us turn then to these arguments.

### *(i) No deception as to gender identity*

The first argument recognises that gender identity fraud prosecutions proceed on the basis that the defendant has committed a fundamental deception concerning his/her gender identity. This claim is one which bolsters cisgender identities while simultaneously denying the gender identities of transgender defendants. In other words, such prosecutions, of necessity, draw us in to a kind of 'truth' or 'authenticity' game, one which implicates power relations. As Judith Butler states, '[h]aving or bearing "truth" and "reality" is an enormously powerful prerogative within the social world' (Butler, 2004, p 27). It is, as she notes, 'one way that power dissimulates as ontology' (Butler, 2004, p 27). In opposition to state sanctioned complainant interpretations of (trans)gender identity, it is argued that from a transgender perspective there is no deception because any assertion of male/female status, either through words or gender performance, is consistent with actual gender identity. In other words, no relevant gap exists between complainant belief concerning the defendant's gender identity and his/her actual gender identity.

In making this argument it is not intended to reproduce some essentialised notion of sex/gender. Rather, the argument takes a strategic form and can be understood in terms of what Spivak describes as 'strategic essentialism' (Spivak, 1990, p 51). This strategy 'empowers previously subordinated groups by providing them a means to self-define, as opposed to being defined by those who would oppress them' (Karaian, 2009, p 378) and is therefore of particular value to gender non-conforming people whose gender identities are so readily fictionalised by law and in broader cultural terms. As Judith Butler has observed, it can be both theoretically and politically necessary 'to invoke [a] category, and hence, provisionally to institute an identity' (Butler, 1993, p 222). Social constructionism does not remove a political imperative to 'mobilise the necessary error of identity' (Butler, 1993, p 229). Thus, and in the present context, the assertion of a male or female identity by those marked 'opposite' gender at birth may prove a legitimate as well as an effective defence strategy.

In developing this point it should be recognised that in cases like *R v Wilson* and *R v Lee (Mason)*, the defendant was clearly a transgender man. In each case, the defendant had identified as male from an early age and, for many years prior to contact with the complainants, had lived as a man.[7] Thus Kyran Lee never lied to the complainant about his gender identity. Rather, and as he put it, 'I was completely myself apart from the fact that she didn't know who I used to be'.[8] Indeed, Wilson had indicated an intention to undergo gender reassignment surgery,[9] and Lee (Mason) had changed his name legally and had undertaken chest surgery to remove or reduce his breast tissue prior to sentencing.[10] To conclude deception in such circumstances is only possible through defining 'man' so as to exclude transgender men. Accordingly, prosecution, conviction and sentence implicate the textual, as well as the actual, violence of law (Sarat and Kearns, 1995). For transgender people, the allegation of deception represents an ontological wound, something which ought to be chalked up for the purposes of calculating harm (see section 4.2 above). Once one starts from the premise that a transgender man is a man, a position which ought to be insisted on in ethical terms (see Chapter 6), it becomes obvious that a conclusion of deception as to gender identity is precluded.

The deception claim presupposes an interpretive act, one performed from a position of cisnormative privilege and power. Thus, the complainants, in the *Wilson* and *Lee (Mason)* cases, having assumed their objects of desire to be cisgender men (assuming they really did), subsequently withdrew this privilege. Both before and after 'discovery' they 'consider[ed] themselves to be the ultimate arbiters of which people are allowed to call themselves women or men' (Serano, 2007, p 166) and they sought, successfully, to write their cisnormative interpretational commitments into law. Accordingly, criminal prosecutions speak to a colonising desire, in the face of which we must emphasise that self-determination of gender identity is non-negotiable. As Judith Butler has reminded us recently, 'we are all

7 *R v Wilson* 7/3/13 (Unrept, Edinburgh High Court, Lord Bannatyne). For media reporting of the case, see J. Morgan, 'Man "Guilty" of Fraud for Not Telling Girlfriend he was Trans', *Gay Star News* 7/3/13 available at www.gaystarnews.com/article/man-'guilty'-fraud-not-telling-girlfriend-he-was-trans070313/ (last accessed: 3/2/17); *R v Lee (Mason)* [2015] Lincoln Crown Court, unrep. For media reporting of the case, see 'Woman Who Used Fake Penis to have Sex with a Woman Avoids Jail', *The Guardian* 15/12/15 available at www.theguardian.com/uk-news/2015/dec/15/woman-who-used-fake-penis-to-have-sex-with-a-woman-avoids-jail (last accessed: 3/2/17).

8 L. Feder, 'How an Online Love Affair Ended with a Trans Man Convicted of Sexual Assault', *BuzzFeed News* 14/10/16 available at www.buzzfeed.com/lesterfeder/how-an-online-love-affair-ended-with-a-trans-man-convicted-o?utm_term=.rnBwkO444#.wgArq5JJJ (last accessed: 3/2/17).

9 Morgan above note 7.

10 Feder above note 8.

ethically bound to recognise another person's declared or enacted sense of sex and/or gender'.[11]

In noting particular biographical details in the cases of *Wilson* and *Lee (Mason)*, it is not intended to suggest that 'authentic' gender identity bears a necessary relationship to surgery, legal name change or length of time in gender role. Rather, information of this kind simply provided cogent evidence of gender identity in these cases making convictions all the more disturbing. If we must play authenticity games, and this may be inescapable for the time being in view of the *McNally* decision, we should place the emphasis on the genuineness or sincerity of present gender identity as evidenced by gender practice or performance, as opposed to relying on biological criteria, psychological assessment or legal status. In other words, and as Talia Mae Bettcher argues, we ought to think of gender identity in existential rather than metaphysical terms (Bettcher, 2009, p 110). While many transgender people would consider themselves men/women in both existential and metaphysical terms, it is the former that ought to assume greater significance in relation to the question of deception. In the absence of some strong reason to disbelieve an assertion of gender identity, it is argued that self-declaration ought to prevail, though in saying this we should recognise self-declaration to be symptomatic of a sense of (dis)embodiment, psychic reality and experiential truth.

Accordingly, CPS guidelines regarding sexual offence prosecution in relation to transgender suspects are especially problematic.[12] This is because evidential and public interest considerations stipulated in the guidelines reproduce the idea that gender truth requires more, and perhaps a lot more, by way of authentification. Thus evidence to be considered includes 'what steps, if any, [a transgender suspect] has taken to live as his/her chosen identity' and 'what steps, if any, he/she has taken to acquire a new gender status'.[13] These factors indicate that a decision to prosecute is more likely in circumstances where a defendant has not taken steps, or is considered to have taken insufficient steps, to live as his/her 'chosen' gender identity. In these respects, the guidelines demonstrate profound ignorance of the difficulties faced by transitioning people, especially those lacking supportive communities and appropriate resources. The problem is particularly acute in relation to transgender youth who, due to their tender age, may feel unable to take the 'necessary' steps prior to becoming sexually active. The guidelines also identify as a public interest consideration, 'whether the offending occurred as a result of the suspect's *uncertainty or ambivalence* about his/her gender identity'.[14] Given that

11 C. Williams, 'Gender Performance: The TransAdvocate Interviews Judith Butler', *TransAdvocate*, 1/5/14 available at www.transadvocate.com/gender-performance-the-transadvocate-interviews-judith-butler_n_13652.htm (last accessed: 3/2/17).

12 Crown Prosecution Service Policy and Guidance on *Rape and Sexual Offences: Chapter 3: Consent*, available at www.cps.gov.uk/legal/p_to_r/rape_and_sexual_offences/consent/ (last accessed: 3/2/17).

13 *Ibid.*

14 *Ibid* (my emphasis).

certainty about gender identity can only be viewed as consistent with its assertion, the relevance of uncertainty or ambivalence can presumably only be of value in casting doubt upon it. This section has highlighted how there can be no deception as to gender identity in the case of transgender people and that an opposite conclusion is inseparable from relations of power, and the epistemologies and ontologies they produce. That is, a conclusion of deception as to gender identity, whether drawn by complainants, prosecutors, judges and/or juries, or indeed as expressed through CPS prosecutorial guidelines, is one premised, and problematically so, on a cisnormative understanding of sex/gender.

### *(ii) No deception as to a material fact*

This section assumes the reality of transgender people's gender identities, but recognises another objection that those who favour prosecution might raise. Thus, while conceding the authenticity of transgender people's gender identities, it might be argued that there has been deception as to other facts concerning gender including gender history, and that such facts, like gender identity, are material. The main difficulty with such an argument is that appears, if indirectly, to amount to a denial, or at least the problematising, of the very gender identities it nominally concedes. After all, it is hard to imagine how historical facts about gender might assume particular significance for a person whose inquiry begins from the premise that transgender men and transgender women are men and women.

In other words, an emphasis on historical facts about gender appears to operate as a second order challenge to gender identity claims. This observation is not only a philosophical one. Rather, it is borne out by complainant narratives in the gender identity fraud cases to have come before the courts. Thus no complainant accepted the gender identity of the defendant, preferring to locate a sense of betrayal and/or an experience of harm in non-disclosure of historical facts about gender. On the contrary, complainants insisted that the defendants were women, and it was precisely this insistence, at least in the case of transgender men like Chris Wilson and Kyran Lee (Mason), that led to distress regarding participation in 'lesbian' sex.

In any event, historical facts about gender ought not to be considered material as a matter of law, so that even if there were deliberate deception it would not bear any criminal law significance. In my view, a conclusion of deception should not be possible because the important fact, namely authentic gender identity, is already in the open and there ought not to be a right to know other personal facts about the body and/or its history. That is, other facts, such as facts pertaining to past (or indeed present) genital and/or gonadal condition, as well as to particular experiences of gender socialisation, should not be viewed as legally material. To view them as such is, of necessity, to imbue them with a weight they ought not to bear, at least not if we wish to take self-determination of gender identity seriously.

### *(iii) No deception at the time of legal liability*

In thinking about gender identity, we need to avoid arriving at a conclusion of deception on the basis of lack of gender constancy. This is an issue which frequently presents itself in actual cases and which has served to call into question the authenticity of defendant assertions of gender identity. Two broad points need to be made here. First, to challenge defendant assertions of gender identity on the basis of lack of constancy is to take gender identity too seriously in metaphysical terms. It is also to prop up the 'heterosexual matrix' which relies on the fantasy of an unwavering nexus between male/masculine, female/feminine and the heterosexual interrelationship of these terms (Butler, 1990, p 35). Second, fluidity and/or 'gender confusion'[15] should not, in any event, be read as deceptive or as inconsistent with assertions of gender identity. The reality is that fluidity and confusion are the staples of, particularly adolescent, gender and sexuality.[16] Moreover, in the case of transgender and other gender non-conforming people, lack of consistency both in articulation and performance of gender is hardly surprising given the conformity demanded by a ciscentric society.

In thinking about this issue of gender constancy there is another quite specific point to be made, one perhaps best illustrated through the case of *McNally*.[17] Justine McNally identified as male at the time of the alleged offences (six counts of assault by penetration).[18] However, at the time of plea and subsequent appeal she asserted a female gender identity, a fact which, in the eyes of both courts, served only to confirm deception, a view replicated by the tabloid and broadsheet media, which variously described McNally as 'posing'[19] as, being in

15 For example, the court in *McNally* (above note 2) referred to the defendant's 'confusion surrounding her gender identity' (para 47).

16 For example, a recent UK YouGov poll conducted in 2015, utilising the Kinsey scale for mapping sexuality, found that 49% of young people aged between 18–24 identified 'as not exclusively heterosexual' ('1 in 2 Young People Say They Are Not 100% Heterosexual', *YouGov*, 16/8/15 available at https://yougov.co.uk/news/2015/08/16/half-young-not-heterosexual/) (last accessed: 3/2/17). A more recent US YouGov poll found that 27% of 2,211 respondents did not identify as exclusively heterosexual, while for the 18–34 cohort, the figure was 33% ('21% of Americans Believe That Being Transgender is a Mental Illness', *YouGov US*, 9/2/17 available at https://today.yougov.com/news/2017/05/17/21-americans-believe-identifying-transgender-menta/) (last accessed: 20/5/17).

17 *McNally* above note 2.

18 s. 2 Sexual Offences Act 2003.

19 M. Robinson, 'Schoolgirl, 18, Pretended to be a Boy Called Scott for Three and a Half Years to get Another Teenage Girl, 16, into Bed and take Her Virginity', *Daily Mail Online*, 21/3/13 available at www.dailymail.co.uk/news/article-2296982/Justine-McNally-18-pretended-boy-girl-bed-virginity.html (last accessed: 3/2/17); A. Shaw, 'Schoolgirl Who Posed as Boy for More Than Three Years to have Sex with Teenage Girl Jailed for Three Years', *Daily Record and Sunday Mail*, 22/3/13 available at www.dailyrecord.co.uk/news/scottish-news/schoolgirl-who-posed-boy-sex-1778083 (last accessed: 3/2/17); H. Dixon, '18-Year-Old Woman Masqueraded as Boy to Get Girl into Bed', *The Telegraph*, 24/3/13 available at www.telegraph.co.uk/news/uknews/crime/9946687/18-year-old-woman-masqueraded-as-boy-to-get-girl-into-bed.html (last accessed: 3/2/17).

the 'disguise'[20] of and as 'masquerading as'[21] a boy. Yet, we should not draw a conclusion of deception too readily. After all, McNally had indicated an intention to undergo gender reassignment surgery[22] and medical evidence suggests that where a person insists on a gender identity contrary to their birth-designated gender after adolescence,[23] persistence rates are extremely high (Wren, 2000; Zucker, 2006; Zucker and Cohen-Kettenis, 2008; Steensma et al, 2011; Steensma et al, 2013). In other words, Justine's 'change of heart' might be explained in terms of media persecution and criminal prosecution of the 17-year-old, rather than in terms of the surfacing of 'truth'.[24]

Crucially, even if McNally's assertion of a female gender identity at the time of plea cannot be explained in terms of an understandable retreat into 'normality', we must insist that 'authenticity' remains compatible with the assertion of different gender identities at different times. That is, gender identity can be fluid for some people. It can change over time. Such an argument not only creates a space for the recognition of gender variance within law, as well as insulating gender non-conforming people from inappropriate and unnecessary criminal law intervention into their sexual lives. It also serves to enable the queering of law from within. To the extent that contradictions arise, this presents less of a problem for queer than it does for liberal law because their respective self-images bear different relationships to economies of order, predictability, determinacy and consistency. If the idea of gender fluidity can be given a legal life, the 'logic' of heteronormativity and cisnormativity can be challenged. Crucially, in the case of Justine McNally, there was evidence to suggest that she believed herself to be a man at the time of the alleged offences and therefore at the moment criminal liability crystallises. This issue, which was given insufficient judicial attention both at the time of plea and appeal, will be taken up in Chapters 5 and 7.

20 *Daily Mail Online* above note 19; *The Telegraph* above note 19.
21 *The Telegraph* above note 19.
22 *McNally* above note 2 at para 10.
23 It should be noted that Steensma et al found that 84% of gender variant children under the age of 12 subsequently desisted in their (trans)gender identification (2011). This study, one often relied on in debates over gender variance in children and the necessity of psychiatric/medical intervention, has been criticised both in terms of its methodology and because actual outcomes were often unknown (H. Webberley, 'Let's Call an End to the 84% Myth' Gendergp 17/11/16 available at https://gendergp.co.uk/lets-call-an-end-to-the-84-myth/?utm_content=buffer18348&utm_medium=social&utm_source=twitter.com&utm_campaign=buffer (last accessed: 3/2/17)). In other words, the persistence rate for gender variant children under 12 may be higher than the Steensma et al study suggests. Indeed, the most recent medical evidence suggests the figure to be much much higher. According to the medical records kept at the Melbourne Royal Children's Hospital for the period 2003–2017, '96 per cent of patients treated for gender dysphoria ... continue to identify as transgender into late adolescence' (*Re: Kelvin* [2017] FamCAFA 258 per affidavit of Dr Telfer, para 160). In any event, in relation to those over 12, and therefore McNally, there is considerable medical consensus in relation to persistence.
24 It is worth noting that even in *R v Newland* 15/9/15 (Unrept, Chester Crown Court, Judge Dutton), the case most explicitly involving a lesbian defendant, transgender themes emerge (see Chapter 2, fn 71).

For present purposes, we need only recognise that deception has a temporality. That is, a statement about gender identity or its performance might be true in a specific time period, without necessarily being true throughout the course of a person's life.

### *(iv) No motivation to deceive*

In addition to the three previous arguments, each of which serves to problematise a claim of deliberate deception, at least in relation to a material fact, we should recognise that deception is not necessarily meant to deceive. Of course, it is appreciated that identifying defendant motive in the cases under discussion might be viewed as somewhat speculative. It is, of course, also true that law is concerned with intention rather than motivation, that is, a person might intend to commit a crime, albeit her motives are good ones.[25] Nevertheless, motivation is considered important to broader questions of criminalisation, social justice and ethics. Thus, if one were to conclude that a transgender man had, prior to sexual intimacy, deceived a cisgender woman regarding his gender identity or gender history (a conclusion that would have to overcome my earlier objections), it should not necessarily be concluded that he did so in order to bed her, a conclusion that tends to be readily made by courts of law. An important counter-narrative to this tendency, one that we ought to take seriously, is that non-disclosure and/or active forms of deception arise in the context of a desire for self-preservation. As Talia Mae Bettcher notes, '[i]n a world that constructs us as either deceivers or pretenders to begin with – invariably denying our authenticity and preventing our existence, surely "gender deception" must be seen as one laudable tactic of attempted survival in what appears to be an exceptionally violent, no-win situation' (Bettcher, 2007, p 60). The point being emphasised here is one made earlier in relation to the calculation of harm, namely, disclosure of gender history can have significant costs for transgender people. Moreover, while law expects transgender and other gender non-conforming people to be forthcoming, it pays little attention to structural and cultural inequalities that constrain transparency, nor to violent consequences associated with revelation.

There is one final issue to be considered under the rubric of deception. A central feature of many of the gender identity fraud cases to come before the courts is prosthetic penetration of the complainant. In relation to oral and/or digital penetration, or indeed penile penetration made possible by phalloplastic surgery, had that been relevant in any of the cases,[26] apparent consent ought to be considered valid, at least in circumstances where gender presentation is consistent with gender identity. To conclude otherwise is only possible through denying gender identity claims, something already considered and rejected. However, in cases

25 For example, a doctor who kills a terminally ill patient in order to relieve suffering (good/benign motive) nevertheless commits murder as she possesses the necessary mental element (an intention to kill) *R v Windle* [1952] 2 QB 826.

26 None of the defendants in the gender identity fraud cases under consideration had undergone phalloplastic surgery prior to the alleged offences.

where a prosthesis is used without the complainant's knowledge (and notwithstanding that this scenario might be considered implausible), it might be argued that there is 'active deception' which does not hinge on the gender identity of the defendant, and that this presents a challenge I have, so far, not met.

In responding to this feature of most of the gender identity fraud cases, I make the following two points, both of which serve to reinforce the centrality of gender identity to the adequacy of any analysis. First, while use of a prosthetic device without complainant knowledge might be viewed as constituting deliberate deception, it must be emphasised that in no case did the complainant seek to ground a claim of deception (or for that matter a claim of non-consent or harm) in the physicality of the sexual encounter. Rather, and consistently, complainants claimed to be distressed, disgusted and/or humiliated because of a kind of gender failure that had befallen them. In other words, after the moment of 'discovery', they claimed to be no longer able to view their object of desire as a man. Thus, the problem here, as understood by the complainants, had little, if anything, to do with the use of a prosthesis. This inanimate object did not motivate prosecution. Rather, complainant motivation is to be understood in ideological terms, that is, as constituted through an interpretative act that conceives of sex/gender only through the prism of cisnormativity, and to that end retrospectively reimagines pleasurable sexual acts. Thus, while a claim of deception might stack up in doctrinal terms, prosecutions remain inextricably tied to the defendant's gender identity. Indeed, had the defendants been cisgender, complaints are perhaps unlikely to have been brought. In other words, it is not doctrinal failure that is being emphasised, but selective enforcement of the law.

Turning to my second point, one which refuses to concede that a finding of deception is a necessary consequence of established legal doctrine, it is important to stress that a prosthetic device is, for at least some transgender men, experienced as an extension of embodied self, as a cock, no different phenomenologically from the fleshy kind (Hale, 2003; Davy, 2011, Chapter 3; Latham, 2016, pp 355–356). As Hale explains, 'inanimate objects – dildoes – sometimes take on some of the phenomenological characteristics of erogenous body parts' (Hale, 2003, p 66). Accordingly, the relationship between its use and a finding of deception is not as straightforward as it might appear. While law proves incapable of re-imagining the male member beyond flesh, other than as monstrous (Sharpe, 2010), the demands of social inclusion and equality require that law's bodily aesthetics be challenged. Certainly, an apparent connection between law's bodily aesthetics and a conclusion of deception provides yet another reason for caution in relation to the criminalisation of gender identity fraud.

## 4.4 Act-omission: a flawed distinction

The objection to prosecuting gender identity fraud to be explored in this section, relates to the way that current legal rules for setting the parameters of criminal liability lack a principled basis. As already noted, since the Court of Appeal's decision in *McNally*, liability for sexual fraud arises only in circumstances where the prosecution can demonstrate active deception as opposed to 'mere' non-disclosure of material information. The act/omission distinction is one long subject to criticism within criminal law jurisprudence (Ashworth, 1989; Elliot and Ormerod, 2008; Herring, 2015, Chapter 2) and more generally (Finnis, 1993; Heyman, 1994; Keown, 1997; Ridolfi, 2000). In this section however, criticism will focus on the particular variant of it articulated by the courts in the context of establishing criminal liability for sexual fraud. In thinking about the merits of the judicial distinction between active deception and non-disclosure there are a number of potential justifications for the criminalisation of the former, but not the latter. This section will focus on three possible justifications for a judicial focus on active deception. These are that active deception (i) involves greater moral culpability, (ii) entails a greater violation of complainant sexual autonomy, and/or (iii) causes more harm than non-disclosure of material information.[27]

To the contrary, it will be argued that lying or actively misleading do not necessarily entail all, or indeed any, of these things or at least not in the ways that might be imagined. To illustrate the difficulty, we will work with four hypothetical scenarios where one of the sexual parties is HIV positive and where the other would not have consented to sexual intercourse if aware of this fact. Until recently, apparent consent to sex with a person infected with the HIV virus operated as valid consent for the purposes of adult sexual offences, irrespective of the judicial distinction.[28] In view of recent cases however, prosecution is now perhaps likely to be viewed as appropriate in circumstances of active deception concerning HIV positive status. The selection of HIV, as the example to work with, is informed by this fact and also by the fact that it is generally considered to be a particularly serious transgression in normative terms (Bryden, 2000, pp 470–471). This can be contrasted with examples of fraud that have generally been given short shrift by the courts in terms of their analysis of consent and harm.[29]

27 There are other possible justifications for the distinction. These include the argument that criminalising active deception does not offend against the principle of liberty, or at least not to the same degree as criminalising omission, and the argument that, unlike active deception, non-disclosure of information lacks a causal relationship to harm. For a detailed discussion, and refutation, of these arguments see Sharpe, 2016, pp 32–33. In relation to the liberty principle see also Ashworth, 1989; Williams, 1991; Herring 2015. In relation to causality see Fletcher, 1978; Hart, 1985; Moore, 1993; Moore, 2009; Mellor, 1995; Herring, 2015.

28 However, non-disclosure of HIV positive status will ground a successful prosecution for non-fatal assault in circumstances where the virus is transmitted: *R v Dica* [2004] EWCA Crim 1103; *R v Konzani* [2005] EWCA Crim 706. For a critique of criminalisation of HIV transmission generally see Weait, 2007.

29 Thus courts have insisted that many deceptions do not vitiate consent because they do not relate to facts considered legally material. Examples of non-material facts include wealth or social status. This judicial position was articulated most recently by Leveson LJ in *McNally* above note 2 at para 25.

***Hypothetical scenarios (A–D)***

(A). D, aware V would not have consented to sex had D disclosed his HIV+ status, had sex with V

(B). D, aware V would not have consented to sex had D disclosed his HIV+ status, lied when asked and then had sex with V.

(C). D, aware V would not have consented to sex had D disclosed his HIV+ status, had sex with V. Sexual intercourse was unprotected and D was not on ART (anti-retroviral treatment).

(D). D, aware V would not have consented to sex had D disclosed his HIV+ status, lied when asked and then had sex with V. D was on ART, had a very low viral load, and used a condom.

*(i) Moral culpability of the defendant*

It has been noted that the act/omission distinction is 'deeply rooted in the common law' (Fleming, 1992, p 146; see also Glazebrook, 1960), and that over time the courts have tended to restrict the criminalisation of omission (Norrie, 2001, p 120). In doing so, they have been quite explicit in 'espousing moral differences between acts and omissions' (Elliot and Ormerod, 2008, p 53).[30] Indeed, they have perhaps persisted with the distinction 'precisely because of [their] belief that the distinction reflects an important moral distinction' (Elliot and Ormerod, 2008, p 53). However, while the courts place emphasis on the moral importance of the distinction, this appears to be more a matter of judicial 'common sense', than the product of rigorous analysis. The failure of the courts to articulate a clear rationale does not, of course, mean one is lacking. Accordingly, in thinking about the moral culpability of defendants, we should recognise the claim that there are morally significant differences between acting and omitting to act.

Stephen Wilkinson has argued that there are moral distinctions between lying, actively misleading and non-disclosure (Wilkinson, 2000). He contends that 'lying is worse than other ways of not telling the truth' because 'lying does more damage to relationships of trust' (Wilkinson, 2000, p 7). This may or may not be true. It is an empirical question as Wilkinson recognises. An emphasis on trust however, proves problematic for a number of other reasons. In the first place, Wilkinson develops his claim in the medical context of the doctor–patient relationship where the element of trust is especially recognised. A focus on trust in the criminal law context may be less appropriate because of the different and non-professional nature of the relationship and because of the implications for liberty that necessarily attend the criminal law. In *McNally*, the Court of Appeal refused to characterise the defendant's 'active deception' as a breach of trust, precisely because the relationship between defendant and complainant lacked this professional quality.[31]

30 See, for example, *R v Lowe* [1973] 1 QB 702.

31 In this regard, the court distanced itself from the view of the trial judge, and this factor proved significant in sentence reduction. The court also noted that s. 21 of the Sexual

Alan Wertheimer suggests that, while the question of criminal liability for sexual fraud must be resolved 'by moral argument as to what the parties who engage in sexual relations owe to each other by way of intentional falsehood and disclosure of information' (Wertheimer, 1996, p 105), it would 'probably be a mistake to apply a strong fiduciary model to sexual relations among competent adults' (Wertheimer, 1996, p 109). However, application of such a model to sexual relations has its supporters. Thus Herring contends that 'sexual partners owe to each other heightened standards of obligation of a fiduciary nature' (Herring, 2005, p 515). Of course, Herring would insist on a heightened standard irrespective of whether a defendant acts deceptively or fails to disclose material information. Importantly, even if we were to concede that a fiduciary model of sexual relations is an appropriate one for establishing criminal liability, any assumption that the active deception/non-disclosure distinction expresses, or indeed is even consistent with, the underlying rationale of that model is dubious. That is to say, it is difficult to conclude that lying, more than non-disclosure of material information, necessarily constitutes a more serious breach of trust. This claim can be demonstrated through considering the hypothetical scenarios involving HIV.

Thus application of the distinction would lead to convictions in scenarios B and D, but not A and C. Yet, such outcomes contradict any claim that the distinction satisfactorily distributes defendants in terms of moral culpability. In all four scenarios, the defendant was unwilling to disclose his HIV positive status and was aware that the victim would not have consented had she been aware of his HIV positive status. In this regard, the scenarios are not distinguished by an intent/recklessness divide. That is, none of the scenarios involve *only* risk-taking. Two differences between scenarios B and D, and scenarios A and C, are that in scenarios B and D the victim is proactive in asking about the defendant's HIV status and the defendant lies. However, in relation to the culpability question, only lying is relevant. Of course, lying is a more active form of deception than non-disclosure. But this does not, of itself, demonstrate greater culpability. Indeed, while the defendant in scenario B may be more morally culpable than the defendant in scenario A, it is certainly not the case that active deception in scenario D is more morally culpable than non-disclosure in scenario C. This is because, in scenario D, lying needs to be considered in relation to other features of the scenario.

The specific features that ought to be valued here are that the defendant is (i) on anti-retroviral drugs and has a low viral load and (ii) used a condom. While the

Offences Act, while not directly applicable, 'defines "position of trust" for the purposes of ss. 16–19 of the Act as covering relationships such as teacher and pupil or doctor and patient' (*McNally* above note 2 at paras 49–51). In the more recent case of Gayle Newland above note 24, His Honour Judge Dutton made clear in his sentencing remarks (12/11/15) that what he considered to be 'a callous breach of trust' on the part of the defendant did not involve 'the kind of trust relationship' (p 3) covered by sentencing guidelines, a conclusion rendered inevitable in view of the Court of Appeal's remarks in *McNally* (paras 49–50). Document provided by Nigel Power QC, defence and appellant counsel for Newland, 7 Harrington Chambers, Liverpool.

defendant's actions might be viewed as unethical,[32] they do demonstrate a quite different relation to risk, harm and care, one that might be viewed as lessening culpability. Certainly, in scenario C, the defendant exposes the victim to a significant risk of serious harm, whereas in scenario D, though the defendant lies, the risk of harm to which the victim is exposed is minimal.[33] Moreover, while the defendant in scenario C is highly likely to be aware of a risk of serious harm to the victim, the defendant in scenario D is likely to be aware of the exceptionally low risk of transmission of the virus. It is true in scenario D, that while lying might not be motivated by a desire to have sex,[34] the defendant is aware of the absence of consent. However, this is true in all four scenarios. What is problematic, is the fact that the defendant who took responsibility for his own sexual health, practised safe sex, and who accordingly exhibited some degree of care and concern toward the 'victim', is more likely to be convicted of a sexual offence under the judicial distinction under consideration. This appears to be intuitively wrong. Reasoning by analogy in this way suggests that the assumption that active deception necessarily involves a greater breach of trust than non-disclosure of information is misplaced, at least in some plausible cases. As Ashworth has reminded us, 'the act-omission distinction should not be used as a cloak for avoiding the moral issues' (Ashworth, 2009, p 100).[35]

### *(ii) Violation of the victim's sexual autonomy*

In Chapter 3, we considered the claim that criminal prosecution for gender identity fraud finds its justification in encroachment on the right to sexual autonomy. While recognising sexual autonomy to be an important right, I rejected this claim and detailed my reasons for doing so. Here however, I am concerned to address the question of whether it can be said that the manner of encroachment matters in terms of the degree to which the right to sexual autonomy is violated. In essence, the question becomes: if we assume violation of sexual autonomy in cases of deception, can it be said that the violation is any greater in cases of active deception than it is in cases of non-disclosure of material information? While there are scholars who would support/oppose prosecution in either case, the point here is to express

32 A person's actions should not necessarily be viewed as unethical here. Rather, questions of ethics need to be considered in the context of associated harms and an analysis of power. In Chapter 6, we will return to such questions in the context of transgender/cisgender sexually intimate relations.

33 ART (antiretroviral treatment) reduces the HIV viral load in blood, semen and vaginal and rectal fluids to very low levels reducing the risk of HIV transmission. A study by Cohen et al, found the risk to be reduced by 96% (Cohen et al, 2011) and follow up studies have confirmed very low infection rates (see, for example, Baeten, 2012).

34 Lying may be motivated by many factors. For transgender people, a desire not to disclose gender history might be read as an act of self-preservation rather than as a strategy to effect sexual intimacy.

35 See also Elliot and Ormerod, 2008; Tadros, 2005, Chapter 7.

scepticism concerning any claim that the right to sexual autonomy can justify the judicial distinction.

Turning to the hypothetical HIV scenarios, it is clear, assuming the victim has a right to know about the defendant's HIV positive status,[36] that consent is lacking in all four scenarios. This is so because the victim would not have had sex with the defendant in any of the scenarios had she known the truth. However, in order to make the case that active deception is more problematic than non-disclosure it would be necessary to conclude that the *source* of our ignorance or error matters. Yet, as Claudia Mills points out: '[a]ll that really seems to matter, for evaluating the autonomy of my choice, is what I know or do not know, not how I came by my state of knowledge or ignorance' (Mills, 1999, p 5).

### *(iii) Harmful consequences*

If lying cannot be described as more culpable than non-disclosure of information, or at least not sufficiently so to justify a different criminal law response, and if sexual autonomy is about informed consent rather than how information is acquired, it might still be argued that active deception produces greater harm than non-disclosure and that this justifies differential treatment. However, a number of difficulties arise here. Putting to one side debate over whether fraud in sexual contexts produces harm sufficient to justify resort to the criminal law (an issue we considered in section 4.2 in the context of gender identity fraud), we are still left with the problem of explaining how active deception involves a surfeit of harm. In my view, while sexual fraud might lead to harm (psychological or emotional)[37] and does entail harm in the sense of a set-back to a rights-based interest (Archard, 1998, p 97) or public good (sexual autonomy) (Gardner, 2007, p 31), it is hardly convincing to suggest that harm is magnified in the case of lying, as opposed to non-disclosure of facts that bear such psychological/emotional significance.

Thus, if we consider our hypothetical scenarios involving HIV status, it is hardly plausible to argue that the active deception in scenarios B and D led the victim to experience a greater degree of psychological or emotional harm than non-disclosure in scenarios A and C. In all four scenarios, assuming that the victim learns of the defendant's HIV positive status subsequent to sexual intimacy, there is either anxiety about the possibility of HIV transmission or there is not. Indeed, in terms of possible psychological harm, non-disclosure might actually be more harmful than active deception. While this might seem counter-intuitive, we should recognise that in the case of non-disclosure, the victim who proceeds with sex draws a false

36 It is not clear that HIV positive people should necessarily bear a moral obligation to disclose. This is especially so where the risk of transmission is exceptionally low.

37 Hyman Gross has challenged the idea that sexual fraud produces harm sufficient to justify invocation of the criminal law, and has accused those who argue for expansion of the sexual fraud category of 'legal moralism' (Gross, 2007, pp 225–227). Jonathan Herring has insisted that sexual fraud may and does produce 'serious harms' (Herring, 2007, p 228).

conclusion regarding the HIV status of the other party. Accordingly, she might feel more responsible for her role in the sexually intimate encounter than had she been the recipient of a lie.

Another example that illustrates the difficulty of the active deception/non-disclosure distinction, at least if harm is the benchmark of its intelligibility, is one that compares HIV scenario C[38] with the case of *R v Devonald*.[39] In this case, a middle-aged man was convicted under s. 4 of the Sexual Offences Act on the basis that he had caused a young man to masturbate in front of a webcam as revenge for what he believed to be the man's mistreatment of his daughter. Yet, the potential for harm evident in HIV scenario C, a scenario which according to the logic of the active deception/non-disclosure distinction would not lead to a criminal conviction, appears to be out of all proportion to the 'harm' occasioned in the active deception case of *Devonald*.

## 4.5 A public policy objection

The aim here is to highlight a tension between prosecution and the liberal state's commitment to its equality and diversity obligations to transgender people and, in particular, to the amelioration of transphobia.[40] This tension also serves to redirect our attention to the fact that complainant sexual autonomy is only one, though a very important, interest in gender identity fraud prosecutions. In order to clarify my argument and to tease out the legally and socially embedded nature of cissexism and transphobia, I will compare two scenarios leading to a sexual offence allegation, one involving a mixed-race defendant, the other, a transgender man.

Let us begin with race because once we shift our attention from facts concerning gender identity to facts concerning racial/ethnic identity, our concern for sexual autonomy tends to wane.[41]

> A white woman and a man of mixed-race, who outwardly appears white, meet in a wine bar. They flirt with each other. The woman invites the man back to her apartment where mutually satisfying sexual intercourse takes place. Subsequently, the woman discovers the mixed-race background of the man and claims to feel violated. She reports the matter to the police and requests that he be charged with a sexual offence on the basis of his failure to disclose his racial/ethnic background.

38 *R v EB* [2006] EWCA Crim 2945.
39 *R v Devonald* [2008] EWCA Crim 527.
40 I refer here, in particular, to the state's obligations under ss. 7 and 149 of the Equality Act and Article 14 of the European Convention on Human Rights.
41 It is recognised that successful prosecutions for sexual fraud on the basis of ethnicity/nationality have been brought in Israel. However, such cases are to be understood in the specific context of the Israeli State and Jewish/Arab relations (Gross, 2000, Gross, 2015).

There are some criminal law scholars (Herring, 2005; Herring, 2007; Herring and Madden-Dempsey, 2007; Madden-Dempsey, 2010) and feminist activists (Estrich, 1986; Chamallas, 1988; MacKinnon, 1989)[42] who would consider a rape charge an appropriate, or at least legitimate, outcome on these facts, and especially in circumstances where the defendant was aware of the complainant's racist feelings.[43] In my view, such a conclusion is not only counter-intuitive, but disturbing, if not bordering on the absurd. To the best of my knowledge, such a charge has never been brought in the UK. In theory, it might be successfully prosecuted if the defendant was asked about his racial/ethnic background and 'lied'. However, putting to one side the arbitrariness of race as a category (Anderson, 1997; Blunt, 2001; Polaszek, 2010),[44] and the insuperable mens rea difficulties to which racial/ethnic identity gives rise (for example, the defendant might identify as white despite his mixed-race parentage),[45] as well as the fact that legal doctrine, with its emphasis on 'active deception', makes conviction impossible on these facts, it seems politically inconceivable that such a prosecution would be brought, and if it was, it would almost certainly fail to pass muster with a jury.

A difficulty here is that prosecution would involve a right to sexual autonomy, even in circumstances of desire-led intimacy and mutual pleasure, trumping a public policy concern to counter racism. In other words, law would be implicated in privileging non-consent even where its apparent absence has its basis in racism. In short, if we were to take consent this seriously, it appears we must take prejudice seriously in equal measure. A consent argument here is a weak one and not worthy of defending when measured against the public policy interest in countering racism. Now consider a different scenario:

42 This is not a monolithic view, cutting across all strands of feminism, but it is certainly one that has traction, especially within 'carceral' or 'governance' feminism. For a critique of this feminist approach see Brown, 1995; Halley et al, 2006; Bernstein, 2007, 2012; Gruber, 2009.

43 In relation to the view that sexual preferences based on race are racist, see Stember, 1978. An Australian study found people with sexual preferences based on race correlated strongly with general racist attitudes (Callander, et al, 2015).

44 The view that racial categories are socially constructed and lack a biological basis (Appiah and Gutmann, 1998) has been reinforced by the advent of, and advances made in, the study of DNA (Marks, 1995).

45 Indeed, a person might identify culturally with a particular ethnic group without having any genealogical connection to it, either because of adoption or due to some other affinity. Thus a person might identify with a group's social, political and historical struggle and become acculturated into the group. This appears to be how Rachel Dolezal explains her identification as black, albeit her claim has provoked both controversy and scepticism, especially within African-American communities (A. Yuhas, 'Rachel Dolezal Defiantly Maintains "I Identify as Black" in TV Interview' *The Guardian* 16/6/15 available at www.theguardian.com/us-news/2015/jun/16/rachel-dolezal-today-show-interview (last accessed: 3/2/17)). Moreover, census studies suggest that a significant number of people change their racial classification over time (Liebler et al, 2014a; Liebler et al, 2014b).

> A cisgender woman and a transgender man meet in a wine bar. They flirt with each other. The man returns with the woman to her apartment where mutually satisfying sexual intercourse takes place. Subsequently, the woman discovers the man is transgender and claims to feel violated. She reports the matter to the police and requests that he be charged with a sexual offence on the basis of his failure to disclose his gender history.

While I imagine my comments concerning the mixed-race example proved uncontroversial to most, if not all readers, I know from experience that the second scenario is likely to lead to a more complicated and variegated set of emotional responses. The comparison is designed to tease out such different responses and encourage reflection upon them. What I want to suggest is that an appropriate response to this scenario ought to be informed by the preceding analysis concerning race. It might be objected that equating transphobia with racism in this context only works if minding about gender history is as transphobic as minding about race is racist. This is precisely my argument. The fact that it provokes resistance reveals not the falseness of the argument but society's failure to take transphobia as seriously as it does racism in this particular sexual context.

## 4.6 Conclusion

This chapter built on Chapter 3 by offering four further objections to prosecution of gender identity fraud. First, it argued that we need to think carefully in terms of an appropriate analysis of harm. Specifically, it argued, that in determining whether a case gives rise to harm sufficient to justify the intervention of criminal law, we should consider the source of complainant harm, and we should ensure that calculations of harm consider properly the position of transgender and other gender non-conforming defendants. That is, we should recognise that complainant harm is an ideological affair, not rooted in the pleasures of the flesh or in real time, but rather the effect of a retrospective and cisnormative reconstruction of both events and the defendant's gender identity. And in thinking about harm in sexually intimate scenarios we should ensure our analysis reflects the significant costs for transgender people associated with disclosing gender history.

Second, it was argued that deception, at least in relation to gender identity, is not a neutral category but rather an effect of power, one which serves to constitute epistemological and ontological limits regarding sex/gender. In responding to this dilemma, and while recognising that deceptions are not necessarily intended to deceive, the chapter argued that there can be no deception where gender presentation accords with gender identity, that other facts about gender, historical or otherwise, should not be considered legally material, and that a later rearticulation of gender identity by a defendant does not establish deception because an earlier articulation may be genuine and it is at the time of offence commission that legal liability falls to be determined. In considering these issues the chapter sought not only to contest legal constructions of gender identity. It also emphasised that it can be mobile or fluid, features which law seeks to erase.

Third, it was argued that legal doctrine developed for the purposes of establishing criminal liability for sexual fraud, namely a particular kind of act/omission distinction, lacks a principled basis. Finally, it was argued that prosecution undermines important public policy interests concerning the realisation of equality and the amelioration of transphobia. In the following chapter, we will turn our attention away from questions of principle toward some socio-legal realities of prosecuting, especially young, gender non-conforming people. In other words, we will move from consideration of abstract jurisprudential questions to more urgent ones of defendant vulnerability, and to possibilities for obtaining justice for transgender and other gender non-conforming people within the criminal justice system.

Part III

# Practices

Chapter 5

# From principle to practice

## 5.1 Introduction

In Chapters 3 and 4 we considered a series of principled objections to prosecutions for gender identity fraud. This chapter will build on an anti-prosecution case. It will do so through moving beyond legal principle in order to critique legal practice. In doing so, it will identify three legal issues, each of which invokes a form/substance problem. In other words, the chapter will focus less on questions of legal principle, and more on moments of law's application as well as the tensions to which the form/substance dichotomy gives rise. The three issues to be considered are (i) the decision to prosecute, (ii) the question of plea and (iii) the application of substantive law. In considering these important matters, we move from abstract jurisprudential questions to more urgent ones of defendant vulnerability, and to possibilities for obtaining justice for transgender and other gender non-conforming defendants within the criminal justice system. While each of these three issues raises some distinct problems, we will see that application of the law in each case is informed by cisnormativity and therefore implicates relations of power.

The chapter will begin, chronologically, with the decision to prosecute. Decisions to prosecute made by the Crown Prosecution Service (CPS) will be challenged because they fail to accord with prosecution guidelines, especially those pertaining to consideration of the credibility of complainant evidence. In exploring these issues, the chapter will first consider CPS interpretation of prosecution guidelines and the apparent ease with which the credibility question is satisfied in gender identity fraud cases. It will then consider the more complicated issue of how prosecution findings of complainant credibility on the consent question are not only implausible, but also presuppose an understanding of ignorance and knowledge as two mutually exclusive cognitive domains. In opposition to this view, the chapter will consider the possibility that ignorance, far from being part of some 'originary dark' (Sedgwick, 1988, p. 104), is a laboured affair, the product of cultural and psychological forces that raise questions concerning the boundary between consent and non-consent.

Second, the chapter will consider the issue of plea. All but one (Newland) of those convicted of sexual offences on the basis of gender identity fraud pleaded guilty. While this might be viewed as undermining an anti-prosecution stance, the chapter will highlight how this pattern of pleading might be understood in the context of structural and cultural inequalities that attend the legal regulation of intimacy between cisgender and transgender or other gender non-conforming people. This issue is also important because few criminal cases are appealed and because success is much more likely at trial than on appeal.[1] Crucially, the guilty plea requires attention because of the social and psychological forces that produce it, namely transphobia, homophobia and cis-sexism (Serano, 2007), which are both pervasive and often internalised by defendants. A guilty plea can, as we will see, also be linked to poor legal representation and deficits in legal representation may, at least in part, be connected to cisnormative readings of the facts. Finally, guilty pleas require examination because they represent moments where power produces effects beyond findings of liability and attendant questions of disposal. In transgender contexts, a guilty plea requires not only confession to a crime, but the adoption of a position of complicity in relation to one's own ontological undoing. Moreover, each plea and finding of guilt contributes to a dominant cultural narrative, one that equates transgender with artifice and deception.

Third, the chapter returns to a dyad considered in the previous chapter, namely the distinction between non-disclosure of information and active deception. The previous chapter highlighted how this particular act/omission distinction lacks a principled basis for determining liability. Here we shift our focus to emphasise how the distinction actually unravels in its application, at least in the context of prosecution of transgender and other gender non-conforming people for gender identity fraud. In other words, in these contexts, the distinction proves to be insufficiently clear-cut to avoid analytical collapse and therefore criminal law overreach. Consideration of this issue will entail a particular focus on the Court of Appeal's decision in *R v McNally*,[2] a case where the distinction has received its clearest expression and enjoys its highest authority. It is then to these three moments of legal practice that we now turn.

## 5.2 The decision to prosecute

This section of the chapter will do two things. First, it will challenge CPS decisions to prosecute in gender identity fraud cases, and second, and relatedly, it will adopt a position of scepticism in relation to complainant evidence upon which those decisions are based. In relation to CPS decision-making, it will argue that decisions to prosecute conflict with prosecutorial guidelines. In relation to complainant claims of ignorance of defendant gender history, it will problematise the distinction between ignorance and knowledge upon which prosecutions rely. Thus we will begin by placing CPS interpretation of prosecutorial guidelines under the microscope.

1 In bringing a criminal appeal it is generally necessary to appeal on a point of law. There can no retrial of the facts (Hungerford-Welch, 2014). However, there is limited scope for the Court of Appeal to hear new evidence (s. 23(1)(c) Criminal Appeal Act 1968).
2 *R v McNally* [2013] EWCA Crim 1051.

We will then proceed to tease out the complexities of the relationship between complainant ignorance and knowledge, complexities which prosecutions belie.

### *(i) Interpreting prosecution guidelines*

Before detailing CPS guidelines which, at least ostensibly, condition prosecution, we should recognise that gender identity fraud prosecutions, as well as the media hysteria they always appear to generate, presuppose a collective 'suspension of disbelief' regarding complainant accounts of the facts. Indeed, the most surprising and counter-intuitive aspect of these cases lies not in legal conclusions as to where consent ends and deception begins, important though these questions are, but precisely in this abeyance of doubt, in the fact that prosecutors accept so readily and unproblematically, stories so fantastic in their improbability.

The phrase, 'suspension of disbelief', was first coined by the poet and aesthetic philosopher, Samuel Taylor Coleridge. It was used to suggest that if a writer could inject a 'human interest and a semblance of truth' (Coleridge, 1907, Chapter XIV, p. 6) into a fantastic tale, the reader would suspend judgment concerning the implausibility of the story. The 'semblance of truth' in the gender identity fraud cases lies in complainant claims of ignorance regarding the gender history of defendants. After all, no matter how otherwise implausible an account may be, young heterosexual cisgender women do not, apparently, willingly choose to become sexually intimate with transgender or other gender non-conforming people. In other words, while cisgender/transgender relationships are empirical realities, and while there are clearly some 'girls who like their boys to [be] genetic girls' (Halberstam, 1994, p. 220), we pretend otherwise. It is perhaps, this suspension of disbelief, and the resolution of cognitive dissonance which suspension effects, that helps explain decisions to prosecute, which might otherwise be viewed to be in conflict with prosecution guidelines which set 'evidential' limits to the bringing of prosecutions.

According to the Code for Prosecutors, the CPS are only supposed to initiate prosecution in circumstances where they are 'satisfied that there is sufficient evidence to provide a realistic prospect of conviction'.[3] To conclude that this test is met requires a conclusion that 'an objective, impartial and reasonable jury … or judge … properly directed and acting in accordance with law, is more likely than not to convict the defendant of the charge alleged'.[4] More specifically, prosecutors are directed to 'consider whether there are any reasons to question the reliability of the evidence, including its accuracy or integrity' and 'whether there are any reasons to doubt the credibility of the evidence'.[5] Further, the Code states that a case that does not meet these tests 'must not proceed, no matter how *serious* or *sensitive* it may be'.[6]

3 Crown Prosecution Service, *Code for Prosecutors* at para 4.4 available at www.cps.gov.uk/publications/code_for_crown_prosecutors/codetest.html (last accessed: 3/2/17).
4 *Ibid*, para 4.5.
5 *Ibid*, para 4.6.
6 *Ibid*, para 4.4 (my emphasis).

It appears difficult to square at least some, if not all, prosecutions for gender identity fraud with these prosecutorial rules. It may be that concerns over *seriousness* and *sensitivity*, especially in relation to sexual offences, are, at least in some cases, serving to override the need to be satisfied in evidential terms that a realistic prospect of conviction exists. This may be connected to the post-Savile environment in which we live, and in which prosecutorial decisions are now made, and relatedly, to a tendency to understand gender non-conforming defendants in terms of deviance and predation. However, a disjunction between prosecutorial rules and their application is almost certainly also an effect of cisnormative interpretations of the facts, whereby transgender and other gender non-conforming people's accounts are rendered unintelligible.

In thinking about questions of complainant 'credibility', let us recall some of the evidence put forward in three of the cases. In the *Gayle Newland* case,[7] the complainant, who claimed to believe Newland was a man, admitted having sex with Newland on a least ten occasions and spending over 100 hours in her company, sometimes at the complainant's apartment, sometimes at a local hotel.[8] She was apparently unaware of the truth about Newland's lesbian identity due to a blindfold worn on all occasions at Newland's request, claims Newland disputed.[9] Her other senses, apparently, also deserted her. Thus her sense of touch proved insensitive to the contours and smooth surface of Newland's body,[10] which had not been masculinised through testosterone administration, to Newland's long hair which reached the mid of her back, and to the prosthetic penis which Newland used, while her sense of hearing proved impervious to Newland's voice which falls within the female range.[11]

7 *R v Newland* 15/9/15 (Unrept, Chester Crown Court, Judge Dutton). For media reporting of the case, see 'Woman Who Pretended to be Man to Trick Friend into Sex Jailed for Eight Years', *The Guardian* 12/11/15 available at www.theguardian.com/uk-news/2015/nov/12/gayle-newland-sentenced-eight-years-prison-duping-friend-having-sex (last accessed: 3/2/17). Newland's conviction was set aside after the Court of Appeal found it to be 'unsafe' due to the summing up of the trial judge. However, she was convicted for a second time at the retrial (*R v Newland* 29/6/17 (Unrept, Manchester Crown Court, Judge Stockdale)). For discussion of the retrial, see S. Hattenstone, '"I was Pretending to be a Boy for a Variety of Reasons": The Strange Case of Gayle Newland', *The Guardian* 15/7/17 available at www.theguardian.com/uk-news/2017/jul/15/gayle-newland-retrial?CMP=share_btn_tw (last accessed: 15/7/17).

8 Summing Up of His Honour Judge Dutton, 14/15 September 2015 at Chester Crown Court, p. 12. Document provided by Nigel Power QC, defence and appellant counsel for Newland, 7 Harrington Street Chambers, Liverpool.

9 *Ibid*, p. 72.

10 *Ibid*, p. 58.

11 The complainant sought to explain this sensory deficit, as well as Newland's lack of body hair by emphasising that Newland, through her online male persona, Kye Fortune, had represented herself as a half-Filipino, half-Asian man (p 36) and, somewhat more bizarrely, claimed that Newland had explained Fortune's higher pitched voice as the effect of strangulation as a child at the hands of his mother (p 63). The defendant

Moreover, the complainant became 'best friends' with Newland, as Gayle, while simultaneously conducting a boyfriend/girlfriend relationship with Newland, in the guise of Kye Fortune, Newland's Facebook avatar.[12] While there was dispute concerning how the complainant first met Newland as Gayle (the complainant claiming that it was due to an online introduction from Kye Fortune,[13] Newland claiming that it occurred earlier at a nightclub where the complainant worked and where Newland had disclosed her lesbian status and online male profile to the complainant),[14] what is not disputed is the incredible fact that the complainant, according to her own evidence, continued to see both her 'best friend', Gayle (Newland), and her boyfriend, Kye Fortune (Newland), on a regular basis and for a period of at least 18 months without ever appreciating they were the same person. Moreover, and according to Newland, her first meeting with the complainant as Gayle took place on the nightclub's 'gender bender night'.[15] This evidence might be viewed as consistent with Newland's claim that the complainant knew about her sexuality from the time of their first face-to-face meeting. The complainant's belief that Newland was Kye also appears to have survived the fact that so many of Gayle's biographical details were the same as Kye's (for example, her date of birth, musical and cinematic interests, and even the name of her dog, Gypsy).[16]

In the earlier case of *Gemma Barker*,[17] complainant evidence appears even more incredible. Thus one of the complainants, who knew Barker previously as Gemma, claimed not to realise that she had been sexually intimate with Barker even though she had dated Barker in different 'guises' and under different pseudonyms. Thus after the termination of a sexually intimate relationship with Luke Jones (Barker) the complainant became sexually intimate with Connor McCormack (Barker) and at all times claimed to remain ignorant of the fact that Barker, Jones and McCormack were all one and the same person.[18] In the most

did not seek to deny the use of Facebook or having created the online persona of Kye, but insisted that the complainant knew the truth from the outset and was a participant in fantasy role-playing (p 69). Thus, according to Newland, the complainant saw her as Kye Fortune in more intimate moments, but otherwise as Gayle (pp 69–70).

12 *Ibid*, pp. 4–5.

13 *Ibid*, p. 21.

14 *Ibid*, p. 69.

15 *Ibid*, p. 69.

16 *Ibid*, p. 71.

17 *R v Barker* 5/3/12 (Unrept, Guildford Crown Court, Judge Moss).

18 For media reporting of the case, see M. Blake, '"I Felt Repulsed and Dirty and Wanted to Kill Myself": Schoolgirl Victims of Teenage Girl Who Dressed as Boy to Date Them Speak of Their Anguish as She is Jailed', *The Daily Mail Online*, 6/3/13 available at www.dailymail.co.uk/news/article-2110430/Gemma-Barker-jailed-Vctims-girl-dressed-boy-date-speak-anguish.html (last accessed: 2/3/17); E. Stretch, 'My Boyfriend Was Really a Girl: Teenage Victim of Sex Con Woman Tells of Her Horror', *The Mirror*, 6/3/13 available at www.mirror.co.uk/news/real-life-stories/agony-of-teen-victims-of-gemma-barker-752654 (last accessed: 3/2/17); R. Sabey et al, 'Boy-Girl Groper Gemma Barker

recent case of Jason Staines,[19] the family of one of the complainants were adamant that the defendant was a woman, a claim which the complainant refused to countenance.[20] Of course, all of the complainants in these cases might have been 'very gullible and naive', as asserted by prosecuting counsel in the *Newland* case.[21]

But what you have to ask yourself is this: do these versions of the facts not provide 'reasons to doubt the credibility of the [complainant] evidence'? Can it really be said that 'an objective, impartial and reasonable jury … or judge [as opposed to one that is antipathetic toward those at the sexual and gender margins] … is more likely than not to convict the defendant of the charge alleged?' Thus, for example, in the *Newland* case, is it more likely, as Newland alleged, that a complaint was made in the service of lesbian denial ('from the very beginning she knew that Kye was a girl and that it was me. She wanted to be straight, always classified me as a girlfriend, and she had "Kye" as a boyfriend … I was happy to allow her to hide her sexuality')[22] and that the parties had engaged in gender/sexual role play[23] or that the complainant remained oblivious to obvious facts? The fact that Gayle Newland was convicted by two juries should not distract us from this important threshold question regarding the credibility of evidence. That is, her conviction does not establish that 'objectivity', 'impartiality' and/or 'reasonableness' pointed to the likelihood of conviction at the time the

Ruined My Life', *The Sun*, 7/3/13 available at www.thesun.co.uk/sol/homepage/news/4176927/Boy-girl-groper-ruined-my-life.html (last accessed: 3/2/17).

19 *R v Staines* 24/3/16 (Unrept, Bristol Crown Court, Judge Cotter).

20 L. Churchill, 'Woman Posed as Man to have Sex with Teenage Girls', *Bristol Post* 24/3/16 available at www.bristolpost.co.uk/exclusive-woman-posed-man-sex-teenage-girls/story-28979462-detail/story.html (last accessed: 3/2/17).

21 H. Pidd, 'Woman Who Claimed She Was Tricked into Sex with Friend Was Lesbian, Court Told', *The Guardian*, 9/9/15 available at www.theguardian.com/uk-news/2015/sep/09/woman-allegedly-tricked-into-sex-with-friend-pretending-to-be-man-lesbian-court-told (last accessed: 3/2/17). In relation to the prosecution claim of complainant naivety, which appears to have so resonated with judge and jury, the evidence at trial revealed that the complainant had lived by herself since 16, had paid her way through university (Summing Up of His Honour Judge Dutton above note 8 at p. 21) and had had 'eleven or twelve sexual experiences with other men', and 'had touched male penises of various kinds and sizes, texture and shape, with and without a condom' (p 50). In contrast, Newland asserted that she was a virgin prior to her involvement with the complainant (p 71, 81).

22 Summing Up of His Honour Judge Dutton above note 8 at pp. 69–70. This is also reminiscent of the claim made by the defendant in the much earlier case of *Jennifer Saunders* (Smith, 1995). Moreover, in *Saunders*, there was evidence suggesting that complaint was motivated by parental discovery of what might otherwise have been considered lesbian sex (Smith, 1995). This concern perhaps also surfaces in *McNally* (above note 2) as the court noted, in this case, that it was the complainant's mother who first confronted the defendant 'about really being a girl' (para 10) and who first made a complaint, albeit to the defendant's school (para 11). It was this complaint which initially triggered police involvement, rather than some act of the complainant.

23 *Ibid*, p. 4.

CPS weighed the evidence. To conclude otherwise is to put the cart before the proverbial horse.[24]

Ultimately, part of the problem with these prosecutions lies in the state's differential response to cisgender accounts, on the one hand, and to the accounts of transgender and other gender non-conforming people, on the other. That is, while accounts of those at the heteronormative centre provoke state and legal sympathy, the accounts of those at the gender margins produce only scepticism. This is not a new problem. Those at the margins have always encountered difficulty in translating their experiences into believable stories, into ones that resonate in courts of law. In some respects, this problem is analogous to the example of a false allegation by a white woman that she was raped by a black man, a problem particularly apparent in the US throughout much of the twentieth century (Lindquist Dorr, 2004). To the extent that a society, at any given historical moment, considers a consensual encounter of this kind to be inappropriate, wrong, and perhaps even scandalous for the woman concerned, the less likely that a false, or at least dubious, complaint will be filtered out and the more likely a conviction will be sustained. In other words, if we exchange the racism, which is so much a part of this particular and regrettable history, for the cissexism, transphobia and homophobia that are surely part of any adequate explanation of prosecutions for gender identity fraud, then we might begin to make some progress both in understanding and contesting the bringing of prosecutions.

In wondering why (especially heterosexual cisgender) complainant 'gullibility' and 'naviety' resonate so powerfully and consistently with prosecutors, and of course courts and juries, we might ask: is it simply an effect of evidence or is it connected to the legal and cultural conceit that cisgender people would never, other than inadvertently, become sexually intimate with transgender or other gender non-conforming people? The latter view, while increasingly out of step with the way, especially young people identify sexually,[25] appears central to understanding both prosecutions for gender identity fraud and their legal resolution. In relation to the *Newland* case, we might think of the blindfold as a metaphor for all of the gender

24 Indeed, Simon Hattenstone, a journalist writing for *The Guardian*, and other journalists who attended Newland's second trial (above note 7), expressed real doubts regarding Newland's guilt. As Hattenstone explained: 'At the end of each day, the reporters try to disentangle truth from fiction, and find it impossible. But we all agree that if we were on the jury, we would not convict; that there is not proof of guilt "beyond a reasonable doubt"' (above note 7).

25 One recent study found that 49% of young people aged between 18–24 identified 'as not exclusively heterosexual', '1 in 2 Young People Say They are Not 100% Heterosexual', *YouGov* 16/8/15 available at https://yougov.co.uk/news/2015/08/16/half-young-not-heterosexual/ (last accessed: 3/2/17). A more recent US YouGov poll found that 27% of 2,211 respondents did not identify as exclusively heterosexual, while for the 18–34 cohort, the figure was 33% ('21% of Americans Believe That Being Transgender is a Mental Illness', *YouGov US*, 9/2/17 available at https://today.yougov.com/news/2017/05/17/21-americans-believe-identifying-transgender-menta/) (last accessed: 20/5/17).

identity fraud cases. That is, the blindfold might stand for blind in(justice) meted out and perhaps, and as importantly, for disavowal of complainant sexual agency and desire. It is to this latter concern that attention now turns.

### *(ii) Ignorance and/as knowledge*

In challenging the credibility of complainant evidence, the focus so far has been to problematise CPS decision making under prosecutorial guidelines. In this section of the Chapter, I want to call into question complainant claims of ignorance and, more particularly, how we conceive of the relationship between ignorance and knowledge. This is not to suggest that any complainant lied about lacking knowledge of defendant gender history. This may or may not have been the case. Rather, it is to interrogate what we mean by complainant ignorance and how it takes shape.

The central problem can be illustrated by an example from fiction. In Neil Jordan's 1992 film, *The Crying Game*,[26] the character Dil, a transgender woman, inhabits and performs as a singer in the Metro, a queer bar in London. The character Fergus, for reasons that do not concern us here, frequents the bar and eventually gets to know Dil. He subsequently forms a relationship with her which becomes sexually intimate. Ultimately, in Dil's apartment, we arrive at the 'discovery scene' where she reveals her naked body to Fergus. Upon seeing Dil's penis, Fergus slaps Dil across the face, drawing blood, before retreating to her bathroom where he vomits violently into the sink. Importantly, and surprised by this turn of events, Dil says: 'I thought you knew. What were you doing in the bar if you didn't know?' This is a very good question, and it is the type of question which appears to escape prosecutors, judges and occasionally juries in gender identity fraud cases.

Eve Sedgwick has described this type of ignorance in terms of the 'privilege of unknowing' (Sedgwick, 1988; Sedgwick 1993). She is referring to a cultural and psychological process whereby privileged people learn not to see, to a kind of 'careful education' (Sedgwick, 1993, p. 24) which erases difference from view. That is, difference is in plain view, yet remains unrecognised by privileged onlookers. Accordingly, ignorance should not be placed beyond critique. Rather, we should ask after the erotics of its 'human production and distribution' (Sedgwick, 1993, p. 25), which include the 'psychological operations of shame, denial [and] projection' that surround it (Sedgwick, 1993, p. 25). Moreover, as she notes, knowledge does not exhaust power. Rather '[i]gnorance and opacity collude and compete with it' (Sedgwick, 1988, p. 102). '[T]hese ignorances, far from being pieces of the originary dark, are produced by and correspond to particular knowledges and circulate as part of particular regimes of truth' (Sedgwick, 1988, p. 104). Thus, in the film, Fergus remained oblivious to Dil's difference, and to difference in general, because he was not looking for it, not expecting to find it,

26 Channel 4 Films.

despite being surrounded by LGBTQI people at the Metro. In fact, he appears to have been the only, heterosexual cisgender man in the bar![27]

Thus in thinking through gender identity fraud cases we need to recognise issues of privilege and power, ones which structure what is seen, or otherwise sensed, that enable cisgender people to 'unknow' facts about gender difference. Moreover, this 'unknowing', should not be thought to exist only where there is interpersonal distance, something that is necessarily transformed through contact, especially bodily intimacy. Rather, as Sedgwick points out, the production of ignorance has an erotics, one which includes the 'psychological operations of shame, denial [and] projection' (Sedgwick, 1993, p. 25). Thus, if we accept that complainants genuinely believed their object of desire to be a man, a conclusion arrived at in the only case, so far, to go before a jury,[28] we should not conclude that complainant ignorance necessarily equates with non-consent. After all, ignorance is not a default position, it is not arrived at through passivity. It requires labour. Crucially, in a hetero and cisnormative society, in which a sexual encounter with a transgender or other gender non-conforming person can produce a crisis at the level of sexual identity, ignorance may serve to consolidate identity, to keep it in tact. That is, ignorance may operate so as to refuse or repudiate facts, including those that come through our bodies, and our lovers' bodies, wave after wave.

For example, in the *Newland* case, the complainant gave evidence that, due to the wearing of a blindfold, she was unable to see Newland during their sexual encounters, and therefore unable to recognise that Newland is a woman. Yet surely, if we do not see our lover's face, we sense them in other ways? Do we not breath them in, feel their touch, experience the contours of their body, feel their breath upon our skin, the timbre of their voice? And are we not undone in such moments, irrespective of the eyes? How can we claim not to have consented to lesbian sex when the presence of a female lover takes the form of sensory overload?

27 There are a number of differences that lie between this fictional scenario and the actual gender identity fraud cases with which we are concerned. These include the fact that Dil is a woman, whereas all of the defendants in the cases prosecuted presented as men. Interestingly, not a single prosecution has been brought against a transgender woman. While a full explanation of this social and legal reality requires further empirical investigation, it does not seem possible to uncouple from the documented reality of extra-legal violence routinely enacted on the bodies of transgender women. Thus, in the UK context, Whittle et al, found that 'in every sphere of life' transgender people 'are subject to high levels of abuse and violence' (Whittle et al, 2007). See also Morton, 2008. In the US context, see GenderPAC, 1997; Waters et al, 2016. The reaction of Fergus is a case in point. Men may also be reluctant to report an offence because of perceived implications for their masculinity that attend admission of sexual intimacy with transgender women. However, this public/private distinction collapses where the violence proves lethal leading to homicide charges. In such cases, and in order preserve stable heterosexual identities, defendants have typically relied on a defence of so-called homosexual 'advance' or 'panic'. For a critique of the defence see, for example, Comstock, 1992; Tomsen, 1998; Statham, 1999; Steinberg, 2005.

28 *Newland* above note 7. Gayle Newland was convicted by a second jury in 2017 (*R v Newland* 29/6/17 (Unrept, Manchester Crown Court, Judge Stockdale)).

Thus in thinking about the question of complainant credibility, we (and prosecutors) need to recognise that cisgender ignorance is learned, operates as a privileged form of knowledge and, in the context of sexual intimacy with transgender or other gender non-conforming people, enables the disavowal of agency and desire.

## 5.3 Pleading guilty

The previous section challenged the bringing of prosecutions for gender identity fraud on the basis that such prosecutorial decision-making conflicts with CPS guidelines established for prosecuting offences. In this section, we move to a later stage in the pre-trial process, the moment of plea, and consider two principal difficulties which arise in this context for those charged with gender identity fraud. First, we will problematise the guilty plea by considering some reasons why innocent gender non-conforming defendants might plead guilty. Second, it will be argued that a guilty plea, at least in some cases, ought not to have been accepted by the court because this should only occur where it is clear that the facts pleaded guilty to actually constitute an offence in law. With the exception of Gayle Newland, all the defendants convicted in the cases so far prosecuted pleaded guilty, something which renders any future appeal more difficult.[29] Pleading guilty however is not the same thing as being guilty. Sadly, there are many reasons why innocent people plead guilty within our criminal justice system. These include a desire to avoid financial penalties that attach to not pleading guilty, but being found so,[30] and an awareness that pleading guilty at the 'first reasonable opportunity' leads to significant sentence reduction (see Ashworth and Roberts, 2013).[31] In the case of gender non-conforming youth accused of gender identity fraud, we can confidently add to the list, internalised shame and societal disbelief concerning assertions of consensual sex with cisgender people.

Thus, it is hardly surprising that Justine McNally 'just wanted it to be over'.[32] In cultural terms, the odds were stacked against her. That is, how likely is it that a

29 D. Bunting, 'Remedies After Pleading Guilty – Comment on Sadighour [2012] EWCA Crim 2669' *UK Criminal Law Blog* 17/12/12 available at https://ukcrime.wordpress.com/2012/12/17/remedies-after-pleading-guilty-comment-on-sadighour-2012-ewca-crim-2669/#comments (last accessed: 3/2/17).

30 E. Duggan, 'Crippling Court Costs Force Poverty-Stricken People to Plead Guilty to Crimes They Didn't Commit' *The Independent* 21/8/15 available at www.independent.co.uk/news/uk/crime/crippling-court-costs-force-poverty-stricken-people-to-plead-guilty-to-crimes-they-didnt-commit-10466451.html (last accessed: 3/2/17).

31 s. 144 Criminal Justice Act 2003 indicates the appropriateness of a sentencing discount for a guilty plea, though it remains at the court's discretion. See also *Reduction in Sentence for a Guilty Plea: Definitive Guideline* (Revised 2007), Sentencing Guidelines Council available at www.sentencingcouncil.org.uk/wp-content/uploads/Reduction_in_Sentence_for_a_Guilty_Plea_-Revised_20071.pdf (last accessed: 3/2/17). The guidelines stipulate a one-third reduction in sentence for a guilty plea at the 'first reasonable opportunity'.

32 *McNally* above note 2 at para 40.

jury will belief that a transgender/genderqueer body was desired by a young cis-gender woman who claims otherwise? After all, gender non-conforming people occupy a low position in a 'hierarchy of credibility' (Becker, 1967). Another reason why a guilty plea is so typical in gender identity fraud cases may be that defendants received poor legal advice. Certainly, poor legal advice provided a basis for one ground of appeal in *McNally*.[33] And in the case of *Kyran Lee (Mason)*,[34] Kyran insisted in a post-conviction interview, that 'his lawyers told him the prosecution's case was ironclad and fighting the charge would only doom him to a stiffer sentence', a potential consequence which petrified him, and which was exacerbated by uncertainty regarding where he would be placed within the gender segregated prison estate.[35] A guilty plea, and 'just wanting it to be over', may also be connected to media persecution of young transgender and other gender non-conforming defendants.[36] Thus, in considering gender identity fraud prosecutions, it is not enough to critique only substantive legal doctrine and/or its application. Rather, it is necessary to consider the pre-trial process and the way that it contributes to differential outcomes across axes of gender and sexuality.

In any event, whatever the reasons for a guilty plea, a further problem presents itself, namely, the acceptance of a guilty plea. This should only be possible in circumstances where the facts pleaded guilty to actually constitute an offence in law.[37] In at least some of the cases this is far from clear. This is because the relevant gap between the complainant's assumption regarding the defendant's gender identity and his actual gender identity did not exist. Thus, and by way of example, in the *Kyran Lee (Mason)* case, the complainant assumed Kyran to be a man and

33 *McNally* above note 2 at para 13. Discussed at paras 28–46.

34 *R v Lee (Mason)* 16/12/15 (Unrept, Lincoln Crown Court, Judge Heath). For media reporting of the case, see 'Woman Who Used Fake Penis to have Sex with a Woman Avoids Jail', *The Guardian* 15/12/15 available at www.theguardian.com/uk-news/2015/dec/15/woman-who-used-fake-penis-to-have-sex-with-a-woman-avoids-jail (last accessed: 3/2/17).

35 L. Feder, 'How an Online Love Affair Ended with a Trans Man Convicted of Sexual Assault', *BuzzFeed News* 14/10/16 available at www.buzzfeed.com/lesterfeder/how-an-online-love-affair-ended-with-a-trans-man-convicted-o?utm_term=.rnBwkO444#.wgArq5JJJ (last accessed: 3/2/17).

36 For example, Justine McNally was routinely described as having 'posed as', 'pretended to be' or 'masqueraded as' a boy, without any attempt to take seriously her gender identity. See M. Robinson, 'Schoolgirl, 18, Pretended to be a Boy Called Scott for Three and a Half Years to Get Another Teenage Girl, 16, into Bed and Take Her Virginity', *Daily Mail Online*, 21/3/13 available at www.dailymail.co.uk/news/article-2296982/Justine-McNally-18-pretended-boy-girl-bed-virginity.html (last accessed: 3/2/17); A. Shaw, 'Schoolgirl Who Posed as Boy for More Than Three Years to have Sex with Teenage Girl Jailed for Three Years', *Daily Record*, 22/3/13 available at www.dailyrecord.co.uk/news/scottish-news/schoolgirl-who-posed-boy-sex-1778083 (last accessed: 3/2/17); H. Dixon, '18-Year-Old Woman Masqueraded as Boy to Get Girl into Bed', *The Telegraph*, 24/3/13 available at www.telegraph.co.uk/news/uknews/crime/9946687/18-year-old-woman-masqueraded-as-boy-to-get-girl-into-bed.html (last accessed: 3/2/17).

37 *R v McReady and Hurd* [1978] 1 WLR 1376.

given that he is a man (and we must insist on this point, despite the protestations of the Germaine Greers of this world) (Greer, 1999),[38] no relevant mistake was made or fraud perpetrated. Rather, upon 'discovery' of Kyran's transgender status, the complainant concluded that he was not a man. In this respect, she understood 'man' to mean, and to be exhausted by, the class of men we now refer to as cisgender. She is, of course, entitled to act on such a view in the sexual relations she chooses to have. What she ought not to be entitled to do is mobilise the power of the state after having exercised agentic choice. To permit her to do so is to rub salt into the wounds of a prior ontological assault – the denial of gender identity. The fact that Kyran was prosecuted demonstrates that prosecutors adopted this problematic view that he was not a man.

Finally, guilty pleas require examination because they represent moments where power produces effects beyond findings of liability and attendant questions of disposal. That is, a guilty plea cannot, at least in the context of transgender and other gender non-conforming people, be understood as being confined in its effects to the individuals prosecuted. Rather, the performative utterance (Austin, 1961, pp. 233–252. See also Austin, 1955), 'Guilty', has a life of its own, one that reaches out beyond the parties and the courtroom. As a performative, it does what it says and 'exercise[s] a binding power' (Butler, 1993, p. 225), that is, it produces a guilty subject. However, it exceeds this action. For it requires not only confession to a crime, but the adoption of a position of complicity in relation to one's own ontological undoing. Crucially, each plea and finding of guilt contributes to a dominant cultural narrative, one that equates transgender with artifice and deception, and which therefore renders intelligible, and prepares the ground for, future prosecutions.

In the following section, we shift our focus away from questions of prosecutorial decision-making and plea to consider the application of substantive legal rules that now determine criminal liability for sexual fraud. Specifically, we will consider legal deployment of a particular act/omission distinction, namely, the distinction between non-disclosure of information and active deception. It will be argued that this distinction lacks robustness. Indeed, more than that, the distinction proves leaky or permeable, with all the possibilities for criminal law overreach that this entails. In exploring these issues, the section will focus on the Court of

38 Greer has continued to deny the gender identities of transgender people, especially transgender women. For a recent example, see H. Saul, 'Germaine Greer Defends "Grossly Offensive" Comments about Transgender Women: "Just because You Lop Off Your D**k Doesn't Make You a ******* Woman,"' *The Independent* 26/10/15 available at www.independent.co.uk/news/people/germaine-greer-defends-grossly-offensive-comments-about-transgender-women-just-because-you-lop-off-a6709061.html (last accessed 3/2/17). Moreover, and as noted by Julia Serano (Serano, 2007, p. 167), Greer has demonstrated a breath-taking sense of cissexual entitlement. Thus, in her book, *The Whole Woman,* she states: 'No one ever asked women if they recognized sex-change males as *belonging* to their sex or considered whether being *obliged* to accept MTF transsexuals as women was at all damaging to their identity or self-esteem' (Greer, 1999, p. 74, my emphasis).

Appeal's decision in *McNally*. The case is important, both because it represents the clearest judicial expression of the distinction, and because it applies the distinction to a gender non-conforming defendant.

## 5.4 Act/omission revisited: the problem of analytical collapse

In the previous chapter, we considered the judicial distinction between non-disclosure of information and active deception, a distinction which now governs the determination of criminal liability in sexual offence cases where fraud is alleged. This particular incarnation of the act/omission dyad was taken to task on the basis that it lacks a principled foundation. In this section, we turn away from this issue of principle in order to highlight how the distinction, especially in cases involving transgender and other gender non-conforming people, unravels in ways which expose defendants, and their sexual lives, to a greater degree of state regulation and punishment than the logic of the distinction implies. In other words, it will be argued that the distinction, while ostensibly setting a limit to criminalisation through placing 'mere' non-disclosure of information beyond the law, fails to guarantee any boundary.

Thus I oppose the argument that, even if a clear rationale and justification for the distinction between active deception and non-disclosure proves elusive, the distinction offers a clear legal test likely to assist courts in navigating their way through the murky waters of sexual fraud. Such an argument assumes the distinction to be analytically robust. Yet, scholars have highlighted difficulties associated with the so-called 'definition question' (Rosenberg, 2014, p. 393) when contemplating the act/omission distinction. Criticism has, perhaps, been especially pronounced in relation to the criminal law homicide distinction between killing and letting die (Finnis, 1993; Keown, 1997). This is due, at least in part, to the willingness of courts, in this context, to characterise as omission what is, on any logical reckoning, action. Thus in *Airedale NHS Trust v Bland*, the House of Lords defined the turning off of a life support machine as an omission on the basis that it was equivalent to having never turned the machine on in the first place.[39]

In challenging the analytical robustness of the distinction, we will focus on gender identity fraud cases. While problems associated with the distinction are not so confined, such cases, in addition to being our object, serve to dramatise the central problem of categorical permeability. In other words, it will be argued that legal reasoning in cases of this kind evinces considerable slippage between active deception and non-disclosure. Moreover, this slippage is, it will be argued, the effect of the power of 'cissexual privilege' (Serano, 2007, p. 184). Thus, while Elliot and Ormerod have rightly expressed concern that the act/omission distinction is vulnerable to 'judicial manipulation' (Elliot and Ormerod, 2008, p. 42), the argument here is that the problem is not simply one of judicial intent but an unacknowledged, and perhaps unconscious, investment in cisnormativity. In the

39 *Airedale NHS Trust v Bland* [1993] AC 789 (HL).

previous chapter, we considered HIV scenarios as a vehicle for thinking about whether the distinction is an adequate basis for setting the parameters of criminal liability. It is worth stating what might seem obvious, namely that HIV positive status is a fact that may or may not be disclosed and in relation to which active deception may or may not occur. In relation to gender identity however, the 'facts' in question are considerably more complex and contestable and in ways that call the distinction, or at least its practical application, into question.

Chapter 2 detailed the facts concerning legal prosecution of young gender non-conforming people for gender identity fraud. It was noted that since 2012 there have been six successful prosecutions brought in the UK, one in Scotland and five in England. Four of the convicted defendants received prison sentences and all have been placed on Sex Offenders Registers. Turning to the act/omission distinction, it is unclear in most cases whether convictions were sustained on the basis of active deception or non-disclosure of information concerning gender history or whether any consideration was given to such a distinction. In reality, and precisely because the distinction tends to unravel in relation to transgender and other gender non-conforming defendants, it is likely that non-disclosure has proved sufficient for conviction, at least in some cases. This is certainly true in the transgender case of *R v Wilson* where Lord Bannatyne made clear, in his sentencing judgment, that 'deception lay in not disclosing … biological sex'.[40]

In exploring this distinction and its robustness in the context of gender identity fraud, the remainder of this chapter will focus on the English decision of *McNally*. It will do so because, in the UK context, it is the only gender identity fraud case, so far, to be considered by a superior court, and because, unlike other sexual fraud cases, it enshrines the active deception/non-disclosure distinction as the basis for establishing criminal liability. Moreover, and crucially, it seeks to explain conviction, explicitly, by reference to it. In this case, the court held that 'the sexual nature of the acts is, on any common sense view, different where the complainant is deliberately deceived by a defendant into believing that the latter

40 *R v Wilson* 7/3/13 (Unrept, Edinburgh High Court, Lord Bannatyne). A copy of the sentencing judgment is on file with the author. Of course, as a Scottish case, *Wilson* does not undermine the operation of a distinction formulated under English law. For media reporting of the case, see J. Morgan, 'Man "Guilty" of Fraud for Not Telling Girlfriend he was Trans', *Gay Star News* 7/3/13 available at www.gaystarnews.com/article/man-'guilty'-fraud-not-telling-girlfriend-he-was-trans070313/ (last accessed: 3/2/17); C. Pinfold, 'Scotland: Case of Trans Man Facing Jail for Sex "by Fraud" Raises Concerns of Scottish Transgender Alliance', *Pink News* 12/3/13 available at www.pinknews.co.uk/2013/03/12/scotland-case-of-trans-man-facing-jail-for-sex-by-fraud-raises-concerns-of-scottish-transgender-alliance/ (last accessed: 3/2/17). Lord Bannatyne accepted that Chris Wilson, who had lived as a boy since childhood and who had indicated an intention to undergo gender reassignment surgery, genuinely felt that he was male rather than female. Strangely, while his Lordship felt this fact reduced Wilson's culpability, he did not consider it to undermine the deception claim, 'Sex Fraud Woman Put on Probation', *BBC News* 9/4/13 available at www.bbc.co.uk/news/uk-scotland-north-east-orkney-shetland-22078298 (last accessed: 3/2/17).

is a male'.[41] In other words, the legality of conviction is predicated on two judicial findings: (i) the defendant is female, and relatedly (ii) actively deceived the complainant into believing the contrary. It is toward challenging these two findings that we now turn.

### *(i) Determining gender*

On the surface of things it may seem unsurprising that McNally was found to be female. After all, McNally was registered female at birth and had not undertaken gender reassignment surgery. However, and while the Law Commission has previously recommended gender reassignment surgery as the tipping point where 'apparent' consent 'should not be disregarded' (Law Commission, 2000, para 5.33), it is clear, since the Gender Recognition Act 2004, that surgery is not a condition for legal recognition of gender identity in the UK.[42] Moreover, to determine gender status for the purposes of criminal prosecution by reference to legal gender status, would serve to make most young transgender people fair game, given that a condition of gender recognition is that an applicant be at least 18.[43] By the same token, a diagnosis of *gender dysphoria*, a diagnosis which operates as a trigger for everything that happens under the Gender Recognition Act,[44] is unlikely to have been made prior to the time when young transgender people begin to explore their sexuality.

As noted by Reed et al, '[s]ocial pressures, especially within the family and at school, currently prevent all but a few from revealing their gender variance and being referred for medical care, especially in adolescence' (Reed et al, 2009. See also Cohen-Kettinis and Pfafflin, 2003, p. 65). To determine gender by reference to conferral of a Gender Recognition Certificate, surgical intervention and/or a diagnosis of *gender dysphoria* is, effectively, to place transgender youth beyond the protection of the criminal law. Further, while such factors should not be viewed as determinative of gender identity, given their potential exclusionary effects, it should be noted that McNally, at least prior to prosecution, identified as male, felt 'more comfortable' in the male gender role,[45] and indicated an intention to undergo gender reassignment surgery.[46] This is entirely consistent with a view of McNally's gender identity as male and inconsistent with the court's conclusion of female identity.

However, the *McNally* case is complicated by McNally's own contrary statements on the question of gender identity. Thus in a witness statement, McNally stated: 'I accept that [the complainant] did not consent to the sexual activity between us because she did not realise I was a girl and not a boy.'[47] This

41 *McNally* above note 2 at para 26.
42 s 3 Gender Recognition Act 2004.
43 s 1 Gender Recognition Act 2004.
44 s 2(a) Gender Recognition Act 2004.
45 *McNally* above note 2 at para 12.
46 *Ibid*, at para 10.
47 *Ibid*, at para 37.

statement is relevant to the question of McNally's self-understanding of gender identity and to the question of deception. The latter question, which the reader might think the statement resolves, is one we will consider in the next section of this chapter, where a contrary view will be offered. In relation to gender identity, McNally's apparently unambiguous statement should be treated with caution. In the first place, McNally speaks of gender in the past tense, never stating 'I am a girl/woman', but always 'I was a girl'. This might be read as consistent with a particular gender journey and conceptualisation of a gendered past. Second, it is important to recognise that a witness statement referring to female gender identity is not necessarily indicative of actual or authentic gender identity.

It may be that McNally was exhausted by criminal prosecution and the media persecution that followed. Thus, and as noted by the Court of Appeal, McNally, in signing the witness statement, 'just wanted it to be over'.[48] In other words, we should not discount the possibility that such statements, as well as McNally's guilty plea, are effects of the gravitational pull of cisnormativity, rather than indicating anything important about veracity or ontology. Of course, I appreciate that these observations about McNally's gender identity might be viewed as speculative and understand that courts have to deal with evidence as presented. Nevertheless, the idea that McNally might have sublimated identity and desire in the face of a legal and cultural world in which transgender and deception are viewed as synonymous (Bettcher, 2007), is one that finds support in medical evidence dealing with rates of gender persistence. Thus, studies have shown children insisting on non birth-designated gender identities after adolescence have a very high rate of persistence into adulthood (Wren, 2000: Zucker, 2006; Zucker and Cohen-Kettinis, 2008).[49] Thus it may be that McNally, who after all, initially indicated a desire for gender reassignment surgery, has participated in a kind of self-repudiation (Shelley, 2008, especially Chapter 2). This draws attention to a very real danger in prosecuting young transgender people on the basis of their sexually intimate relations with cisgender people.[50] In many respects, *McNally* might be viewed as a hard case producing bad law.

In this respect, we might wonder what the implications of the Court of Appeal's decision are for sexually active transgender people who offer different gender

48 *Ibid*, at para 40.

49 Indeed, the most recent medical evidence suggests that the rate of persistence for pre-adolescent children is also very high (see above Chapter 4, fn 23).

50 This is perhaps especially so given that young transgender people are a very vulnerable group within society and have exceptionally high suicide rates. Indeed, one recent UK study found that nearly half of young transgender people have attempted suicide, P Strudwick, 'Nearly Half of Young Transgender People Have Attempted Suicide – UK Survey' *The Guardian* 19/11/14 available at www.theguardian.com/society/2014/nov/19/young-transgender-suicide-attempts-survey (last accessed: 3/2/17).

narratives at trial. Thus, we might ask, what would be the legal position of a transgender person who asserted their gender identity very clearly and consistently throughout the criminal justice process? Would this lead the court to take the view that consent is valid because of the existence of a symmetrical relationship between the complainant's sexual object choice and the defendant's gender identity, or would the court continue to find a disjunction, serving to vitiate consent?[51] If so, in what circumstances would consent be found to exist? Would possession of a Gender Recognition Certificate and/or having undertaken gender reassignment surgery resolve the gender identity question in a transgender person's favour? The question of how gender identity is to be determined for the purposes of sexual fraud offences is obviously an important one, yet it remains unclear. There is an urgent need here for judicial, and perhaps legislative, clarification. However, even in circumstances where a transgender person's gender identity were to be acknowledged by the courts, the question of active deception would not necessarily disappear. While rejection of a gender identity claim (or in *McNally*, the countermanding of such a claim by the defendant) will bring active deception to the fore, judicial acceptance of gender identity might serve only to kick it down the road. It is to this question of active deception that we now turn.

### *(ii) Finding active deception*

The court's finding of female gender status did not seal McNally's fate. The question of mens rea still had to be faced. Indeed, even resolving the question of consent under s. 74 of the Sexual Offences Act seems to have required consideration of mens rea, given that the active deception/non-disclosure distinction appears to have injected 'a certain degree of knowledge or intentionality' into the provision (Laird, 2014, p. 505). In other words, and according to the court's logic, even if we were to accept that McNally is female, mere non-disclosure of this 'fact' would not, of itself, lead either to vitiation of consent, given judicial reluctance to process sexual fraud cases through s. 76(2)(a), or to proof of mens rea. Accordingly, the court had to find, whether through words or deeds, active deception on the part of McNally.

The Court of Appeal referred to various facts which appear, individually or collectively, to have been interpreted as constituting active deception. Before considering them however, it is necessary to deal with an important matter that the reader has perhaps anticipated. It might be thought, given the court's conclusion that McNally is female, and indeed McNally's own assertion of a female

51 In view of the recent conviction of Kyran Lee (Mason) by an English court (above note 34), it would seem that consistent expression of a male gender identity will not, of itself, preclude a finding that consent is vitiated. In this respect, the English courts have failed to chart a different course to their Scottish counterparts (see *Wilson*, above note 40).

gender identity at the time of plea and subsequent appeal, that active deception is abundantly evident in McNally's male gender performance. The difficulty here is that McNally appears to have asserted a male gender identity prior to and at the time of the alleged offences. As already discussed, we should not conclude that this is disingenuous simply because of subsequent retraction and/or because McNally expressed some 'gender confusion'.[52] It may be that retraction served to conceal rather than reveal authentic gender identity in the case. At a minimum, a masculine gender performance might have been consistent with McNally's gender identity at the time of sexual intimacy with the complainant, and therefore at the moment of criminal liability.

In any event, we should not assume gender flux or playfulness to be evidence of deceit. There is a real danger here, especially given the porousness of the non-disclosure/active deception distinction, that cisnormative understandings of gender, identity and authenticity will expand the net of criminalisation beyond the example of transgender, even on the limited question of gender identity fraud. Thus, for example, a woman who identifies as genderqueer might perform gender in a masculine way. However, her performance is not deceptive. She does not act inauthentically, nor is she motivated by a desire to deceive. On the contrary, genderqueer is precisely the identity position that she occupies and lives. She should not be punished because a sexual partner mistakenly assumes her to be male. Crucially, we should recognise the very real danger of coupling truth with gender performances that faithfully and consistently replicate the gender binary, a binary which is, after all, more ideological than real (Butler, 1990, p. 7, Butler, 1993, p. 5).

Returning to the facts of *McNally*, let us consider the question of active deception. It is important here to begin by reminding ourselves about the degree to which we are expected to suspend our disbelief regarding complainant evidence, a theme we explored earlier in the chapter in relation to gender identity fraud cases more generally. Thus the case involved repeated sexual intimacies over a period of time, culminating in at least six occasions of oral and digital penetration of the complainant. In other words, the complainant's claim that she believed McNally to be a cisgender man appears somewhat implausible on the facts. This is especially so given that McNally was not on testosterone and so had not benefited from its significant masculinising effects.[53] Moreover, McNally claimed that the complainant had 'commented on her breasts and her high pitched voice'.[54] Whether she did so or not, she certainly became intimate with a person possessing these physical features. Leveson LJ's penchant for approaching the evidence in a

52 *McNally* above note 2 at para 47.

53 In terms of changes likely to be visible, transgender men, prescribed testosterone, typically experience increases in muscle mass, body and facial hair, as well some degree of deepening of the voice (World Professional Association of Transgender Health, 2012, p. 36).

54 *McNally* above note 2 at para 84.

broad 'common sense' way seems to have deserted him in these respects. It is contended this is an effect of an underlying cissexist conceit that no cisgender person would knowingly have sex with a transgender person, a conceit which both implicates transphobia and constitutes a 'route by which the unthinkability of homosexuality is being constituted time and again' (Butler, 1991, p. 20). It is true that McNally admitted, despite an earlier contradictory statement, that the complainant was not informed about her gender history, but not being informed is not the same as not knowing. Moreover, an admission of non-disclosure is an inadequate basis for criminal liability according to the logic of *McNally*.

In finding active deception, the court focused on several pieces of evidence. We have already dealt with the issue of McNally's gender performance, which cannot easily be squared with deception, at least not at the time of the alleged offences. However, the court identified two statements made by McNally which relate to facts that might be considered material, and which might therefore be considered to constitute active deception.[55] First, McNally and the complainant discussed 'getting married and having children'.[56] Yet, there is nothing necessarily deceptive about such future speculations. McNally would be able to marry a woman as a man after obtaining a Gender Recognition Certificate and the couple would be able to have children either through adoption or in vitro fertilisation. Second, McNally apparently spoke of a desire to '"[put] it in" which the complainant took to mean [being penetrated by] "his" penis'.[57] This statement, which was made during phone sex prior to meeting in person, was part of an exchange in which both parties spoke 'about what they wanted to do to each other sexually'.[58] A conclusion that McNally's statement indicates deception fails to recognise that some transgender men consider a prosthetic device to be their penis (Hale, 2003; Davy, 2011, Chapter 3; Latham, 2016, pp. 355–356).

The court also attached significance to the fact that the complainant had purchased condoms 'intending that the couple have intercourse'.[59] The inference the court drew from this fact was that McNally's (subsequently retracted) claim that the complainant already knew about McNally's gender identity was false.[60] Yet, even if McNally had lied about disclosure this does not demonstrate 'active' deception. More importantly, for present purposes, there is no necessary logical relationship between the complainant buying condoms and a belief that McNally had a penis. Insistence on such a relationship relies on the view that condoms have

55 *Ibid*, at paras 4 and 5. McNally also used an alias, Scott Hill, while online and subsequently in person-to-person meetings with the complainant (para 3). This deception however, does not go to a material fact. Nor does it cast doubt on McNally's gender identity.

56 *Ibid*, at para 4.

57 *Ibid*, at para 5.

58 *Ibid*.

59 *Ibid*, at para 8. McNally's solicitor also placed emphasis on the fact of condom purchase stating that 'it would be clear to the jury who was telling the truth' (para 35).

60 This problematic inference is also drawn by Laird, 2014, p. 505.

no use in the absence of a penis. Yet, purchase could be explained in terms of a concern over hygiene in the context of potential use of a prosthesis, a device that McNally did possess.[61] Judicial treatment of these various facts reveals the ease with which non-disclosure of gender history can be translated into active deception. In this sense, *McNally* presents and should be read as a cautionary tale.

The predicament of sexually active transgender people, that is, the uncertainty regarding future application of the law, is also evident in the ease with which criminal lawyers conjure up 'problematic' sexual scenarios. Thus Karl Laird offers the example of deception in relation to chromosomes. He raises this example in relation to his analysis of the applicability of s. 76(2)(a) of the Sexual Offences Act, rather than s. 74, though it make little difference for the purposes of my argument. He argues: '[i]f the allegation is that D presented himself as chromosomally male and C believes she is engaging in intercourse with someone who is chromosomally male, then it is not contrary to the legislative language to conceptualise this as a case involving deception as to the nature of the act' (Laird, 2014, p. 509, fn 97). His analysis raises some serious difficulties. Even if the courts were willing to process such a case through s. 76,[62] thereby avoiding having to wrestle with the *McNally* distinction, it would still be necessary to prove that 'the defendant intentionally deceived the complainant'.[63]

Yet, it is not clear from Laird's example where deception would lie. It is also unclear what he means by: 'D presented himself as a chromosomal man.' Perhaps Laird is envisaging a scenario where a complainant makes an assumption about the chromosomal status of her sexual partner. This is little different to scenarios where false assumptions are made about legal or genital status. Transgender men present as the men they are. They do not, in doing so, make any claim about their chromosomal, genital or legal status. The fact that cisgender people routinely make the assumption that all men are cissexual, and therefore are likely to possess an XY chromosome,[64] should not be a basis for finding transgender people deceptive. To find fraud in these circumstances is tantamount to rendering deceptive the very fact of transgender existence. We should also recognise that a transgender person may not even be aware of the significance of the absence of an XY chromosome to a sexual partner. Indeed, we might wonder whether anybody is actually chromocentric, or at least self-consciously so.

61 *McNally* above note 2 at para 7.

62 The courts have proved especially reluctant to do so (*R v Jheeta* [2007] EWCA Crim 1699 at para 28; *Assange v Swedish Prosecution Authority* [2011] EWHC 2849 (Admin) at para 87; *R (on the application of F) v DPP* [2013] EWHC 945 (Admin) at para 26; *R v B* [2013] EWCA Crim 823 at para 24; *McNally* above note 2 at para 18).

63 s 76(2)(a) Sexual Offences Act 2003.

64 We should not assume all cissexual men have an XY chromosome. Some intersex people, who lack an XY chromosome, identify as male, have a male anatomy/penis, and were registered as male at birth. The clearest example of this is Klinefelter Syndrome (see Greenberg, 2012, p. 137).

Conversely, Laird perhaps imagines that a complainant might ask a direct question about chromosomal status. I think this to be rather implausible, and also likely to indicate some degree of knowledge or suspicion regarding chromosomes serving to problematise a claim of non-consent.[65] However, were this not the case, we ought to resist an argument that lying about chromosomes or, for example, some portion of childhood biography, constitutes intentional deception as to the 'nature of the act', for the purposes of s. 76(2)(a), or active deception regarding a material fact, for the purposes of s. 74. This might seem counter-intuitive to some readers. Such is the power of cisnormative ideology. To accept such an argument is to make chromosomes, or a linear gender narrative, critical to the question of determining gender identity. As a matter of law, they are not.[66] Nor should they be. To argue that the nature of the sexual act is different because of a lie of this sort, or that the lie pertains to a material fact, is to collude in the ontological degradation of transgender people.

The question: 'are you a chromosomal man?' cannot be a neutral question. It only makes sense in a world in which a hierarchy of men is imagined. To answer in the negative involves self-dimunition or repudiation. Law ought not, through defining 'the nature of the sexual act', or the materiality of facts, to privilege cis-gender people in sexual relations nor confer upon them a right to define the bodies and authentic gender experiences of others. Moreover, and irrespective of the ethicality of lying, an issue to be considered in Chapter 6, we should not assume its purpose is to deceive. This is a likely inference when the question is posed from a ciscentric perspective. Yet, the sorts of lies detailed here might, more realistically, be read in terms of self-preservation.[67]

Before concluding this chapter, it is necessary to tease out another, more queer, dimension of the non-disclosure/active deception distinction. While it lacks analytical robustness for the reasons already elaborated, its conceptual ambivalence, and its practical application, also provide an opportunity to challenge the notion of fixed and stable gender identities from a position internal to law. That is, the distinction would appear to produce such queer effects. Thus, it produces a situation where recognition of gender identity hinges on the presence/absence of an active defendant. That is, law would appear to recognise the validity of complainant consent to sex, and therefore defendant gender identity, in circumstances where the defendant is constructed as 'passive'. In other words, and in view of the fact that gender identity is clearly treated as a material fact by the courts in the cases prosecuted, a finding that consent is valid presupposes the 'truth' of facts, including the fact of the defendant's gender identity. Accordingly, in addition to determining

65 It is also important here to avoid reproducing the notion that transgender people would want to have sex with transphobic people.

66 s. 3 Gender Recognition Act 2004.

67 I refer here both to physical and psychic survival. In relation to the former, it should be recognised that transgender visibility can, and frequently does, lead to violence (see Whittle et al, 2007; Morton, 2008). In the US context, see GenderPAC, 1997; Waters et al, 2016.

the presence/absence of consent and deception, some form of legal recognition, or at least acknowledgment, of gender identity outside the terms of the Gender Recognition Act appears to turn, somewhat queerly, on whether or not the defendant acted in the world.

Of course, it might be objected that a legal conclusion of valid consent cannot necessarily be squared with the 'truth' of facts represented. Thus, while courts treat lying about wealth or social status in order to have sex as a trivial matter,[68] this does not change the fact that such representations are false. However, in the case of transgender defendants the matter is more complex because a finding of valid consent can hardly be said to follow from an interpretation of gender identity as trivial. Rather, the status of the gender identities of transgender and other gender non-conforming people in gender identity fraud cases proves fundamental. Certainly, it would seem that law, through its formal legal rules, if not their practical application, insulates transgender and other gender non-conforming people from conviction provided that the line between non-disclosure and active deception is not interpreted to have been crossed. At this point, 'authentic' gender identities are trumped by action. Ultimately, and rather bizarrely, legal desire for consistency in thinking about gender identity meets its limit in a formal, and morally bankrupt, jurisprudential distinction.

## 5.5 Conclusion

This chapter has sought to consolidate the case against prosecuting gender identity fraud. In doing so, it built on the principled objections detailed in Chapters 3 and 4. In moving from consideration of matters of principle and abstract jurisprudential thinking to more urgent questions of defendant vulnerability and the (im)possibility of justice, it highlighted some socio-legal realities of prosecuting, especially young, gender non-conforming people. To that end, it focused on three distinct, though related issues. First, it adopted a position of scepticism toward the credibility of complainant evidence and, relatedly, toward the notion that ignorance and knowledge presuppose two mutually exclusive cognitive domains. In doing so, it called into question whether prosecutorial decisions have been properly informed and delimited by CPS guidelines.

Second, the chapter considered two problems associated with plea. First, it considered reasons why transgender and other gender non-conforming defendants might plead guilty to sexual offences in circumstances where complainants were aware of their gender histories. Second, it argued that a guilty plea, at least in some cases, ought not to have been accepted by the court because it remained unclear whether the facts pleaded guilty to actually constitute an offence in law. The fact that courts found the prosecution case to be made out without much

68 The courts have long taken the view that certain kinds of facts are too trivial to vitiate consent for the purposes of sexual offences. This legal position was most recently articulated in *McNally* above note 2 at para 25, per Leveson LJ.

scrutiny serves to highlight the cisnormative frame through which 'facts' were established.

Third, the chapter returned to the distinction between active deception and non-disclosure, explored in the previous chapter, in order to stress how the distinction unravels in contexts of prosecuting gender identity fraud. After all, how does one stay on the right side of the law when, in legal and cultural terms, active deception characterises one's ontological position? That is, how can one avoid liability, when the cultural terms through which one is defined are duplicity, subterfuge and dissimulation? For those who favour criminal prosecution irrespective of whether 'deception' is active or passive, the objections raised to using the distinction for the purposes of establishing liability for sexual fraud may count for little. For the judiciary, it is hoped they encourage caution in this area. In the following chapter, we shift our attention from law to ethics, where we will consider the ethicality of lying and, more importantly, given the actual facts of gender identity fraud cases, the question of what we owe to each other in terms of disclosing information prior to sexual intimacy.

Chapter 6

# From legal to ethical practice

## 6.1 Introduction

In life we are all faced, more or less continuously, with situations where we might choose to reveal, withhold or modify information about ourselves, our pasts and/or our future aspirations. This chapter is interested in the ethical status of such choices and the legitimate expectations of others to know the 'truth'. The specific focus, of course, continues to be occasions of sexual intimacy between cisgender and gender non-conforming people, though for the purposes of this chapter we will focus on transgender people. Accordingly, this chapter moves from considering such moments as an occasion for state regulation through the criminal law, to considering their ethicality. The question of ethical practice is an important one to address because, while many criminal law commentators appear sceptical regarding expansion of the fraud category within sexual offences law, a position that would appear to hold in relation to cases involving gender identity (see, for example, Simester et al, 2010, p. 755; Ormerod, 2011, p. 734), it seems that this same scepticism often evaporates in the face of the ethical characterisation of the role transgender people play in sexually intimate scenarios. In other words, while the liberal distinction between illegality and immorality is insisted upon as a bulwark against the state,[1] the notion that 'lying' about or non-disclosure of gender history, constitute unethical practice/omission proves more resilient. This claim is informed not only by what is implicit in criminal prosecution and by wider community sentiment (Moore, 2016), but by conversations had with numerous legal and non-legal academics over the last few years while researching these issues.[2]

1 The view that not all immoral acts should be subject to the criminal law or, which is the same thing, opposition to 'legal moralism', is well-established within liberalism. In particular, 'immoral' acts that are private, consensual and self-regarding are viewed as being rightly beyond the law, as none of its business (see Hart, 1964).

2 This attitude is one noted by others within the legal academy (S.F. Colb, 'Is There a Moral Duty to Disclose That You're Transgender to a Potential Partner?' *Verdict* 6/18/15 available at https://verdict.justia.com/2015/06/18/is-there-a-moral-duty-to-disclose-that-youre-transgender-to-a-potential-partner (last accessed: 13/2/17)).

In many respects, challenging this view is as, if not more, important as challenging criminal prosecution, albeit under current English law, non-disclosure of information is, at least ostensibly,[3] insufficient to ground prosecution.[4] This is because it is the widespread view that transgender people are quintessentially deceptive, that is most antithetical to the liveability of transgender lives. The fact that many cisgender people feel, almost 'instinctively', that they have a right to know, and transgender people an obligation to disclose, gender history, is something this chapter will contest. In doing so, it will situate ethical thinking within the context of cisgender privilege and power. The view that 'lying' and non-disclosure of information are, in the present context, necessarily unethical is problematic for several reasons which the chapter will explore. However, before considering and challenging the characterisation of transgender decision-making as unethical, the chapter will first attempt to delineate the relevant 'facts', in relation to which ethical conclusions might appropriately be drawn. This is important because this chapter takes as axiomatic the view that transgender men and transgender women are men and women. Indeed, it will argue this to be the only view available consistent with maintaining an ethical relation to transgender people.

Thus, this chapter will begin by approaching the question: *do transgender people have an ethical obligation to disclose the truth about their gender identity?* through an external critique, one which turns that question on its head and reveals how posing the question in this way is both hubristic and demonstrative of a failure to approach moments of cis–trans sexual intimacy in an ethical manner. The chapter will then adopt an internal critique, that is, it will engage with arguments derived from normative ethics. It will do so in order to show that, even when issues of ideology, power and privilege are ignored or suspended, the view that an ethical obligation to disclose ought to exist will not necessarily win the day. Finally, the chapter will look to the future and consider what it might mean to be 'ethically gendered' (Serano, 2013, p. 259), and the implications of being so for the way we think and feel about sexual encounters in world characterised by gender variance.

3 As observed in earlier chapters, especially chapter 5, it is far from clear that the distinction between active deception and non-disclosure of information serves to protect transgender people who simply exercise privacy. In most of the gender identity fraud cases prosecuted it was not made clear whether the basis for conviction lay with acts or omission. In the only case where this was rendered clear at the time of conviction, it was non-disclosure of biological sex, rather than active deception, that proved decisive (*R v Wilson* 7/3/13 (Unrept, Edinburgh High Court, Lord Bannatyne). A copy of Lord Bannatyne's sentencing judgment is on file with the author).

4 As established by the Court of Appeal in *R v McNally* [2013] EWCA Crim 1051. It should be noted however, that non-disclosure may have other legal consequences. Thus, in the context of marriage, failure to disclose 'gender history' prior to a marriage operates as a legal ground for having the marriage annulled (s. 12(h) Matrimonial Causes Act 1973) (for a discussion of this provision see Sharpe, 2012).

## 6.2 Gender, truth and power

Any discussion of what parties might owe to each other in contexts of sexual intimacy ought, from the outset, to acknowledge any underlying assumptions that might influence the process of ethical reflection and the conclusions drawn. Accordingly, we should recognise that 'lying' or non-disclosure of information assumes some factual 'truth' against which the ethicality of conduct/omission might be measured or tested. As Scanlon notes, '[i]f judgments of right and wrong can be said to be true or false, this must be because there is some realm of facts that they are meant to describe, and to which they can correspond, or fail to correspond' (Scanlon, 1998, p. 2). If therefore, we want to describe acts or omissions as unethical, we must first establish the facts to which they pertain.

Let us begin then by stating that the central fact in cases of sexual intimacy between cisgender and transgender people is that transgender men and transgender women who present as men and women, are men and women or, at least, ought to be treated as such. As Judith Butler has noted: 'we are all ethically bound to recognise another person's declared or enacted sense of sex and/or gender'[5] and, of course, it is sex/gender in this sense, rather than any other, that best accords with the ethical conception of being true to oneself and others. As Talia Mae Bettcher explains, in distinguishing metaphysical from existential understandings of gender identity, while there may be dispute concerning the definition of sex and gender, we ought to privilege existential understandings of gender self-identity because they best address who we are in the most meaningful and ethical sense. An existential understanding captures what we are about, what moves us, what we stand for and what we care about the most regarding our gender identity (Bettcher, 2009 p. 110). While this book recognises that gender identities are socially constructed, it also recognises that they are tied to embodied and psychic experiences, that is, to lived (and sadly, for some transgender people, unliveable) realities.

It is these facts we must insist on, in any inquiry about ethicality, and which must inform judgment, at least if judgment is to remain ethical. It is not that other conclusions cannot be drawn. After all, from a social constructionist perspective, claims about gender, sexuality and the body are inevitably part of a 'truth' game which produces them as 'truth-effects' (Foucault, 1980b, p. 132). Rather, it is that ethics demands that we draw this conclusion and act accordingly, at least in circumstances where gender identity claims are non-trivial. In the case of transgender people, such claims are clearly non-trivial because they speak to a sense of (dis) embodiment, psychic reality and experiential truth. Accordingly, this chapter adopts a 'hermeneutics of suspicion' (Ricoeur, 1970, p. 356) in relation to the view that transgender people who do not confess a 'truth' that is not their own are deceptive. This problematic view defines transgender people against their will and

5 C Williams, 'Gender Performance: The TransAdvocate Interviews Judith Butler', *TransAdvocate*, 1/5/14 available at www.transadvocate.com/gender-performance-the-transadvocate-interviews-judith-butler_n_13652.htm (last accessed: 3/2/17).

measures ethical performance against an ability to live up to an imposed gender identity.[6]

There will be those who, while accepting gender identity claims, say that other gendered facts exist in relation to which lying might occur or in relation to which non-disclosure of information might assume ethical importance. This may be so, and it is a matter we will consider in the following section. For now, it should be noted that alighting on such facts always, if indirectly, appears to amount to a denial, or at least the problematising, of the very gender identities such arguments nominally concede. At this stage however, I aim to develop my claim, and article of ethical faith, that assertions of gender identity by transgender people are grounded in lived reality and ought to be respected.[7] It is important to labour this point because the gender identities of transgender people are, to one degree or another, refused by the fact of criminal prosecution, complainant assertions of non-consent, harm and deception, and the foregrounding of an 'ethical' question put to transgender people concerning facts that ought to be disclosed.

If we take seriously assertions of gender identity, we must recognise that no relevant gap exists between a transgender person's actual gender identity and the gender identity some cisgender people assume. Thus, if a cisgender woman believed her object of desire to be a man, a conclusion of unethical deception on his part is only possible if we accept the following propositions: (i) a transgender man's understanding of his own gender identity is trumped by a cisgender woman's interpretation, (ii) her sexual autonomy is, despite the desire-led nature of intimacy, undermined because the privileging of her interpretation produces a gap between her belief about his gender identity and his actual gender identity, and (iii) because of (i) and (ii) she has suffered harm. Accordingly, a conclusion that a transgender man acts unethically in circumstances where he asserts his masculinity, either through statements or through gender performance, is unsustainable. It would be a conclusion, possible only through vacating the space of ethics.

6 The reader may object to the weight I place on assertions of gender identity. It may be asked, where does this leave individuals who are uncertain about their gender identity? However, in ethical terms, how a person identifies is important because it bears down on the question of deception. If a person asserts a male identity and believes the same this is qualitatively different from making the same claim without believing it to be true (or having doubts about its truth) and the two scenarios have different moral/ethical implications, and this is so irrespective of the social construction of gender. Of course, even in a case of gender uncertainty, a lie or non-disclosure of information may not necessarily be unethical because a conclusion of unethicality would still need to overcome potential justifications and certainly those raised in section 6.3(ii).

7 In saying this, I am not suggesting that gender identity be understood in essentialist terms. On the contrary, this book has argued for a social constructionist understanding. Rather, my claim is that the gender identities of transgender people are no less real, and no more constructed, than those of cisgender people. Accordingly, we ought to accept such claims.

To reiterate, in insisting on the reality of the gender identities of transgender people, it is not intended to suggest a pre-discursive subject exists. Rather, we *all* bear the mark of social construction. That is, while transgender people perhaps render the constructedness of gender especially transparent, we are, as Jack Halberstam notes, 'all transsexual' (Halberstam, 1994, p. 212) in the sense that 'gender uncertainty is visited upon us all' and in as much as gender 'is not so much a status but a lifelong project for everyone' (Currah, 2017, p. 441). However, as Judith Butler observes, '[t]hinking the body as constructed demands a rethinking of the meaning of construction itself' (Butler, 1993, p. xi). To emphasise construction is not to deny that bodies are thrown into the world with a particular materiality, or set of body parts. Rather, it is to recognise that 'their irrefutability in no way implies what it might mean to affirm them and through what discursive means' (Butler, 1993, p. xi).

In other words, what matters is not so much raw facts about bodies, as much as how we make sense of, experience and live them. Moreover, making sense, presupposes that we are engaged in constructive activity, that the line between nature and culture has already been crossed, '[a]nd if certain constructions appear constitutive, that is, have this character of being that "without which" we could not think at all, we might suggest that bodies only appear, only endure, only live within the productive constraints of highly gendered regulatory schemas' (Butler, 1993, p. xi). Importantly, these schemas produce hierarchies in which some bodies do not matter, or matter less. This is precisely what we encounter in the context of criminal prosecutions for gender identity fraud and, problematically, it is this not mattering of some bodies which precedes and informs the formation of 'ethical' questions. To put the matter more simply, some socially constructed genders are more likely to be read as 'real' than others and this is an effect of relations of power.

To speak of transgender people as deceptive is immediately to risk implication in a history of oppression and to deny the constructedness of cisgender bodies. It is also a failure on the part of cisgender people to acknowledge the privilege and interpretative power they possess and necessarily, if perhaps unconsciously, bring to the viewing exercise. The cultural means through which transgender and fraud become associated is citation through time, a cisgender communal chant, what Butler has described as 'an imaginary chorus that taunts' (Butler, 1993, p. 226). What needs to be emphasised here however, is the obvious difficulty experienced when attempting to uncouple ethical reflection from ideologies in which it is embedded and from which it issues. It is through posing questions about the obligations transgender people owe to cisgender people that 'cis-supremacy is enacted'.[8] As Natalie Reed notes, the question of transgender obligation 'frames

8 N Reed, 'The "Ethical Imperative" Of Disclosure, or: How to Believe Your Victim Owes You an Opportunity for Abuse' *FreeThoughtBlogs.com* 20/3/12 available at http://freethoughtblogs.com/nataliereed/2012/03/20/the-ethical-imperative-of-disclosure-or-how-to-believe-your-victim-owes-you-an-opportunity-for-abuse/ (last accessed: 3/2/17).

cisgender identity, experience and perspective as … the *yardstick by which ethics and morality themselves are determined*. It extends cis privilege into the concepts of "right" and "wrong" itself, determining morality primarily by how it relates to a cis person's experience of a conflict, cis perceptions of identity, cis perceptions of "truth" and "falsehood," cis perceptions of what are the salient issues in identity and sexual interaction."[9]

This problem is also apparent in the differential value we accord to the feelings of the parties to desire. Thus, and as criminal prosecutions reveal, concern tends to lie with 'harm' experienced by cisgender people, occasioned through 'discovery' of 'unwitting' sexual communion with transgender people. That is, legal and broader cultural conversations about such scenarios tend to focus, almost exclusively, on feelings of hurt, outrage, distress, humiliation and disgust that a cisgender person (understandably) experiences at the moment of 'discovery' and subsequently. Indeed, so seriously do we take cisgender feelings at the moment of 'discovery' that they have frequently served as a basis for a diminished responsibility type defence on occasions when transgender people have been murdered (Steinberg, 2005; Bettcher, 2007, pp. 43–45; Shelley, 2008, pp. 47–48).[10]

Conversely, less, if any, ethical attention is given to the fact that transgender people are, in such circumstances, subjected to considerable shaming and to other forms of degradation. After all, the typical complainant, and subsequent legal and societal, response to knowledge that 'inadvertent' cis–trans sexual intimacy has occurred is to seek to expel what has been experienced as 'polluting' (Douglas, 1966). Through the expression of individual and collective disgust transgender people are literally abjected (Kristeva, 1982), that is, 'treated like "shit"' (Cavanagh, 2013, p. 428) and, of course, this process is integral to their very constitution as Other (Butler, 1990, p. 133). The point here however, is not to reintroduce a harm calculus, to attempt to weigh relative harms, an issue we explored in Chapter 4 and one we will return to in the following section where we will consider the demands of normative ethics, nor is it to highlight how the ever-present threat of such shaming and othering practices serves to preclude disclosure, though this point certainly stands repetition. Rather, it is to highlight how the perspectives and feelings of cisgender people tend to condition ethical thought itself.

The tendency to approach ethical questions from a cisgender perspective, one that proceeds from the assumption that everyone is cisgender, an assumption that is clearly unwarranted and demonstrably false, must be avoided if proper ethical characterisation of sexual conduct/omission is our object. Indeed, we might focus on the cisgender demand to know as the proper object of ethical scrutiny. Posing the question in this way shines a light on those who would otherwise sit in

9 *Ibid.*

10 In the US, defence counsel have relied on 'trans-panic' (Steinberg, 2005), a variant on the so-called 'homosexual panic' (Comstock, 1992; Tomsen, 1998; Statham, 1999) defence to murder. However, the notion of 'panic' tends to pathologise and therefore individualise reactions to discovery, thereby masking the social and historical forces which produce them.

judgment and whose sexual ethics normally escape our attention. Further, it brings into sharp relief the question of burden and who should bear it. After all, it is peculiar that those for whom particular facts are apparently fundamental, are relieved from having to make any effort to ensure that sexual scenarios conform with those facts. Surely, refusing to bear any responsibility for the possibility that actual sex might differ from imagined sex is questionable in ethical terms.

Placing the obligation on transgender people produces a situation where the one who has no problem with his/her identity/body (why would s/he), is required to disclose personal information to the one who has a problem. On this account, the ethical characterisation of sexually active transgender people becomes an effect of a willingness to respond to and endorse the (cis)sexism and (trans) phobia harboured by others. Indeed, the transgender person who wishes to remain ethical must not only respond to prejudice, but must, in order to do so, have already internalised it. In this respect, the truly ethical transgender person emerges as a self-loathing individual who cannot legitimately imagine him/herself to be the object of another's desire. It seems to me that if inquiry is to proceed from such 'givens', it can hardly be described as ethical.

Indeed, we might consider it ethical for a transgender person to withhold information in circumstances where it is feared a cisgender sexual partner may be transphobic. Not because of potential violence, though this is an important issue we will return to in the following section. But because dehumanised people might first want to give others the opportunity to get to know them as fully human before potentially being dismissed as 'freaks'.[11] Indeed, and while recognising that fear of transphobic reactions might not be based on knowledge or even suspicion of their likelihood in the context of a specific sexual encounter, but on prior experiences and internalised transphobia, we might even choose to characterise a person who is willing to love in the face of another's prejudice, to run that risk, as laudable or even heroic.

Of course, I recognise that, in the same way that most Jews would not want to become sexually intimate with an anti-semite, and most black people would not want to become sexually intimate with a racist, most transgender people would not want to become sexually intimate with a transphobe. It is revealing nevertheless, how those transgender people whose love might survive an encounter with prejudice are likely to be read in terms of deception rather than virtue. This observation becomes especially pronounced once we recognise the virtual silence concerning the dubious relationship between ethical selfhood and failure to disclose a transphobic mindset prior to sexual intimacy with a person who, after all, may be transgender.

Having marshalled my position on the 'authenticity' of gender identity, and having teased out the conundrum that questions of authenticity present for establishing ethical first principles, I now turn to addressing the concerns of those who, while accepting gender identity claims, might argue that other facts about

11 Reed above note 8.

gender exist in relation to which lying or non-disclosure of information might assume ethical importance. In my view, such arguments always seem to pull the rug from under the very identities they nominally concede. Nevertheless, while I adopt a sceptical position in relation to such arguments, it is important to address them, at least strategically, because in a cisnormative society they have acquired traction in ethical debates (see, for example, Laird, 2014, p. 509).

## 6.3 Engaging with normative ethics

In this section we turn to consider the demands of normative ethics. It is recognised that ethical inquiry within philosophy also encompasses *applied, meta* and *descriptive* ethics (van der Burg, 2010, p. 5). Moreover, thinking about 'deception' in the specific context of cis-trans sexual intimacy, necessarily entails these other avenues of ethical inquiry. Thus our inquiry involves applied ethics, given the specific focus adopted. It is meta ethical given our interest in what it means to be ethically gendered, a theme we will explore in depth in section 6.4, and it covers descriptive ethics in that it covers actual and widespread moral beliefs held by cisgender people. Nevertheless, it is primarily the normative ethical question of what we owe to each other in sexual contexts, and specifically prior to sexual intimacy, with which we are concerned. So far, we have proceeded on the basis that we should accept gender identity claims, except in rare circumstances where they are demonstrably false.[12] It might be argued however, that while a person's gender identity cannot be considered a lie, nor can it call for disclosure because it is already on show performatively, lying about other facts which bear a gendered character or not disclosing such facts might constitute unethical deception.

The kind of facts likely to be identified here are those pertaining to the body, to its past and/or present (especially genital) state, to gender history and/or legal status, and perhaps gender socialisation.[13] As already noted, any attempt to disaggregate such facts from gender identity must be treated with caution given that such information seems to have little value beyond its use in challenging gender identity claims. In this sense, the ethical significance of a distinction between gender identity and other facts concerning gender is less analytically distinct than might be imagined. Nevertheless, and while bearing this important caveat in mind, let

12 *R v Devonald* [2008] EWCA Crim 527. For a discussion of the case see Chapter 4.

13 Gender socialisation has assumed relevance in the context of the importance given to it by some radical feminists for the purposes of determining whether a person is a woman. For these feminists, described as Trans Exclusionary Radical Feminists (TERFs), a pejorative but nonetheless accurate term, gender socialisation as a girl/woman is fundamental to being classified as a woman. Indeed, this particular feminist position serves to redraw our attention to the way in which facts about gender tend to prove important for the purpose of calling into question gender identity itself. For a critique of the TERF position, see A. Sharpe, 'The Poverty of Gender Critical Feminism' *Inherently Human: Critical Perspectives on Law, Gender and Sexuality* 17/5/16 available at https://inherentlyhuman.wordpress.com/2016/05/17/the-poverty-of-gender-critical-feminism/ (last accessed: 3/2/17).

us turn our attention to considering the ethical significance of lying about or not disclosing other gendered facts.

Let us begin by noting that the phrase 'unethical deception' presupposes that deception, either through acts or omission, is not necessarily unethical. This point is perhaps easier to grasp in relation to non-disclosure of information, because characterisation of omission as unethical requires first establishing a duty to act. However, even in relation to lying, while we perhaps bear a general moral duty to refrain from doing so (Mill, 1979), there are clearly cases where lying is less easily described as unethical.[14] As Carson observes, '[i]f we say that lying is always wrong no matter what, then we are claiming that the duty not to lie is always more important than any conflicting duties. However, on reflection this claim is very dubious. There is no good reason to think that the duty not to lie is always and necessarily more important than the duty to prevent harm to others' (Carson, 2010, p. 85). If it were it would produce some perverse results. For example, it would lead to a conclusion that a Jewish woman, who lied about her Jewish status to a Nazi officer in order to avoid being sent to a concentration camp, acted unethically (Carson, 2010, p. 85). As Judith Butler has noted, such moments are 'not the time to go Kantian' (quoted by Harrison, 2013, p. 54).

In developing my argument, I reject the notion that there is an overriding duty-based obligation not to lie about or to disclose facts pertaining to gender, though accept that such an obligation may arise if telling the truth or disclosing information can be shown to produce the best overall consequences. In other words, I am adopting a consequentialist approach to the problem facing us and will argue that lying and/or non-disclosure may, and typically will, produce the best overall result.[15] Accordingly, I will focus on consequential harm arising, or potentially arising, out of a decision to lie about or not disclose facts about gender, and argue, at least for the purposes of this part of the chapter, that this ought to prove decisive in any evaluative exercise. Emphasis on harm, and the need to balance harms, as central to proper ethical characterisation of decision-making, ensures analysis remains grounded in social reality and embodied experience. It also reveals, indeed heightens, what is at stake for parties to desire. While harms can clearly be disaggregated from wrongs (Gardner, 2007), and while complainants in gender identity fraud cases identify both as a source of complaint, it remains the case that harms or potential harms occasioned by discovering facts pertaining to gender must be balanced against those harms arising, or likely to arise, from having to disclose those same facts. Indeed, within a consequentialist framework, wrongs are rendered unimportant, or at least important only to the extent that they identify harms. In proceeding in this way, the chapter will not consider the right to sexual

14 Indeed, even Kant appears to have recognised situations where lying would be permissible (see Carson, 2010, Chapter 3).

15 To be more precise, I am adopting rule consequentialism (Carson, 2010, Chapter 5) concerning information provision, at least for this part of my argument. In assessing consequences, it is harm that will be used as the measure.

autonomy which some ethicists clearly see as determinative of the issue and as favouring disclosure (Archard, 1998; Wertheimer, 2003; Dougherty, 2013). This was an issue considered in depth and rejected in Chapter 3.

Before proceeding further, and in order to ensure that ethical analysis remains tied to real life situations, it will be helpful to clarify what is envisaged by 'unethical deception'. To begin with, let us remove from the table a whole series of rather abstract and somewhat unreal situations. To begin with, we are not dealing with scenarios where a transgender man announces that he is, or has always been, legally or chromosomally male. Nobody makes statements of this kind because there is no need to do so, and because to make such a statement is immediately to call into question, in the mind of the addressee, the authenticity of the claim. Equally, nobody asks questions along these lines, and if they did it would appear to suggest that they have knowledge, or at least suspicion, concerning the gender history of their intended sexual partner.

Indeed, when one stops to think about it, it is actually quite difficult to imagine the content of a lie that might actually be told or the content of a question that might actually be asked and which might produce a lie by way of response. This claim is borne out, not only by common sense, but by the gender identity fraud cases prosecuted.[16] Moreover, given the difficulty of identifying a lie that a transgender person might tell or a question his/her sexual partner might plausibly ask, it would seem that the substantive ethical issue relates to information and its disclosure. In other words, it is non-disclosure or omission which provides the substance around which practical moral reasoning needs to be organised. An emphasis on omission is also appropriate because the central objection complainants make in such cases is not that they have been lied to but that information they feel they have a right or legitimate expectation to know has been withheld. Accordingly, and while much of the analysis that follows applies equally to lying, especially the arguments made in section 6.3(ii), the remainder of this section will focus on non-disclosure, and will argue that non-disclosure of facts about gender, beyond the fact of gender identity itself, is not necessarily unethical for at least two reasons. First, a conclusion that non-disclosure constitutes unethical omission depends on the existence of a prima facie moral obligation to disclose information, and second, if such an obligation exists, it presupposes that non-disclosure cannot otherwise be justified according to normative ethical considerations. It is to these matters that we now turn.

### *(i) A moral obligation to disclose information*

While it is generally accepted that there exists a prima facie moral obligation to refrain from lying, there is a lack of consensus as to the moral status of non-disclosure of information. Certainly, non-disclosure of information is typically thought to be less morally problematic than lying (Ross, 1930; Wilkinson, 2000). As Scanlon

16 Thus none of the defendants claimed to be chromosomally or legally male, and no complainant asked a question along these lines.

argues, '[a] principle forbidding one to lie (or to give intentionally misleading information) is, obviously, easier to argue for than one requiring the provision of information' (Scanlon, 1998, p. 318). Importantly, and emphasising liberal ideas of autonomy and privacy, many, if not all (Wasserstrom, 1978; Posner, 1978), philosophers consider non-disclosure to fall outside the sphere of ethical condemnation altogether. Thus, Schoeman observes that provided that 'a person does not misrepresent himself to those who, within the relevant domain, reasonably rely on his projected image, that person is not acting deceptively' (Schoeman, 1984, p. 409). Others have articulated this position more strongly. Thus, according to William Ross (Ross, 1930), and as noted by Carson, while there is generally 'a duty to refrain from lying' there is 'no duty to tell the truth or reveal information' (Carson, 2010, p. 103).

Moreover, a duty to reveal information, if it does exist, presupposes that the party who chooses not to reveal, appreciates the importance of the information either to the other sexual party, or in general normative terms. In the present context, this presents some difficulties which we will consider before addressing justifications for non-disclosure that might operate in any event. In essence, what we are considering here is the question of knowledge, as distinct from motivation. While both bare down on questions of ethicality, it should be recognised that knowledge that particular facts hold importance to the other sexual party does not demonstrate that non-disclosure was motivated by a desire to deceive, either in order to have sex irrespective of consent or at all, an issue to be considered later in the context of justification. As Sissela Bok notes, '[t]o confuse secrecy and deception is easy, since all deception does involve keeping something secret … But while all deception requires secrecy, all secrecy is not meant to deceive' (Bok, 1998, p. 7).

Thus, for the purposes of this section, my argument is that a duty to disclose, if it arises at all, can only arise in circumstances where a person has knowledge, or ought to have knowledge, of the importance of particular gendered facts to his or her sexual partner. One of the problems, in the present context, lies in the tendency to assume that cisgender people would consider it important to know that their sexual partner is transgender, and transgender people therefore must have knowledge of the importance of this information. While one might argue, as Ross does, that a duty to disclose information does not, or ought not, to arise in any event, if one were to accept that a duty does arise with knowledge, then a duty might be said to arise here. The difficulty, of course, rests with assumptions about what cisgender people consider important and what transgender people are assumed to know, or ought to know, about what cisgender people consider important.

First, the assumption that transgender status is an important fact for cisgender people to know proceeds from and reinforces the cissexist notion that a cisgender person's consent would not be forthcoming if she were aware of the other party's gender history. This outlook, one that flies in the face of the empirical reality of successful unions between cisgender and transgender people, renders transgender people and their bodies undesirable,[17] and therefore sexual congress with us unimaginable. By the same token, we should not assume transgender people to be self-loathing individuals, incapable of imagining ourselves to be the proper object of cisgender desire. In other words, if duty presupposes knowledge, a conclusion that omission constitutes ethical failure must rely on actual knowledge, or at least knowledge one ought to possess, rather than on non-empirically based assumptions concerning cisgender desire or transgender self-repudiation (Shelley, 2008). Crucially, a duty to disclose cannot be founded on the manufacture of knowledge out of prejudice.

In any event, if there is a prima facie obligation to disclose gendered facts, non-disclosure may nevertheless be justified. While the burden of proof must rest ultimately with those who sit in judgment, I will argue that there are at least two broad justifications for not disclosing facts about gender history or past or present anatomical or legal gender status, justifications which, if persuasive, ought to uncouple non-disclosure from moral censure. These justifications are to be found in the value of privacy, both in relation to individual well-being and human intersubjectivity, and in a concern to preserve the self, both in physical and psychic terms. It is contended that in determining the ethicality of decision-making, such factors must be considered and weighed, at least if the ethical bar is not to be set too high, and that these factors, when properly considered, demonstrate, at least in some and perhaps most cases, that non-disclosure produces the best overall consequences. Both of these justifications, in addition to providing support for characterising non-disclosure as ethical, point to motivational forces for non-disclosure other than a desire to have sex irrespective of the other party's consent. While this latter motivation tends to be readily assumed, consent, as Moira Carmody argues, 'remains a limited concept without some consideration of how individuals as sexed and gendered bodies constitute themselves as ethical' (Carmody, 2004, p. 45).

### *(ii) Justifications*

#### *(a) Privacy*

In Chapter 3, we considered the right to privacy as one objection to criminalisation of gender identity fraud. While there is some overlap, the focus here lies not with legality or public policy, but with the proper ethical characterisation of conduct or omission. Privacy is an important value and one compromised by an obligation either to disclose information or to always tell the truth. As already noted, the focus here lies with non-disclosure of information. In making an ethical case for not disclosing historical or present facts bearing a gendered character, I will argue

17 While this section of the chapter assumes the possibility of unethical omission, in order to refute it, the fact that what is really at stake is the desirability of bodies, might be viewed as involving the ethical collapsing into the aesthetic. That is, we might view knowledge as not bearing ethical import, but rather as something that can alter an aesthetic value, and therefore as something trivial when it comes to the ethics of relationships. I am indebted to my colleague, Anthony Wrigley, for this perceptive insight.

that privacy constitutes a significant good in the consequentialist weighing exercise. While privacy is clearly a right that comes with some baggage, as feminist scholars have long pointed out (see for example, Pateman, 1983; Okin, 1989; Gavison, 1992; Chinkin, 1999),[18] it remains necessary to recognise its importance and to carve space for an inner life. After all, as Charles Fried has argued, privacy is essential to the formation of relationships, including those of love and friendship, for relationships between self and others are based on an individual's ability to share and control personal information (Fried, 1984, p. 290).

Indeed, for Fried, without privacy, such relationships 'are simply inconceivable' (Fried, 1984, p. 205). This is a view shared by Thomas Nagel who insists that 'the boundary between what we reveal and what we do not, and some control over the boundary, are among the most important attributes of our humanity' (Nagel, 1998, p. 4). Moreover, the need to exercise some control over personal information is perhaps especially marked in relation to identity. As Bok notes, in relation to personal identity, secrecy guards its central aspects (Bok, 1998, p. 13). Indeed, for Bok, 'without perceiving some sacredness in human identity, individuals are out of touch with the depth they might feel in themselves and respond to in others' (Bok, 1998, p. 21). Accordingly, and in this sense, privacy or reticence with regard to the sharing of personal information might be viewed as a necessary ground of ethics, of ethical decision-making, of an ethical relation with others.[19]

### *(b) Self-preservation*

As noted in earlier chapters, female complainants in gender identity fraud cases speak of distress, humiliation and disgust when describing their experience of 'discovering' that their sexual partners are not cisgender men. It is not my intention to trivialise such experiences. However, it is important to recognise that they are inextricably connected to homo/trans phobias which they sustain. As Cressida Heyes notes, it is inadequate to identify harms without first recognising as an ethical problem, disciplinary practices that produce harms, that render practices meaningful in terms of harm. In other words, any theory that presents itself as ethical must both acknowledge and challenge normalisation, lest it contribute to the very harms it identifies and on the basis of which presumes to judge (Heyes, 2007). Thus, while harms cisgender women experience are real and significant, they cannot easily be separated from the power and privilege cisgender status confers and through which experiences are interpreted to be harmful.[20]

18 Feminist critiques of liberal privacy emphasise, among other things, how the private realm has long functioned as a site of gendered violence, and it is recognised that state intervention into this realm is, in many contexts, warranted.

19 In Foucauldian terms, '[t]he care of the self is ethical in itself ... and the ethos of freedom (which it implies) is also a way of caring for others' (Rabinow, 1998, p. 287).

20 In emphasising relations of power, I recognise that in cases prosecuted female complainants were typically younger than defendants, and in several cases were 15 and therefore below the age of lawful consent. While this may raise criminal law issues

Moreover, and more pertinently for present purposes, harms which cisgender people identify need to be balanced against the harms transgender people face, and experience on a fairly regular basis, whenever we expose our transgender status. As we will see, these harms, ones which are effects of relative powerlessness, appear to be more significant than cisgender disgust, and therefore support maintaining privacy as a consequentialist rule. In a passage that has particular resonance for transgender people, Thomas Nagel argues that '[s]ome forms of reticence have a social function, protecting us from one another and from undesirable collisions and hostile reactions. Other forms of reticience have a personal function, protecting the inner life from a public exposure that would cause it to wither, or would require too much distortion' (Nagel, 1998, p. 10). In essence, Nagel, while referring to people generally, captures both sides of the dilemma transgender people face in trying to negotiate their way in a cissexist and transphobic society. In relation to protecting the inner life from a public exposure that would cause it to wither, for many transgender people, disclosing highly personal information concerning chromosomal status, earlier or present gonadal and/or genital condition, as well as a history of coerced gendered performance is a source of pain and trauma.

It is perhaps difficult here to specify the most appropriate analogy. However, secrecy, or the maintenance of privacy, in relation to gender history might be compared to the control of information exhibited by some victims of child abuse. We would not demand that a victim of child abuse disclose details of the abuse or even the fact of abuse within the context of an intimate relationship. Indeed, even in the context of a lengthy marriage, it would be hard to insist on an ethical obligation to disclose a history of child abuse. The reader might respond that this is because (a) an intimate partner would remain unaffected by such personal information and (b) it would be intolerable to demand disclosure in these circumstances. In relation to (b) the point is well made. In relation to (a) however, it is far from clear that an intimate partner would remain unaffected over the course of a relationship. A history of child abuse might make its presence felt in numerous ways (Berenson and Andersen, 2006). The important point here is to recognise the relationship between non-disclosure of core personal information and psychic survival. If ethics requires sacrifice, this surely cannot encompass the abandonment of a desire to preserve the self or amount to psychic suicide. That is, we ought not to demand a supererogatory kind of ethical performance.

Moreover, the force of an ethical demand to disclose information would, if it is not to be diluted, have to overcome, not only a legitimate desire to stave of

(though no charges in relation to sex with a minor were brought), it is contended that the ethical analysis adopted holds. In my view, while youth, and especially minority, are relevant to an analysis of power, non-coercive desire-led intimacy between young people close in age should not be viewed as an abuse of power or otherwise unethical simply because one party is 15. In the cases under consideration, it is contended that the key element of power is not age, but rather, a legally and culturally sanctioned interpretive power to refuse the gender identities of others.

psychological harm, but also a concern to avoid physical, including lethal, violence. Yet, violence against transgender people is pervasive and well-documented (GenderPac, 1997; Whittle et al, 2007; Morton, 2008; Waters, 2016). In fact, it is worth emphasising that a more typical outcome of non-disclosure of gender history prior to sexual intimacy is not criminal prosecution, but the hospitalisation or burial of transgender people.[21] In this respect, and in terms of political theory, the ethical demand to disclose would appear to sit uncomfortably with the state's failure to meet its first obligation to its citizens, namely to provide physical protection.[22] To argue for an ethical demand to disclose then, is literally to put lives on the line. It is also indicative of a failure to recognise the 'double-bind' (Bettcher, 2007) in which transgender people are placed. On the one hand, transgender people are expected to be invisible, to disappear into binary gender (Green, 2006, p. 501; Enke, 2013, p. 238). In doing so, we reassure cisgender people about the proper relationship between and the naturalness of their own sex, gender and sexuality. On the other hand, whenever cisgender people express desire toward transgender people, we are expected to reappear quick smart, and irrespective of the always present dangers that accompany disclosure.

Ultimately, we have to wonder whether 'gender deception' is best understood as 'one laudable tactic of attempted survival in what appears to be an exceptionally violent no-win situation' (Bettcher, 2007, p. 60). After all, isn't telling the 'truth' 'only to acquiesce to the morality of oppression' (Bettcher, 2007, p. 60) and isn't 'disclosure discourse', a discourse 'used to justify real violence against transgender people', also 'one of the primary grounds on which cis-supremacy is enacted'.[23] As Wilchins observes, in posing the Foucauldian question, *what does it cost to tell the truth?* (Foucault, 1989, p. 252), some of us bear a different and costlier relationship to telling the 'truth' about our gender than others. For those whose sense of gender self matches their anatomy it perhaps costs little. For 'the rest of us, though, it can cost a great deal' (Wilchins, 2006, p. 551).

This section of the chapter has sought to engage with normative ethics in order to demonstrate that within these philosophical terms non-disclosure of gender history can be justified. To that end, it relied on rule consequentialism and demonstrated how this approach is, in the present context, capable of doing the necessary work, albeit such an approach necessarily sacrifices claims about

21 This violent reality, though commonplace, is dramatised by the film, *Boys Don't Cry* (1999), which depicts the life, and tragic death, of a young transgender man, Brandon Teena. The allegation of 'deception' also proved central in the equally tragic case of Gwen Araujo (see Bettcher, 2007) depicted in the film, *A Girl Like Me: The Gwen Araujo Story* (2006). In both cases, the defendants asserted ignorance of the victims' transgender status and relied on a 'trans-panic' defence. In both cases, defendant claims of ignorance were dubious, a theme that this book has sought to emphasise throughout.

22 As Hobbes made clear, the first duty of government is to protect individuals from private violence or from violence emanating from outside the sovereign body (Hobbes, 2008).

23 Reed above note 8.

individual justice and rights. However, ultimately, ethical analysis about what we owe to each other in contexts of cis–trans sexual intimacy cannot be reduced to a cost-benefit analysis or to an assessment of what produces the greatest good, albeit such an analysis appears to favour non-disclosure. Nor, for that matter, can it be reduced to questions of duty or right. Rather, if ethical thinking in this context is to avoid impoverishment, it must engage more seriously with the complexity of gender and sexuality, of the body and desire. In other words, we must move beyond a concern with normative ethics in order to deal with meta-ethical concerns, principally the matter of how we conceive of and make ethical judgments about gender, and in doing so we necessarily return to the social-relatedness of ethical issues, that is, to questions of privilege and power. In the present context, to act and think ethically first requires that we assume a position which Julia Serano has described as 'ethically gendered' (Serano, 2013, p. 259).

## 6.4 To be(come) ethically gendered: beyond cisnormativity

In this section, we turn away from the concerns of normative ethics in order to venture into the territory of what it might mean to be(come) ethically gendered in a cisnormative society. As Tim Dean notes, 'it is not the recognizable other but the unrecognizable other … that most urgently calls for an ethical attitude' (Dean, 2001, p. 131). Ultimately, ethical thought in the context of sexual intimacy between cisgender and transgender people requires reflexivity and openness. Of course, it requires recognition of cis privilege or gender entitlement, something which, in the present context, means never having to 'come out' or declare one's gender identity, or even consider what this might mean, and which, in addition to producing a sense of intelligible gender that requires no explanation, encourages a view that cissexuality exhausts sexual desire, an outlook, it should be emphasised, that fails to conceive of the possibility of other forms of consensual intimacy. It requires recognising 'how a culturally central concept like public/private is organized so as to preserve for [cissexuality as well as] heterosexuality the unproblematicalness, the apparent naturalness, of its *discretionary* choice between display and concealment' (Sedgwick, 1993, p. 10). But it requires more than acknowledging privilege, it requires self-examination.

As Serano argues, it requires 'gender-anxious cissexuals to look deep within themselves and ask why they *choose* to view transsexual bodies as unsettling or disturbing' (Serano, 2007, p. 92). Crucially, being 'ethically gendered … requires us to engage in personal reflection and questioning' (Serano, 2013, p. 259). As Serano suggests, 'this process might begin by critically examining that [to] which we are not attracted' (Serano, 2013, p. 259). Thus we might ask: '[i]f we do not desire a particular type of person or sexual practice, why is that? Does it simply not pique our interest? Or do we have a strong visceral reaction against it? Do we find it abhorrent? Or do we experience some level of attraction, but we are reluctant to act on it because we would be too embarrassed if someone else were to find out?' (Serano, 2013, p. 259). Thinking about these and other questions ought to be central to any enterprise that aims to draw conclusions about ethical selfhood.

Crucially, we 'must stop projecting what we wish were true about gender and sexuality onto other people, and instead learn to yield to their unique individual identities, experiences and perspectives' (Serano, 2007, p. 113). The first step in this process perhaps, is to disabuse ourselves of the ludicrous assumption that everybody is cisgender. While this assumption is demonstrably false, it continues to structure the approach of most, if not all, cisgender people to the sexual life-world. However, 'seeing' transgender people, or overcoming 'the killing pretense that a culture does not know what it knows' (Sedgwick, 1988, p. 121), is not enough. We must also resist the tendency toward what Ann Cahill has described as 'derivitization' (Cahill, 2011). To derivatise is to treat another as a thing, rather than a self. Not to derivatise 'requires encountering a person, even a person one might want to have sex with, without asking what this encounter says about me. ... Not to derivatize another person means not confusing my encounter with her for a horrifying portrait of myself, an event that is entirely about me' (Parker, 2017, p. 113).

As Judith Butler explains, the task is to understand how 'we encounter the difference that calls our grids of intelligibility into question without trying to foreclose the challenge that the difference delivers' (Butler, 2004, p. 35). It is to ask, '[w]hat might it mean to learn to live in the anxiety of that challenge, to feel the surety of one's epistemological and ontological anchor go, but be willing, in the name of the human to become something other than what it is traditionally assumed to be' (Butler, 2004, p. 35). As Adriana Cavarero points out, with a nod to Arendt, the question we pose is 'who are you?' (Cavarero, 2000). This question, though simple, is unanswerable (Butler, 2004, p. 35). But in the face of it we can at least avoid, or attempt to avoid, violence. As Butler explains:

> The violent [and, of course, the unethical] response is the one that does not ask, and does not seek to know. It wants to shore up what it knows, to expunge what threatens it with not-knowing, what forces it to reconsider the presuppositions of its world, their contingency, their malleability. The non-violent response lives with its unknowingness about the other in the face of the Other, since sustaining the bond that the question opens is finally more valuable than knowing in advance what holds us in common, as if we already have all the resources we need to know what defines the human, what its future life might be (Butler, 2004, p. 35).

## 6.5 Conclusion

This chapter has concerned itself with ethical rather than legal questions in thinking about occasions of sexual intimacy between cisgender and transgender people. While earlier chapters focused on, and strongly opposed, criminalisation and criminal prosecution of gender identity fraud, this chapter has sought to consider broader ethical questions which arise and to challenge some of the assumptions upon which they are founded. A focus on ethics is considered especially important because, while liberal scholars have generally exhibited scepticism regarding the use of criminal law in the context of desire-led intimacy, and certainly in the present context, such scepticism was noted to often evaporate when attention turns to the proper ethical characterisation of non-disclosure of gender history. In view of this tendency to view non-disclosure as unethical deception, the chapter began by considering the relationship between gender, truth and power. In doing so, it recognised the contested nature of 'truth' about gender identities and the bodies to which they (sometimes uneasily) correspond. While the posing of some 'ethical' questions appears to problematise the gender identities of transgender people, it was taken as given that transgender men and transgender women are the men and women they claim to be. Indeed, insistence on this point was considered unavoidable if analysis was to be properly described as ethical.

In taking this position, it was not suggested that identity should be understood in some essentialised way. Rather, throughout this book, identity has been understood through the lens of social constructionism. The important point that the chapter emphasised however, is that the gender identities of transgender people are no less, albeit no more, real than those of cisgender people. Accordingly, they should be taken as seriously and receive the same degree of respect. In developing this theme, the chapter highlighted how questioning gender identity is an effect of the power and privilege cisgender people enjoy. Moreover, it was argued that cisgender identity, experience and perspective actually operate to frame ethical thinking itself in relation to these particular kinds of desire-led intimacy. Indeed, an 'ethical' focus on an assumed obligation to disclose gender history perhaps gives the game away. That is to say, scrutiny of a cisgender demand to know rarely, if ever, receives proper attention. Yet, it is precisely this demand that ought perhaps to preoccupy us if it is to the ethical that we wish to appeal, that is, if we wish to approach cis–trans sexual intimacies through an appropriate moral grammar.

The chapter then considered the possibility that it might constitute unethical deception to lie about or to fail to disclose facts relating to gender beyond the fact of gender identity itself. While recognising that such a distinction is always vulnerable to analytical collapse, given other facts about gender tend to prove relevant only to the extent that they cast doubt on gender identity, the chapter first considered whether a duty to disclose exists and, if it does, argued that non-disclosure of gendered facts might nevertheless be justified in normative ethical terms. That is, and while recognising that deception is not necessarily unethical, the chapter sought to defend what might be considered deception against precisely this charge. To this end, it argued that non-disclosure of highly personal information can be viewed as consistent with ethical selfhood because of the considerable costs disclosure involves. This argument entailed consideration of the importance of a private life and the threat disclosure can pose to preservation of self, both in psychological and physical terms. In these latter respects, the chapter emphasised that ethical significance attaches to the fact that the costs of disclosure are unevenly distributed across the cis–trans divide.

Finally, the chapter returned to questions of privilege and power. In opposition to kinds of ethical framing which centre the experiences and perspectives of cisgender people, it asked instead what it might mean to be ethically gendered. Drawing on transgender and queer theories it called on cisgender people to not only recognise their privilege, but to engage in self-examination. Importantly, this requires abandoning the gender fiction that cisgender people exhaust the categories of men and women. It also necessitates some introspection concerning the nature and sources of anxieties held about communion with transgender bodies. And it most certainly requires assuming a degree of ownership for desires that are pleasurably acted out and only retrospectively reimagined as disgusting and/or harmful, and this is perhaps especially so where gender ambiguity lies at the heart of a desire-based encounter (Butler, 1990, p. 123). Ultimately, as Butler contends, we must all learn to feel the surety of our epistemological and ontological anchor go, at least if we wish to maintain ethical sexual relationships with gendered others.

In the following chapter, the legal and ethical issues considered so far in this book will culminate in the writing of a counter-judgment to the judgment of Leveson LJ in *R v McNally*. The counter-judgment will constitute an act of ethical reimagination. It will write transgender and other gender non-conforming people into legal existence, and will provide an alternative legal interpretation and resolution of the case, one actually available to the Court of Appeal at the time. In other words, it will argue not only that *McNally* could have been decided differently, but that it ought to have been decided differently.

Chapter 7

# Queering legal practice: re-writing *McNally*

## 7.1 Introduction

This book has taken issue with the prosecution of young gender non-conforming people for gender identity fraud. To that end, it has offered a series of principled objections (Chapters 3 and 4) and an analysis that seeks to ground consideration of the relevant legal issues in certain socio-legal realities which precede, and which are apparent in, the application of substantive legal rules (Chapter 5). In Chapter 6, it extended the analysis to ethics, where it problematised the widespread view that gender history ought to be disclosed prior to sexual relations. Throughout, an attempt was made to tease out issues of privilege and power and to centre the experiences and perspectives of gender non-conforming people. In this chapter, one which develops the theme of resistance, I will provide an alternative judgment to the one handed down in *R v McNally*[1] by Leveson LJ. I have selected *McNally* because it is one of only two gender identity fraud cases to have reached the Court of Appeal. In relation to the other, more recent case of *R v Newland*,[2] the court has not yet published its reasons for quashing the appellant's conviction. In any event, the focus of appeal in *Newland* was confined to the trial judge's summing up to the jury.[3]

In contrast, the Court of Appeal's decision in *McNally* has emerged as a leading authority in relation to establishing liability for sexual fraud generally, and gender identity fraud specifically. It is also the decision that has most developed the

1 *R v McNally* [2013] EWCA Crim 1051.

2 *R v Newland* 15/9/15 (Unrept, Chester Crown Court, Judge Dutton). After the Court of Appeal found Newland's convictions to be unsafe, she was convicted for a second time and of the same sexual offences (*R v Newland* 29/6/17 (Unrept, Manchester Crown Court, Judge Stockdale)).

3 S. Nelson, 'Prosthetic Penis Case: Gayle Newland Conviction Overturned' *Huffington Post* 12/12/16 available at www.huffingtonpost.co.uk/entry/prosthetic-penis-case-gayle-newland-conviction-overturned_uk_57fe32dcc4b08e08b93d6149 (last accessed: 3/2/17); 'Gayle Newland: Woman Accused of Impersonating a Man in Blindfold "Sex Attack" Has Conviction Quashed' *The Telegraph* 12/12/16 available at www.telegraph.co.uk/news/2016/10/12/gayle-newland-blindfold-sex-attacker-accused-of-impersonating-a/ (last accessed: 3/2/17).

distinction between non-disclosure of information and active deception, as well as most explicitly applying this distinction to the facts of a case. The chapter will proceed as follows. First, it will preface the counter-judgment with an explanation of why an exercise in academic judgment-writing is valuable. In writing an alternative judgment, the chapter will draw significantly on feminist judgment-writing projects (Hunter et al, 2010; Hunter, 2012; Rackley, 2012). Second, the chapter will consider a queer approach to law, and will detail some queer principles around which the counter-judgment will be organised, while at the same time highlighting tensions between queer theory and engagement with law and judgment. Third, the chapter will present the counter-judgment which will suggest *McNally* was wrongly decided.

## 7.2 The value of counter-judgment writing

While the judgment to be offered is more properly described as queer, and while its aim is to queer or trouble *McNally*, it shares much with the approach taken by feminist legal scholars who have attempted to imagine, and express in judgment form, what a judgment might look like if it were animated by a desire to achieve substantive equality, overcome gender bias, privilege context over abstraction, avoid (at least non-strategic kinds of) essentialism and further other feminist principles (Hunter, 2010). In a similar fashion, the alternative and dissenting judgment to be offered here, a kind of queer missing voice, constitutes an act of ethical reimagination, one that aims to centre-stage the experiences and perspectives of gender non-conforming people, accommodate their differences and address their historical disadvantage. As Erika Rackley has put it, such judgments aim to 'challenge the majority's story and weaken its hold on our collective imagination' (Rackley, 2010, p. 33).

Writing a queer or feminist judgment, or indeed a judgment informed by some other set of alternative ethical principles, involves the writer in 'a kind of hybrid form of critique and law reform project' (Hunter, 2012, p. 137). As Rosemary Hunter observes, engaging in such a task is 'not done simply as an academic exercise or for an academic audience' (Hunter, 2012, p. 137). Rather, the aim is to have the counter-judgment 'taken seriously', to influence activists, lawyers and judges, and therefore, if indirectly, 'to change the law or at least to contribute to its development' (Hunter, 2012, p. 137. See also Marjury, 2006, p. 6). Value also lies in the fact that:

> by appropriating legal personas and forms, [counter-judgments] powerfully demonstrate that, at the time these cases were decided and with the legal and other materials then available to the court, the cases could have been reasoned and/or decided differently (Hunter, 2012, p. 137).

Accordingly, re-writing a judgment from another perspective represents an intervention in law's production of 'truth'. It serves to 'expose the contingency and biases of existing decisions and disrupt the unique authority of the courts and legal decision-making' (Hunter, 2012, p. 137) or, as Margaret Davies has put it, we dress up as judges, dress ourselves in law, 'in order to expose or reveal it' (Davies, 2012, p. 172). And as Leslie Moran explains, in considering feminist counter-judgments, they 'reveal the contested nature of what are presented in the original judgments as the "facts" of the lives of the women who have come to courts for justice under the law' (Moran, 2012, p. 298). In other words, they re-imagine the real (Geertz, 1983). As Clifford Geertz has noted, law is not, and cannot be, 'a bounded set of norms, rules, principles, values ... from which jural responses to distilled events can be drawn'. It is also, and inevitably, 'a distinctive manner of imagining the real' (Geertz, 1983, p. 173). The implication, of course, is that the law/fact distinction is unsustainable, at least to the extent that it assumes legal rules can be applied to pre-existing objective facts. For the 'facts', as judicially described, are always the 'legal facts', that is, the facts that have survived an encounter with law, with pre-trial filtration and judicial or jury interpretation. Stating the facts then, as they are understood by those at the sexual and gender margins, goes to the very heart of counter-judgment. It writes outsiders into law as intelligible subjects.

Of course, in adopting legal judgment-writing as a particular form of praxis, legal form or legal method go essentially unchallenged (Marjury, 2006, p. 6; Hunter et al, 2010, pp. 5–6). From feminist or queer perspectives this obviously raises some difficulties, ones which I will address below. However, for present purposes, it is important to emphasise that in order for counter-judgment to be taken seriously and therefore have legal and political purchase, external critique must be circumscribed. While weaving external critique into counter-judgment is essential if the exercise is not to become pointless, the degree and extent to which this can be done must be limited by fidelity to precedent, to judicial custom and to the practices of judges in the English appellate courts.

Thus, the re-writing of *McNally* will be a constrained exercise. That is, the counter-judgment offered will be one that might actually have been written while remaining faithful to existing legal principles, including the need not to go beyond the issues actually raised in the case (Paterson, 1982, p. 127). It will stretch legal principle, but only within the confines of its own elasticity. Within these confines, judgment-writing offers possibilities to 'manipulate the tools of legal reasoning, categorisation, precedent and statutory interpretation' (Hunter, 2012, p. 139). While legal form might be viewed as too restrictive in the context of pursuing progressive, and especially more radical politics, through curtailing critique in this way it becomes possible 'to demonstrate the porosity of legal method' and therefore 'the possibility and the legitimacy of taking a feminist [or queer] approach to legal analysis' (Hunter, 2012, p. 140).

Moreover, in addition to the stated aim of influencing law reform, or at least engendering a dialogue with the judiciary and the wider legal profession through providing a '[mirror] reflecting back onto judicial practice' (Moran, 2012, p. 289), counter judgment-writing provides alternative histories, recovers 'subjugated knowledges' (Foucault, 1980a, p. 81) and 'remind[s] us that law is a process of decisions, actions, choices, relationships and values, and not simply a set of abstract or hypostatised doctrines' (Davies, 2011, pp. 2, 6). In other words, judging is not a 'disinterested' practice (Hale, 2008, p. 320). Accordingly, counter-judgments can be viewed as 'a form of parodic – and hence subversive – performance' operating to 'powerfully denaturalise existing judicial and doctrinal norms, exposing them as contingent, and as themselves (the product of) performances' (Hunter et al, 2010, p. 8), thereby opening up new possibilities for queer advocacy and intervention.

Another benefit that judgment-writing offers 'lies in the discipline of putting one's theoretical insights into judgment form' (Rackley, 2012, p. 397). As Jack Balkin explains:

> the task of putting one's views in the form of a judicial opinion requires an intellectual discipline that has its own distinctive values. It is one thing to offer academic theories ... It is quite another to have to ... demonstrate that one's views ... really are consistent with a successful and acceptable judicial performance (Balkin, 2005, p. xiii, quoted by Rackley, 2012, p. 397).

This not only serves to convey the practicality of theoretical arguments, it also 'works to validate and give authority to the arguments deployed in reaching the alternative decision' (Rackley, 2012, p. 398). As Erika Rackley notes, an academic argument may be seen 'as stronger, or more persuasive, *for being presented in judgment form*' (Rackley, 2012, p. 398). This is because a legal judgment 'must, without exception, not only come to a conclusion but also in the process leave "no room for doubt, and no room for argument, about what has been decided and why"' (Rackley, 2012, p. 398).[4] Of course, this definitive moment is confined to an immediate set of facts. It remains subject to possible appeals and the revisiting of the relevant legal issues by appellate courts in the future. However, while common law decision-making is always postponed or deferred in this important sense, providing a counter-narrative in the form of a bounded judgment, at least in relation to the key legal questions which fall to be decided, strengthens its persuasive power because finality is integral to a particular instance of legal judgment.

Moreover, and importantly, in order to be properly effective, a judgment should be 'a combination of judicial rhetoric and persuasion which ensures that the reader arrives at the same conclusion as the judge' (Rackley, 2012, p. 400). Judicial rhetoric, narrative style and tone are important as techniques of persuasion, as means of establishing affective relations between judge and reader. They are matters to which the counter-judgment will pay attention. Judges clearly have different

4 Rackley is quoting from *OBG Ltd v Allan, Douglas v Hello! Ltd (No. 3), Mainstream Properties Ltd v Young and others* [2007] UKHL 21 at para 303, per Baroness Hale of Richmond.

writing styles ranging from the technical to lucid prose.[5] It is important however, especially when writing with the marginal in mind, to write in a style that draws on the reader's sense of pathos and empathy, that is, in a style that strikes an emotional chord. As Benjamin Cardozo recognised long ago, a judgment 'need[s] persuasive force, or the impressive virtue of sincerity and fire, or the mnemonic power of alliteration and antithesis, or the terseness of proverb and the maxim. Neglect these allies, and it may never win its way.'[6] Whether judges always recognise the significance of these features, one or more of them are often present, demonstrating the importance of, amongst other things, the relationship between cultural imagery and judicial rule choice (Kennedy, 1997, p. 405).

They can be deployed in ways which either further or hinder progressive social change. Thus, in the context of transgender jurisprudence, we might contrast Aubin J's invocation of the Jekyll and Hyde story (Stevenson, 1986) in the New Zealand marriage case of *M v M*[7] and Handler J's reference in the earlier New Jersey marriage case of *MT v JT*[8] to 'an exhibit in a circus side show',[9] in distinguishing 'pre' from 'post' operative transgender bodies,[10] with Street CJ's observation in the Australian criminal law case of *R v Harris and McGuiness*[11] that 'Mr Bumble would give chromosomes short shrift'.[12] While all these judges were engaged in carving out some legal space for 'post' operative transgender people, Street CJ's choice of a Dickensian figure embodying 'common sense' is to be preferred to the figure of the monster.

5 Lord Denning is perhaps the most notable example of a judge writing in this latter style (Nourse, 2005).

6 Cardozo, 1947 quoted in Rodger, 2002, p. 240. Anglo-American common law judgments are replete with literary references, especially to Shakespeare, but also to Lewis Carroll, Kafka, Balzac, Dickens, Faulkner, Orwell, Huxley, Melville and many others (Skilton, 1991). See also 'Why Lawyers Love Shakespeare' *The Economist* 8/1/16 available at www.economist.com/blogs/prospero/2016/01/literature-and-law (last accessed: 3/2/17). This tendency is increasingly apparent in the jurisprudence of the European Court of Justice (e.g. Balzac) and European Court of Human Rights (e.g. Kafka, Faulkner) (Gadbin-George, 2013).

7 *M v M* [1991] NZFLR 337 at 347.

8 *MT v JT* 355 A 2d 204 (1976).

9 *Ibid*, 207.

10 The terms 'pre' and 'post' operative are problematised because in medico-legal discourse they tend to be used to indicate a transgender person's temporal relationship to genital surgery (specifically vaginoplasty/phalloplasty). While surgery is not necessarily sought, nor is it required by the Gender Recognition Act 2004 for the purposes of legal recognition, many transgender people do undergo various forms of non-genital surgery, including castration, penectomy, facial feminisation (trans women) and mastectomy and hysterectomy (trans men). Medico-legal usage of the term 'pre-operative' presents a problem both because it is descriptively inaccurate and because it suggests a particular and teleological relationship between 'authentic' gender identity and genital surgery.

11 *R v Harris and McGuiness* (1989) 17 NSWLR 158.

12 *Ibid*, 161.

Returning to the theme of fidelity to the law, it is noted that judicial judgment-writing often, and increasingly, draws on context and extraneous material. This might appear to conflict with the earlier observation that appellate courts should confine themselves to matters raised by the parties at trial or before them on appeal, and should not consider matters upon which the parties have not had an opportunity to comment (Hunter, 2010, p. 39). However, a judge can introduce material of her own motion. To do so, she must rely on the doctrine of 'judicial notice'. This doctrine permits judges to have regard to 'matters which are so notorious, or clearly established, or susceptible to demonstration by reference to a readily obtainable and authoritative source, that evidence of their existence is unnecessary' (Archbold, 2010, principle 10–71). Judicial notice may also be taken of principles of international law and courts are bound to have regard to European human rights law. Moreover, 'it is also permissible for a judge to make inquiries and consult sources "to which it is proper to … refer"' (Hunter, 2010, p. 39).[13] It is unclear how wide such an ambit might be, though it certainly appears to cover 'sources which are publicly available, reasonably widely known, and unlikely to be the subject of serious dispute' (Hunter, 2010, p. 39). Accordingly, it would, for example, be appropriate for a judge to refer to well-documented patterns of discrimination and violence experienced by transgender and other gender non-conforming people (Keogh et al, 2006; Whittle et al, 2007; Morton, 2008), and to exceptionally high rates of suicide within transgender communities (Clements-Nolle et al, 2006).[14]

Finally, judgment-writing responds, in one particular way, to the criticism that feminist, queer and other critical legal scholars are removed from the struggles of marginalised communities, and to the charge, or at least the perception, of irrelevance (Rackley, 2012, p. 401). Of course, in taking up judgment-writing as a form of resistance to heteronormativity and cisnormativity, it is not pretended that the authority acquired in doing so is that of an appellate court judge. Obviously, academic judgment-writing does not operate in the same 'field of pain and death' (Cover, 1986, p. 1601) as that of the judiciary. Its power therefore 'lies not in its manifestation of authority' (Rackley, 2012, p. 408) but in its demonstration of the contingency in the way that judges arrive at judgment and in 'the degree to which the [academic] judge is able to push the boundaries of legal convention' (Davies, 2012, p. 175). Ultimately however, value lies in offering a more ethically palatable solution to the controversy at hand and in emphasising not only the fact that *McNally* could have been decided differently, but that it ought to have been decided differently.

## 7.3 A queer approach

In approaching legal judgment-writing from a queer theory perspective it is necessary to confront the charge that such an endeavour, as an engagement with

13 Hunter quotes from *Commonwealth Shipping Representative v P & O Branch Service* [1923] AC 191 (HL) per Lord Sumner at 212.

14 However, the counter-judgment will not rely on a discrimination argument as one was not put before the court in *McNally*.

law, is distinctly unqueer. As Fineman et al note, queer legal theory is 'something of a paradox given the tension between "queer" and "legal"' (Fineman et al, 2009, p. 190). This is a matter I will turn to shortly. First, however, it is important to outline the approach to be taken. A queer approach assumes that judgment-writing is guided by what might be described as an important set of queer principles. These include, challenging dominant and binary understandings of the categories of sex, gender and sexuality, deconstructing ideas of normalcy and deviance, defending desire (Valdes, 1995, pp. 368–370), and placing at the centre of analysis and critique, those located at the sexual and gender margins. The queer approach is indebted to postmodern philosophical approaches to notions of power, knowledge and the subject (Lyotard, 1984, 1989; Derrida, 1977, 2001), and especially to the writings of Michel Foucault (Foucault, 1970, 1972, 1980b), as well as to sociological theories that also foreground social constructionism in accounting for identity categories (Goffman, 1959; Berger and Luckman, 1966; Plummer, 1981; Weeks, 1985, 1991). It deploys these various theories, and insights that might be derived from them, specifically on the terrain of gender and sexuality.

In terms of an explicitly queer theoretical approach, it can perhaps be dated to the writings of Judith Butler (1990, 1993) and Eve Sedgwick (1990), though a queer corpus has expanded considerably since (for example, see Halberstam, 1998; Warner, 1991, 2000). This approach has also been taken up within legal scholarship (Robson, 1992, 1998; Stychin, 1995b; Fineman et al, 2009; Zanghellini, 2009). A queer approach is of particular value in the present instance because the counter-judgment to be written is one that must deal with a set of facts where questions of sex, gender and sexual identity lie at the heart of any legal resolution. Thus Justine McNally's personal story crosses sexual and gender lines. It does so in the sense that she 'performed' straight masculinity.

However, we need to be careful here. First, it must be acknowledged that, while queer theory and trans theory overlap significantly (Bornstein, 1994; Feinberg, 1996; Cromwell, 1999; Namaste, 2000; Stryker, 2004; Stone, 2006; Serano, 2007), and while one can be both transgender and queer, there are tensions existing across this theoretical and political divide. In particular, there has been resistance to queer theory's emphasis on gender 'performance', and its frequent failure to take the materiality of the body seriously (see, for example, Prosser, 1998; Rubin, 1998; Namaste, 2000). Thus, Jay Prosser, has argued that queer theory '[elides] the experience of "trans" embodiment' (Prosser, 1998, p. 6), the way in which '[t]he body is crucially and materially formative of the self' (Prosser, 1998, p. 65). This problem is perhaps especially troublesome given that queer has tended to take trans to be emblematic of its theoretical position. As Prosser has put it, in his critique of Judith Butler's *Gender Trouble* (Butler, 1990), trans has been presented 'as the concrete example' of the 'performativity of gender' (Prosser, 1998, p. 28).

However, my focus in re-writing *McNally* remains queer for two related reasons. First, not all of the gender non-conforming defendants in the gender identity fraud cases identify as transgender and, in the case of Justine McNally, she later countermanded her earlier male gender identification. It should also be noted that in relation to those who do, none had commenced cross-sex hormones or undertaken any surgeries prior to the time of the alleged offences. Second, and, most importantly, especially in the context of criminal prosecution and sanction, it is desirable to approach judgment in a way which does not diminish or render inauthentic the gender experiences of gender non-conforming people, irrespective of whether they identify as transgender or not. For this book is against prosecution of gender non-conforming people generally. It is not confined to any subset.

In thinking of gender as *performative* in the Butlerian sense, that is, as 'a reiteration of a norm or a set of norms' which '[conceal] or [dissimulate] the conventions of which it is a repetition' (Butler, 1993, p. 12), the notion of a deceptive performance immediately becomes problematic. After all, how can there be fraud if represented gender has no ontological referent? However, while we *all* perform gender, some performances are more likely to be read as 'artificial' or as drag in contradistinction to the 'natural' genders of others, for whom they act as mirror or ontological prop. This is, of course, given dominant ideologies of heteronormativity and cisnormativity, more likely for those who perform their genders at odds with birth-designated scripts. This issue is important because a claim of fraud goes to the heart of the prosecution case and tends to reinforce the notion that while gender identity can be legally recognised (at least in the case of some transgender people),[15] gender 'authenticity' depends on, if not total stasis, then a one-off relocation within a binary gender system. This raises difficulties for many of the defendants in the gender identity fraud cases prosecuted. In relation to *McNally*, any attempt to overcome a hegemonic reading of gender identity, and therefore deception, becomes immediately complicated by the fact that Justine, having initially identified as male, subsequently asserted a female gender identity from the time of plea. In writing a counter-judgment, I will, though constrained by the nature of the judicial exercise, attempt to render legible the complexity, variance and fluidity of this category we call gender identity.

I now turn to addressing the concerns of those who would refuse a queer/law nexus. In trying to stage an encounter between queer and law, and perhaps especially so in the context of legal judgment-writing where, as already noted, one necessarily proceeds into the fray with one hand tied behind one's back, such are the demands of the legal exercise, it is understandable that some queer, feminist and other critical legal scholars might adopt a position of scepticism. Nor is such scepticism an idle affair. The danger that law will reproduce, and thereby entrench, the very problem to which queer theory is now offered as partial solution, or at

15 The Gender Recognition Act 2004 makes provision for legal recognition of gender identity subject to particular medico-legal conditions. While it does not require surgical or hormonal interventions, it does require a diagnosis of 'gender dysphoria' which operates as a trigger for everything which happens under the Act (s. 2(1)). For a critique of the legislation, see Sandland, 2005; Cowan, 2005; Sharpe, 2007a; Sharpe, 2007b.

least strategic intervention, is acknowledged. It is, of course, a danger emphasised long ago by Carol Smart in the context of feminist engagements with law (Smart, 1989). As she put it, law cannot 'provide the solution to the oppression that it celebrates and sustains' (Smart, 1989, p. 49). Certainly, an encounter with law is always a risk or wager. This is true both in the sense of adverse instrumental outcomes and in terms of negative discursive fallout for those at the sexual and gender margins. Ultimately, for Smart, law's power to construct 'truth' and the consequent power-effects of its 'truth' claims, make law a risk not worth taking.

Moreover, these dangers, the instrumental and the discursive, are not confined to those who seek out law or who find themselves caught up in its clutches. Rather, they are also apparent in the potential conflict defending such cases provokes between individuals and wider constituencies of which they may be members. That is, while we must exhibit pathos to the actual circumstances of gender non-conforming defendants, and recognise a lawyer's duty to defend her client, both the legal outcome and the narrative structure of judgment in gender identity fraud cases may prove antithetical to the interests of other gender non-conforming people. Thus, and by way of example, as we saw in earlier chapters, self-understandings of gender identity differ across the cases prosecuted. While all defendants performed masculinity, some identified as men (Chris Wilson, Kyran Lee (Mason) and Jason Staines) while at least one identified as lesbian (Gayle Newland). In relation to other defendants, the specificity of their gender identity proved more opaque (Jennifer Saunders and Gemma Barker). *McNally* involved a defendant who identified as male, but later reasserted a female gender identity. Accordingly, in attempting to give voice to an individual, in rendering one embodied experience legible, there is a danger of producing a judgment that might operate to the detriment of other gender non-conforming people in the future. This is an important concern, but not one that precludes judgment-writing. Rather, it points to a need to be conscious of this difficulty when engaged in the task. The key thing is to endeavour to ensure that judgment is 'sufficiently contextualised so as not to foreclose the possibility of a different outcome for [the] differently-situated' (Hunter, 2012, p. 141). In other words, judgment-writing should seek to avoid, to the extent possible, rendering unintelligible the narratives and embodied gendered experiences of others, including those to come.

Having acknowledged some of the dangers of engaging law, attention now turns to queer theory's failure to express normative commitments and to make normative arguments (Bamforth, 1997). As Aleardo Zanghellini argues, queer legal theoretical scholarship must transcend a preoccupation with the 'conceptual' at the expense of the 'normative' in mapping out jurisprudential space (Zanghellini, 2009). As he explains, while counter-normativity, 'the repudiation of dominant norms', is important, it should not succumb to antinormativity, which would commit us to a 'renunciation of prescriptive projects' (Zanghellini, 2009, p. 1. See also Jagose, 2015). Rather, 'the primary motor of queer incursions into conceptual jurisprudential ground ... must be political in nature – in the sense of its connection with a concern for justice for sex and gender outsiders' (Zanghellini, 2009, p. 4). While some might view such an approach to be anything but queer, it remains a truism to say that it is 'the normative commitments from which they proceed' that make queer critiques 'ultimately worthwhile' (Zanghellini, 2009, p. 6).

Thus, while it is important to chart disciplinary power and its normalising effects, it is equally, if not more, important to recognise how they 'constrain personal autonomy' (Zanghellini, 2009, p. 6) and counter diversity. Moreover, and importantly, despite queer's anti-humanist rhetoric, one tends to find, as Zanghellini contends, 'a general commitment to liberal humanist values ... such as ideas of respect, value pluralism and personal autonomy' (Zanghellini, 2009, p. 8. See also Seidman, 1997, p. 157; Turner, 2000, p. 17; Ball, 2002, pp. 457–458). Thus, while queer, influenced by poststructural thought as it is, conceives of the concepts of power, knowledge and the subject and their interrelationship, differently than liberalism, broader values of tolerance, pluralism and respect for agency (a queer and feminist version of liberal autonomy) belie some common and worthwhile ground. Moreover, as Sandland notes, deconstruction and law reform are not mutually exclusive, that is, the latter might be accomplished by the former (Sandland, 1995, p. 28). Ultimately, '[t]he question of whether some forms of resistance are more effective than others is a matter of social and historical investigation and not of a priori theoretical pronouncement' (Sawicki, 1991, p. 26).

What we must do however, in approaching law from a queer perspective, is 'be prepared to consider our evaluative and prescriptive analysis potentially provisional and always capable of being revised or superseded' (Zanghellini, 2009, p. 11). While judgment-writing requires finality, at least in relation to present facts, subject to appeal, it is important to construct a judgment, to the maximum extent possible, in such a way that sexual and gender futures are not foreclosed. I do not pretend this to be an easy task. And, no doubt, any attempt at judgment-writing will fall short of this ideal. Ultimately, while justice is a concept which is perhaps unattainable in any pure sense, we ought nevertheless to move toward it, toward its horizon. Moreover, if queer (or feminism) renunciate judgment, then the space of judgment will continue to be monopolised by the judiciary and therefore is likely to be animated by hegemonic discourses. The judgment to be written in this chapter will attempt to write into legal existence transgender and other gender non-conforming people in a manner that qualifies their knowledge and experience as legitimate.

## 7.4 A dissenting judgment: *R v McNally*

[COURT OF APPEAL]
REGINA V McNALLY
2013 June 27
SHARPE J.

### *Introduction*

1 I have had the benefit of reading in draft the judgment of Leveson LJ. However, I reach an entirely different conclusion based on my reading of the facts. As Oscar Wilde observed, '[t]he truth is rarely pure and never simple' (*The Importance of Being Earnest*, Act I). This certainly seems to be true in this case, in which young love appears to have gone awry.

2 On the 4 December 2012, the defendant was convicted of six counts of assault by penetration contrary to s. 2 of the Sexual Offences Act 2003, and on 21 March 2013, was sentenced to three years in a young offender institution. In relation to sentence, Leveson LJ recommends reducing the sentence to a term of 9 months, suspended for two years, together with a suspended sentence supervision order. While sentence reduction is, in my view, to be welcomed, I do not intend otherwise to address the question of sentence because I consider the conviction to be unsafe for reasons I shall detail.

3 It appears from the evidence that the complainant was significantly and detrimentally affected by discovering that the object of her affections, whom she apparently believed to be a boy, was in fact a girl. It was precisely this discrepancy, and the 'deception' implicit therein, that led the trial judge, His Honour Judge Patrick, to consider that the elements of the offence were made out. In his judgment, Leveson LJ rightly pointed out that if, on any version of the facts, the elements of the offence were not made out, the appellant's conviction would undeniably be unsafe and would fall to be quashed even though she had pleaded guilty (see *R v McReady and Hurd* [1978] 1 WLR 1376). I state from the outset that I am not satisfied the Crown discharged this burden on the basis of the facts presented. My concerns relate both to the actus reus and mens rea elements of the offences prosecuted, though I shall base my conclusions on a failure to establish the latter under current law. I will come to my reasons for so concluding in due course.

4 It is important also to emphasise the vulnerability and marginality of the appellant as a gender non-conforming person, considerations which, in my view, received insufficient attention before the trial judge and Leveson LJ in their treatment of the issues. In particular, there appear to be considerable dangers associated with 'coming out' as transgender in our society. These include high rates of violence, discrimination and suicide (see S Whittle et al, *The Equalities Review: Engendered Penalties: Transgender and Transsexual People's Experiences of Inequality & Discrimination*, London: Press for Change, 2007). I do not draw my conclusions on the basis of these observations, though they do provide some colour and context to the general approach I adopt.

### *The facts of the case*

5 The facts of the case are detailed by Leveson LJ and can be summarised here, though whether they are 'undeniably unusual', as he contends, is perhaps

more properly an empirical question. In this respect, I note only that dating, and other forms of social interaction, are increasingly occurring through the internet, and that this is perhaps especially true for young people for whom such technologies appear to be de rigueur. Another difficulty with viewing the facts as 'unusual' is that it presumes young people struggling with gender identity to be few in number, and that non-disclosure of their birth-designated gender, prior to sexual intimacy, to be unjustifiable. It appears to me that the first presumption has, in recent years, been shown to be demonstrably false. Indeed, a study by the Gender Identity Research and Education Society has put the UK transgender population at 300,000 (B Reed et al, *Gender Variance in the UK: Prevalence, Incidence, Growth and Geographic Distribution* (GIRES) 2009, p. 13). In relation to the second presumption, it is important to reiterate the serious problem of prejudice faced by transgender and other gender non-conforming people in our society, a problem, sadly, that only a cursory acquaintance with our daily newspapers attests.

6 Turning to the facts, the appellant, who lives in Scotland, met the complainant, who lives in London, on the internet through the social networking game, 'Habbo'. She used the male name 'Scott' for the purposes of her online presence. At the time of first meeting, the appellant was aged 13 years, while the complainant was a year younger, aged 12–13 (there appears to be uncertainty on this point). In using female pronouns in referring to the appellant, I am simply respecting her assertion of a female gender identity at the time of plea and subsequently. For reasons I will make clear however, this does not serve to preclude the alternative legal conclusion that I have arrived at regarding the claim of deception.

7 The internet relationship developed over the following three and half years with the parties considering themselves boyfriend and girlfriend respectively. They communicated, mainly by the online messenger service, MSN, and spoke of getting married and having children. They also communicated by mobile phone conversations and the complainant saw the appellant as 'Scott' on a web cam.

8 As the couple moved further into adolescence, their interest in one another became increasingly sexual and they settled on an exclusive romantic relationship. They engaged in phone sex and spoke of what they wanted to do to each other sexually. Apparently, 'Scott' spoke of what he wanted to do to the complainant with 'it', and also spoke of 'putting it in', which the complainant took to mean 'his' penis. These are important parts of the evidence. However, I consider them to be open to an interpretation at odds with deception, a point I will develop later. Shortly after the complainant's 16th birthday in March 2011 the parties met in London at the complainant's home. The appellant, who by this time was aged 17 years, presented as a boy. Under her trousers, she wore a penile prosthesis. In the months that followed, the appellant visited the complainant on four subsequent occasions.

9 On the second visit, they watched a movie together and they kissed. They then went to the complainant's bedroom. In the dark, the appellant rubbed the complainant's vagina with her fingers and performed cunnilingus. The complainant then went to get condoms which she purchased for the purpose of sexual intercourse. The appellant remained dressed and refused the complainant's offer to perform fellatio. On the third visit the appellant orally and digitally penetrated the complainant on multiple occasions. On the fourth visit the parties spoke about having sex but did not do so, partly because they were experiencing some relationship difficulties. On the final visit in November 2011, the complainant's mother confronted the appellant and insisted 'Scott' was really a girl. At this point, according to her own evidence, the complainant felt devastated and physically sick after having being 'lied' to for four years. At this stage, the appellant spoke of a desire to undergo gender reassignment surgery. This latter piece of evidence was, in my view, not given proper regard or weight in considering the broader issues.

10 After this final visit the relationship ended, though there was some limited communication between the parties thereafter. The complainant's mother made a complaint to the appellant's school and the police became involved after she admitted to her head teacher that sexual acts had taken place. On 30 November 2011, the complainant made a full statement to the police detailing the alleged offences. While some of her answers were perhaps equivocal, the substance of her statement was essentially that she viewed herself as heterosexual, and had only consented to sexual acts with 'Scott' because she believed the appellant to be a boy.

11 For her part, the appellant offered the following account to the police by way of a prepared statement. She met the complainant through the internet using the avatar 'Scott'. She claims to have done so because she felt more comfortable presenting as male. She also claimed that as early as December 2009, the complainant discovered or at least suspected that she had been designated female at birth, and that this led to an argument. According to the appellant they started speaking to each other again after this point and the relationship continued. In his judgment, Leveson LJ expressed the view that the claim that the complainant knew or had suspicions regarding the appellant's birth-designated gender was inconsistent with the evidence presented.

12 He did so, not because of its later retraction and the appellant's subsequent guilty plea, but because he appears to have interpreted two pieces of evidence as pointing to only one conclusion. Thus he expressed the view that the appellant's claim regarding complainant knowledge or suspicion was incompatible with the alleged argument, and with the complainant's subsequent purchase of condoms at the time of the second visit. I do not share Leveson LJ's view that complainant knowledge or suspicion is necessarily or logically inconsistent with the occurrence of an argument or indeed the complainant's purchase of condoms. I will provide reasons for so concluding but at this stage simply note the existence of alternative interpretations that are open on

the evidence, ones which raise difficulties for the view that the appellant necessarily acted deceptively.

### *Grounds of appeal*

13 Counsel for the appellant raised three grounds of appeal against conviction: (1) the appellant's legal advisors failed to advise her correctly on matters which went to the heart of her plea because (2) the elements of the offence were not made out and the appellant could not have been convicted with the result that (3) the appellant's plea was equivocal. In his judgment, Leveson, LJ has dealt in detail with each of these interrelated grounds of appeal. I propose to focus on (2), which if correct, as counsel for the appellant asserts, leads logically to (3). In my view, and on the basis of the evidence, I do not think it can be said that the elements of the offence were made out. For this reason I agree with counsel's claim that the appellant's plea was equivocal. I also note in this regard, that the appellant stated before this court that, at the time of signing witness statements, she 'just wanted it to be over'.

14 However, before turning to consider the second ground of appeal, I will address the first ground and to that extent proceed in the same manner as Leveson LJ. However, unlike Leveson LJ, I would uphold this ground of appeal. My reasons are specific, but linked to the more substantive objection raised by counsel under the second ground. In the first place, Mr Thomas, the appellant's barrister prior to appeal, while insisting that he did not tell the appellant she had no defence and that she should plead guilty, made the following statement before this court: 'In view of [the appellant's] replies I was satisfied in my own mind she (and her parents) knew all the constituent elements of the offence *and that these were made out*' (my emphasis).

15 In my view, and for reasons to be provided in my consideration of the second ground of appeal, it is not at all clear on the basis of the evidence that the prosecution case was made out. Further, Mr Thomas appears to have drawn the same conclusion as Leveson LJ regarding the significance of the complainant's purchase of condoms, and in terms emphasising the difficulty of the appellant's position. He also stated that the versions of events provided by the complainant and appellant 'could not live in the same world', a claim I consider to be over-blown, at least in some respects and, more importantly, that 'it would be clear to the jury who was telling the truth'. While the appellant may have lied about some matters, and although her case possesses some obvious evidential weaknesses, the difficulty I have with the legal advice she received lies in the fact that it failed, in my opinion, to recognise that the appellant may have had a good defence had the central issue of her gender identity at the time of legal liability been properly addressed.

16 Indeed, one of the central difficulties of this case is the fact that several pieces of evidence used to support a conclusion of deception are also entirely

consistent with the view that the appellant actually believed herself to be male at the time of the alleged offences. This possibility appears to have been discounted because of the fact that the appellant subsequently, that is, at the time of plea and this present appeal, asserted a female gender identity. In other words, the question becomes: must gender identity be static in order to be authentic? In my view, it is the assumption that it must that goes to the heart of this case. It is perhaps the elephant in the room and, in my view, failure to recognise it as such places gender non-conforming people at great peril within our criminal justice system. I now turn to the second ground and therefore to the substance of this appeal, where I will flesh out some of the concerns to which I have alluded.

### *The substantive legal issues*

17 Counsel's second ground of appeal is that the elements of the offence were not made out. The elements of the offence of assault by penetration are threefold: (i) sexual penetration occurred (ii) the complainant did not consent, and (iii) the appellant possessed the necessary mens rea. In this case (i) is an agreed fact. It is (ii) and (iii) to which I shall devote attention, and consideration of (iii) upon which I shall base my judgment. However, before proceeding further, it is necessary to recognise that in relation to proving mens rea it is not sufficient for the Crown to establish only that the appellant lacked a reasonable belief in consent. This is because the present case involves not a claim of coercive sex, but deceptive sex. In relation to the latter, the Court of Appeal has made clear that there is no obligation to disclose personal information, even in circumstances where a defendant is aware that a complainant would not consent to sexual intimacy if she knew this information. Rather, the mens rea for sexual fraud is to be established by proof also of some form of 'active deception' (see *R v EB* [2006] EWCA Crim 2945, *Assange v Swedish Prosecution Authority* [2011] EWHC 2849 (Admin), *R v Bingham* [2013] EWCA Crim 823, *R (on the application of F) v DPP* [2013] EWHC 945 (Admin)). In my view, this is the central issue and difficulty for the prosecution and it is one to which I shall return and consider in some detail.

18 Unfortunately, the matter is more complicated still because the Court of Appeal in earlier decisions, and Leveson LJ in this case, have muddied the waters of actus reus and mens rea. Thus, the notion of 'active deception', while clearly an element of mens rea, appears also to have been imported into the actus reus element of non-consent so that consent, amongst other things, turns on whether deception is considered to be of an active kind. In my view, this development of criminal law doctrine is regrettable and is reminiscent of the 'wrong turn' taken by the House of Lords in the case of *R v Morris* [1984] AC 320 (HL) (dicta of Lord Roskill not applied in *R v Gomez* [1993] AC 442 (HL); *R v Hinks* [2001] 2 AC 241 (HL)). In

*Morris*, the actus reus element of *appropriation* in s. 1 of the Theft Act 1968, which is defined to mean, 'any assumption by a person of the rights of the owner' (s. 3), was interpreted by the majority, and in particular Lord Roskill, as 'adverse interference'. This led his Lordship to distinguish the 'practical joker' from the 'rogue' and to insist that only the latter could be said to have *appropriated*. In my view, proof of actus reus and mens rea elements should be kept analytically separate. That is, whether a defendant deliberately deceived the complainant and whether he did so in an active manner ought to be matters considered only in the context of establishing mens rea. However, if proof of non-consent now requires proof of active deception, which the authorities suggest it does, then my conclusion that active deception is not made out would also mean that there has been a failure to establish non-consent. Before turning to the mens rea, where I will consider the concept of active deception and its application to the facts, I will first consider the actus reus element of non-consent where, for the reasons already stated, I will chart the emergence of a distinction between non-disclosure of information and active deception.

### *Non-consent*

19 This case appears to be one in which two young people who had reached the age of consent participated in desire-led intimacy on multiple occasions. The claim that consent was absent is based on s. 74 of the Sexual Offences Act which provides that:

> 'For the purposes of this Part, a person consents if he agrees by choice and has the freedom and capacity to make that choice'.

It was made clear by the Crown that the evidential presumptions to be found in s. 75 are not relevant on the facts and that the conclusive presumptions in s. 76 are not relied on. While intentional fraud as to 'the nature and purpose of the sexual act' might be considered relevant under s. 76(2)(a), the Court of Appeal has proved extremely reluctant to find consent absent on this basis (in particular see, *R v EB* [2006] EWCA Crim 2945, *R v Jheeta* [2007] EWCA Crim 1699, *R v Bingham* [2013] EWCA Crim 823, *R (on the application of F) v DPP* [2013] EWHC 945 (Admin)), though it has done so on occasion (*R v Devonald* [2008] EWCA Crim 527, though in *R v Bingham*, judicial notice was taken of academic criticism of the case (para 14)). This general reluctance is due to what the presumption conclusively concludes in addition to an absence of consent, namely, 'that the defendant did not believe that the complainant consented to the relevant act'. This is an approach I wholly endorse.

20 In cases of sexual fraud, it is clear that a finding of non-consent under s. 74 presupposes that deception pertains to a fact that is considered legally material. The courts have long considered some deceptions to be so trivial that

consent is deemed valid. In his judgment, Leveson LJ offers the example of deception as to wealth, and notes that this 'will obviously not be sufficient to vitiate consent'. Accordingly, the courts have taken the view that sexual autonomy, while an important right, is not an unlimited one, at least not in fraud contexts. Thus, the language of s. 74 and, in particular, the words 'choice' and 'freedom', are not understood in some philosophically pure sense, but rather as circumscribed in normative terms, or as Lord Judge CJ put it in *R (on the application of F) v DPP* [2013] EWCA 945 (Admin), they 'must be approached in a broad commonsense way' (para 26). In contexts of desire-led, as opposed to coerced intimacy, it is clearly important to set limits to the reach of the criminal law, lest it become uncoupled from the community in which it is to take root. Such an approach not only accords with basic liberal principles, but also with the need to recognise the special vulnerability of some individuals in our society due to widespread prejudice and discrimination. The present case, dealing with a young gender non-conforming person as it does, is a case in point. While I have every sympathy for the complainant in this case, and for other women in her position, there are other interests at stake, as well as important public policy considerations that must be taken into account.

21 In saying this, I do not mean to suggest, as a matter of law, that deception as to gender be considered a trivial affair. In this respect, I stop short of endorsing counsel for the appellant's contention to that effect. As Leveson LJ stated, 'depending on the circumstances, deception as to gender can vitiate consent'. While it is unclear from his judgment which kinds of deceptions as to gender would vitiate consent and which would not, I accept that if a defendant, prior to sexual intimacy, deliberately deceived a complainant about his gender identity, knowing that gender status was fundamental to her consent, then consent would be invalid. At some point in the future, being a man or woman might cease to possess such importance. If so, deception as to gender identity might be more readily analogised to Leveson LJ's example of fraud concerning wealth. For the present however, the view that being a man or woman is important in sexual contexts is one which accords with community sentiment. However, while Leveson LJ appears to leave the matter open, I do not consider facts about gender to be legally material beyond the immediate fact of gender identity. To treat them as such would be to imbue transgender people's bodies and histories with legal significance. It might be argued that all sorts of facts relating to gender are material, including chromosomes, past and present genital status, legal gender status and gender socialisation experience. However, to my mind, a line in the sand must be drawn between gender identity and such other matters. Failure to do so would, in effect, be to confer on a non-transgender person a right to determine a transgender person's gender identity. It would also come perilously close to subverting the very act/omission distinction on which the Court of Appeal has founded liability.

22 In the present case, the view that consent is lacking is based on the claim that the complainant was unaware of the appellant's 'true' gender identity and that this was due to active deception perpetrated by the appellant. That is, the complainant claimed that she believed the appellant to be the boy, 'Scott', the appellant had represented herself to be. This question of representation is one I will address in some detail when considering mens rea. However, I express reservation concerning the apparent ease with which the Crown Prosecution Service, prosecuting counsel and His Honour Judge Patrick accepted that the actus reus element of non-consent was met.

23 The concern I have here pertains to the way in which the complainant's claim of ignorance regarding the appellant's birth-designated gender resonated so easily despite the following facts: the parties spent considerable time in each other's company; had penetrative sex on multiple occasions; the appellant has breasts, a voice within the female range; and although expressing a desire for gender reassignment surgery (a point to which I shall return), had not benefited from the masculinising effects of testosterone. In other words, accepting the complainant's account, not something a jury were called on to do, seems to require, to quote one of England's great poets, Samuel Taylor Coleridge, that we 'suspend our disbelief' (*Biographia Literaria,* 1817, Chapter xvi), and in my view, to a quite extraordinary degree.

24 I also note that the Crown Prosecution Service's *Code for Prosecutors* requires prosecutors to 'consider whether there are any reasons to question the reliability of the evidence, including its accuracy or integrity' and 'whether there are any reasons to doubt the credibility of the evidence' (para 4.6). Further, the Code states that a case that does not meet these tests 'must not proceed, no matter how *serious* or *sensitive* it may be' (para 4.4) (my emphasis). I would encourage the Crown Prosecution Service to look again at the Code when prosecuting these kinds of cases.

25 Having expressed these reservations, I now turn to providing a summary of relevant case law decided under s. 74. For reasons already given, this will entail reference to the concept of active deception. In considering the scope of this legal concept, I will suggest that existing authorities might be distinguished from the present facts. The interpretation of s. 74, as it applies to sexual fraud, as opposed to sexual coercion, has been considered in a series of cases beginning with *R v EB* [2006] EWCA Crim 2945. In this case, counsel for the prosecution suggested that a failure to disclose HIV positive status prior to sexual intercourse served to vitiate consent. The suggestion was roundly rejected by the Court of Appeal. While consent would be vitiated in such circumstances in relation to charges brought under the Offences Against the Person Act 1861, Latham LJ insisted that:

> 'Where one party to sexual activity has a sexually transmissible disease which is not disclosed to the other party any consent that may have been

> given to that activity by the other party is not thereby vitiated. The act remains a consensual act'.

In other words, non-disclosure of HIV positive status was considered 'not relevant to the issue of consent under s. 74 in relation to the sexual activity'.

26 In the later case of *Assange v Swedish Prosecution Authority* [2011] EWHC 2849 (Admin), the Divisional Court emphasised that *EB* 'goes no further than deciding that a failure to disclose HIV infection is not *of itself* a relevant consideration under s. 74' (my emphasis). In other words, the court left open the possibility that, for example, lying about HIV status might be a relevant consideration. In hearing the extradition case brought against Julian Assange, the court found that consent would be lacking if a jury accepted the complainant's evidence that the defendant had sexual intercourse without a condom, or continued sexual intercourse after removing, damaging or tearing a condom, after it had been made clear to him that consent was conditional on condom use.

27 In the more recent decision of *R (on the application of F) v DPP*, a case which involved judicial review of a decision by the Crown Prosecution Service not to prosecute, the court found ejaculation in the defendant's wife's vagina to be inconsistent with consent under s. 74 in circumstances where she had made clear to him that sexual intercourse was conditional on non-ejaculation, and ordered a review of the case.

28 It is important, in my view, to make a number of observations about these cases, observations I consider relevant in determining the boundaries of consent under s. 74. In the first place, the cases of *Assange* and *R (on the application of F) v DPP* involved an express condition. That is, consent was subject to condom use in *Assange* and non-ejaculation in *R (on the application of F) v DPP*. There was no express condition in the case before us and any suggestion that a condition was or ought to be implied would raise difficulties for the Crown because to give legal effect to an implied condition would be tantamount to criminalising non-disclosure of personal information. This would be clearly at odds with the developing jurisprudence of this court. It would also potentially conflict with legal obligations under European and international law. Certainly, criminalisation of non-disclosure of information may conflict with privacy rights protected under Article 8 of the European Convention on Human Rights and Article 17 of the International Covenant on Civil and Political Rights. Indeed, the *Yogyakarta Principles* 2007, which articulate principles on the application of international human rights law in relation to sexual orientation and gender identity, state that:

> '[t]he right to privacy ordinarily includes the choice to disclose or not to disclose information relating to one's sexual orientation or gender identity, as well as decisions and choices regarding both one's own body and consensual sexual and other relations with others' (*principle 6*).

In relation to Article 8, the Law Commission has expressed reservation concerning its compatibility with prosecution of transgender people for non-disclosure of their gender history:

> 'an apparent agreement to a sexual act by another should not be disregarded merely because it is given under the impression that the other is male whereas the other is in fact female [sic], or vice versa, where the other has undergone sex reassignment surgery' (Law Commission, *Consent in Sex Offences: A Policy Paper: Appendix C of Setting the Boundaries* (London: Home Office, 2000) vol 2, para 5.32).

Indeed, and putting to one side the Law Commission's clumsiness in describing transgender people's actual gender identities, since the Gender Recognition Act 2004 and the Equality Act 2010, nothing now hinges, if it did previously, on whether a person has undergone gender reassignment surgery. This is entirely consistent with a right to privacy and with recognising the importance of self-determination.

29 With the exception of *R v Devonald* [2008] EWCA Crim 527, a case where a father pretended to be a 20-year old woman on the internet in order to seduce a young man to masturbate in front of a webcam as revenge for what he believed to have been the man's mistreatment of his daughter, other cases that have come before the Court of Appeal, and through which legal liability for sexual fraud has been expanded, involve the element of coercion. Thus in *R v Bingham* EWCA Crim 823 the defendant, having created false identities on a social media website, blackmailed a female victim into engaging in sexual activity through the threatened use of sexually explicit photographs shared between the parties. In the earlier case of *R v Jheeta* [2007] EWCA Crim 1699 the Court of Appeal came to the same conclusion in relation to a fabricated threat of police sanction against the complainant. I note that the present case does not involve any element of coercion. *Devonald*, a case which, it should be noted, did involve deception as to gender identity, can also be distinguished from the present facts. While there was neither coercion nor an express condition insisted on by the complainant, the interaction between the parties occurred entirely online and therefore an opportunity to verify the defendant's credentials was more limited. Moreover, unlike the present facts, the deception in *Devonald* was unequivocal and the representation of female gender identity, trivial.

30 In my view, and in accordance with these authorities, it is open to this court to conclude that vitiation of consent for the purposes of sexual fraud requires, not only active deception, but also either an express condition or the element of coercion, at least in circumstances where the parties meet face to face. Indeed, I favour such an approach, which has the virtue of limiting criminal liability in relation to sexual relations which are desire-led and where alleged harm arising consists in the retrospective reimagining of pleasure. However, I do not base my decision on such a demarcation of consent.

### *Active deception*

31 I now turn to what I consider to be the crux of the case and, correspondingly, to my reasons for allowing the appeal. In order for the Crown case to be made out mens rea must be established. This requires proof not only that the appellant lacked a reasonable belief in consent but also that she acted deceptively. The former, by itself, is clearly insufficient in establishing liability because a person who chooses not to disclose particular information cannot for this reason alone be convicted, even if aware that a sexual partner would not become intimate with her if in possession of the information. Proof of active deception, by itself, is also insufficient. For a person who acts deceptively, whether through statements or deeds, may nevertheless believe that the complainant consented and this belief might hold when measured against the required standard of reasonableness.

32 In view of the evidence put before His Honour Judge Patrick and this court, it would appear that the claim of active deception refers, in the main, to a series of allegedly false representations made by the appellant: the appellant's use of the male pseudonym, 'Scott Hill', both as an online avatar and subsequently in face to face meetings with the complainant; the appellant's expression of a desire to marry and have children with the complainant; the appellant's stated desire to 'put it in' the complainant, which the complainant took to mean a reference to the appellant's penis; and the appellant's use of female pronouns in her witness statements. In addition to these representations, legal significance also appears to have been attributed to the fact that the appellant expressed 'gender confusion' and to the fact that the complainant purchased condoms.

33 If any of the representations constitute 'active deception', as opposed to mere non-disclosure of information, it is because they deliberately and actively misrepresent the appellant's gender identity. In my view, it is, on the basis of the evidence, more than possible to conclude that they do not. I shall deal with each of these matters separately.

34 First, the use of the male pseudonym, 'Scott Hill', while deceptive in the sense that this was not the appellant's legal name, was not necessarily deceptive in terms of the appellant's gender identity. Indeed, the name is entirely consistent with a male gender identity and it is perhaps understandable that a transgender or gender non-conforming person would, or at least might, adopt such a name.

35 Second, the appellant's assertion that she wanted to marry and have children with the complainant was not necessarily false. Marriage to the complainant as a man would be possible if the appellant obtained a Gender Recognition Certificate and the couple would be able to have children either through adoption or in vitro fertilisation. The notion that the appellant might be transgender might seem surprising, and perhaps misplaced, given her present articulation of a female gender identity. However, and this goes to the heart

of the case, the moment of legal liability arises not at the time of plea or this appeal, but at the time of the alleged offences, and there is evidence at this time to suggest the appellant identified as male. I shall come to this important evidence shortly.

36 Third, it appears to have been assumed that the appellant's statement to the complainant, that she wanted to 'put it in' the complainant, referred to a penis and is therefore deceptive. Yet, it is not deceptive as to gender identity as men are not defined by this anatomical part. If they were, legally recognised transgender men would not be considered men, nor, for example, would some of our injured soldiers returning from conflict zones. However, there is also an issue as to whether the statement is deceptive at all. The fact that the complainant appears to have assumed that the statement referred to a fleshy penis should not equate with the view that this was the appellant's intent. Perhaps the appellant was referring to a prosthetic penis, which the evidence showed she possessed, and perhaps she experienced this device as other men would a fleshy penis. A serious difficulty I have with what appears to have been the treatment of this piece of evidence is the tendency to approach it, and questions of gender identity and embodiment more generally, from a perspective alien to the appellant.

37 Fourth, the appellant's use of female pronouns in witness statements does not necessarily establish deception for legal purposes. This is because the appellant may have been referring to her birth-designated gender rather than her actual gender at the time. In any event, and despite the appellant's present assertion of a female gender identity, there was evidence before His Honour Judge Patrick and this court, evidence I shall detail shortly, to conclude that the appellant did in fact identify as male at the time when criminal liability crystallises.

38 Turning to the other evidence which might be considered to support a conclusion of deception, the appellant's expression of 'confusion' regarding her gender identity did not take the form of a statement made to the complainant, and indeed only surfaced subsequent to the alleged offences. In any event, given the prejudice and misunderstandings gender non-conforming people face in our society, confusion may not be uncommon. I certainly do not think that confusion should lead to a conclusion of fabrication. In relation to the final piece of evidence listed above, the complainant's purchase of condoms assumed importance because purchase was considered inconsistent with the appellant's (later retracted) statement that the complainant either knew or suspected that the appellant's birth-designated gender was female. Yet, this interpretation of the evidence, from which inferences appear to have been drawn regarding the appellant's veracity, is not the only interpretation available. Thus, the complainant may have purchased condoms, not because she assumed the appellant to have a fleshy penis, which appears to have been what the Crown argued, but out of a concern over hygiene in the context of the intended use of the appellant's prosthetic penis. Of course, we cannot

know which interpretation is true. What appears clear however, is that all of these pieces of evidence can be interpreted in ways other than as supporting a claim of deception, and this raises the possibility, if not the likelihood, that a jury would have struggled to have been persuaded beyond reasonable doubt.

39 In drawing attention to these possible alternative interpretations of the evidence, which, in my view, would be open to a jury, I recognise they depend on evidence that the appellant actually believed herself to be male, a transgender man that is, prior to and crucially at the time of the alleged offences. Evidence for this is not insignificant. Thus, the fact that the appellant presented as male, both online and throughout her face to face meetings with the complainant, and therefore for a period of some three to four years, might be viewed as consistent with a male gender identity, rather than as evidence of inauthenticity or fraud.

40 Further, the appellant had stated that she felt 'more comfortable' in the male gender role and, prior to her assertion of a female gender identity before His Honour Judge Patrick, had stated an intention to undergo gender reassignment surgery. I note that according to recent medical studies, children continuing to express a gender identity opposite to their birth-designated gender after adolescence, are highly likely to persist with their gender identification (K Zucker and P T Cohen-Kettenis, 'Gender Identity Disorder in Children and Adolescents' in D L Rowland and L Incrocci (eds) *Handbook of Sexual and Gender Identity Disorders* (London: John Wiley & Sons 2008) 376–422; T D Steensma et al, 'Desisting and Persisting Gender Dysphoria after Childhood: A Qualitative Follow-Up Study' (2011) 16(4) *Clinical Child Psychol Psychiatry* 499–516). Such medical findings introduce a further concern about prosecution in these types of cases and, in particular, about satisfaction of the mens rea requirement. While we cannot know why the appellant now asserts a female gender identity, it is possible it is associated with criminal prosecution as well as the negative media portrayal that, sadly, appears to attend coverage of the lives of transgender people caught up in our criminal justice system and more generally. In other words, I express concern that the appellant may have, so to speak, retreated into a cocoon of 'normality'. However, I do not base my judgment on evidence that the appellant is a transgender man. Rather, however the appellant identifies, and it appears that there is some fluidity in her gender identification, the crucial thing in establishing criminal liability is proof that she deceived the complainant at the time of, or prior to, sexual intimacy. However she identifies today or at the time of plea, if she genuinely identified as male at the relevant time then she ought to be acquitted.

41 Indeed, even if she did not identify as male, but as a masculine woman, presenting as such and preferring to use a name traditionally associated with the male gender, as long as this was not done in order to deceive, then it does not follow that a deception has occurred as a matter of law. To conclude otherwise, would be to implicate law in unnecessary and unwarranted

state intrusion and regulation of gender and sexuality. Such an approach would give the imprimatur of law to the idea that gender non-conforming people are, by definition, duplicitous and/or that other people have a right to know intimate details about their personal and private lives.

42 In my view, uncertainty as to whether active deception has been established according to law renders the appellant's conviction unsafe. However, I also express concern regarding the conclusion that the appellant lacked a reasonable belief in consent. Of course, we cannot know what was in her mind at the relevant time. Nevertheless, I harbour concern regarding the difficulties both the appellant and other gender non-conforming people are likely to face in meeting a legal standard of 'reasonableness'. I suspect that a claim made by, for example, a young transgender man, that he believed his sexual partner's desire for him would have been unaffected by knowledge of his gender history, is one unlikely to resonate in normative terms and therefore with a jury. In this respect, I express concern that the truthful transgender or gender non-conforming defendant is likely to be equated with some kind of self-loathing individual who can never legitimately or convincingly claim to be the object of another's desire. While I do not base my decision on a failure to prove lack of reasonable belief in consent, I do think these sorts of concerns point to very real dangers in regulating sexuality through the fraud mechanism, and certainly in the present context.

43 Ultimately, law, and especially criminal law, ought to respect the self-determination that is implicit in gender identity claims unless it can be clearly established that they are fabricated. For my part, I do not consider gender identity to be fabricated because it differs from birth-designated gender or because it is not static, or because it creates alarm in others.

### *Conclusions*

44 Accordingly, and for the reasons given, I consider the convictions in this case to be unsafe. For this reason, I would order a re-trial where a jury can consider the Crown's case as well as other possible interpretations of the evidence.

## Chapter 8

# Conclusions

This book has sought to interrogate the regulation of intimacy and desire by the liberal state in one specific context, that of sexual relations between cisgender and gender non-conforming people in circumstances where the former claim to lack knowledge of the latter's gender history. This is no abstract question, as a series of successful sexual offence prosecutions brought against young transgender and other gender non-conforming people attests. Moreover, and as we saw in Chapter 2, expansion of sexual fraud law, occasioned through judicial interpretation of the consent provisions in the Sexual Offences Act 2003, has had a disproportionate impact on gender non-conforming people. Indeed, the jurisprudence of the courts has culminated in a Court of Appeal decision[1] that would be infamous if non-cisgender bodies were bodies that mattered (Butler, 1993).

Chapter 2 also expressed concern regarding 'carceral' or 'governance' feminism (Estrich, 1986; Chamallas, 1988; MacKinnon, 1989; Falk, 1998; Gotell, 2015) and its absolutist approach to sexual autonomy, an approach which appears increasingly to animate both judicial thinking around consent, and broader discourses concerning sexually intimate relations. These social forces, along with the 'sacralisation of childhood' (Zelizer, 1994, Chapter 1), which now, at least culturally, seem to extend beyond the age of majority, appear to operate to the considerable disadvantage of transgender and other gender non-conforming people. This is because an absolutist conception of cisgender female sexual autonomy leaves no room for consideration of conflicting rights and interests of sexually active transgender and other gender non-conforming people, and because discourses of childhood are readily translated into the problematic dichotomy of cisgender innocence and transgender knowingness and predation.

In response to this state of affairs, the book offered, in Chapters 3 and 4, a series of principled objections to criminal prosecution. In Chapter 3, it argued that criminal prosecution for gender identity fraud constituted significant criminal law overreach according to liberal principles; it challenged the notion that a cisgender right to sexual autonomy should mandate prosecution and sought to erect limits to the supposed absoluteness of this right; it highlighted significant

1 *R v McNally* [2013] EWCA Crim 1051.

legal inconsistencies in determining the materiality of facts and therefore questioned the ground upon which a finding of non-consent might be reached; it recognised the discriminatory effects of prosecution on gender non-conforming people; and it considered conflicting rights claims and, in particular, the right to privacy.

In Chapter 4, further objections were articulated: the claim that cisgender people are harmed by 'inadvertent' sexual intimacy with gender non-conforming people was taken to task both in the sense of problematising the notion of 'harm' and its ideological (cissexist, transphobic and homophobic) sources, and in the sense of introducing a harm calculus to ensure that any weighing of harms takes proper account of harms associated with disclosing gender history, as well as those associated with non-disclosure; the claim of deception was refracted through the Foucauldian prism of power/knowledge in order to tease out the relationship between deception discourse and the 'truth games' (Foucault, 1980b, p. 132) it inevitably produces, especially in relation to questions of identity; the distinction between active deception and non-disclosure of information, which now plays a pivotal role in determining criminal liability for sexual fraud, was laid bare in terms of its lack of any convincing justification for its distribution of defendants; and finally, a public policy objection to prosecution was identified, namely inconsistency between prosecution and the state's commitment to equality and diversity, and the need to ameliorate transphobia.

In Chapter 5, these more formal objections to prosecution were supplemented by an analysis and critique of legal practice. In exploring this distinction between legal form and legal substance, the chapter considered the decision to prosecute, the question of plea, and the application of substantive law in cases involving transgender and other gender non-conforming defendants. In doing so, it moved beyond abstract jurisprudential questions in order to consider more urgent ones of defendant vulnerability and the possibilities for justice within our criminal justice system for gender non-conforming people. In relation to these specific issues of legal practice, the chapter emphasised how complainants, prosecutors, judges and sometimes juries approach them through an interpretational lens that foregrounds cisnormative perspectives, experiences and truths.

In Chapter 6, our attention shifted from law to ethics and consideration was given to the question of what we owe to each other in contexts of sexual intimacy by way of truth telling and information disclosure. It was contended that the issue of ethical characterisation of the acts/omissions of transgender people, prior to moments of sexual intimacy, assumes tremendous significance because the fundamental difficulty arising lies not in criminal prosecution per se, but in what makes prosecution possible, and indeed what problematises the lives of transgender people more generally, namely, the underlying cisnormative assumption that transgender people are quintessentially deceptive, that we are synonymous with artifice. The chapter insisted on acknowledging the truth of gender identity claims, except in rare circumstances where they can easily be demonstrated to be false, such as in the *Devonald* case.[2] To do otherwise, is to constrain ethical thinking within a cisnormative frame.

Beyond this, chapter 6 considered the possibility that there may be other gendered facts in relation to which lying or non-disclosure of information constitute unethical deception. To this extent, the chapter engaged with normative ethics in order to demonstrate that within these philosophical terms, non-disclosure of gender history can be justified. To that end, it relied on rule consequentialism and demonstrated how this approach is, in the present context, capable of doing the necessary work, albeit such an approach necessarily sacrifices claims about individual justice and rights. However, ultimately, the chapter argued that ethical analysis about what we owe to each other in contexts of cis–trans sexual intimacy cannot be reduced to a cost-benefit analysis or to an assessment of what produces the greatest good. Rather, ethical thinking in this area must foreground a call to cisgender people to be(come) 'ethically gendered' (Serano, 2013, p. 259). That is, it must begin with recognition of cisgender privilege and power and how their enjoyment and/or exercise sustain gender and sexual hierarchies. In the end, we must all learn to live in the face of the anxiety gender difference generates and be willing, as Butler argues, to let our 'epistemological and ontological anchor[s] go' (Butler, 2004, p. 35) in the name of forging ethical relationships, and yes, even those of the most intimate kind.

In Chapter 7, the book's attempt to reframe the legal and ethical debate surrounding gender identity fraud shifted, more explicitly, to legal and political intervention. It did so through re-writing the *McNally* judgment from a queer legal perspective. The counter-judgment provided contains two virtues. First, it served to write transgender and other gender non-conforming people into legal existence as fully human and second, it highlighted, not only that the Court of Appeal could have decided the case differently, consistent with existing legal principles, but that it ought to have done so.

In addition to being against prosecution, and seeking to foster a reimagined ethical relation between cisgender and transgender people, this book has been animated by a series of themes, which not only elucidate the predicament of gender non-conforming people within our criminal justice system and society more generally, but also offer important insights in relation to broader questions and debates within criminal justice and sexual politics. The remainder of this chapter will highlight the ways in which this study of criminal prosecution of gender non-conforming youth and the ethical problematisation of their 'choices', especially their decision to keep personal information private, contributes to broader knowledge within, and raises some serious questions for, liberal, feminist and queer legal scholarship. It is to this contribution that attention now turns.

While the book considered several themes (ideology, agency, ignorance/knowledge, act/identity, resistance, law's bodily aesthetics, act/omission), and while they are clearly interrelated, it is the particular triangulation of the concepts

2 *R v Devonald* [2008] EWCA Crim 527.

of consent, harm and deception, around which these other themes coalesce, that I will focus on. A study of the legal regulation of sexually intimate relations between cisgender and transgender people contributes both to a more nuanced understanding of these concepts, and to an appreciation of desirable limits. These three concepts are central within criminal law, especially in relation to sexual offences, and equally loom large in feminist debates. In relation to consent, it is 'the moral magic of consent' (Alexander, 1996, p. 165) that renders sex both non-criminal and ethical. However, in law it is clear that the validity of consent does not depend either on the materiality of facts, as subjectively understood, or on operative deception per se. Rather, the courts have insisted that deceptive sex only vitiates consent where the deception relates to a fact considered legally (and therefore normatively) material, and where it is 'active' rather than passive.[3] While the appropriateness of both these legal stipulations is open to contestation, what is of interest here is the way their application, in the context of gender non-conforming defendants, sheds light on law and, given the obligations created, the way we conceive of ethics.

First, the question of fact materiality proves to have a cisnormative foundation. That is, facts about sex, gender, the body and desire prove important only to the extent that they are considered important for cisgender people. This poses a problem on a number of fronts. It serves to re-centre the problem of normativity itself and the way it is given legal effect. After all, if we are concerned about issues of equality, diversity and social justice we cannot uncritically endorse or allow free rein to norms that marginalise the experiences and perspectives of gender non-conforming people. This point ought to apply both to questions of criminalisation and, as a matter of public policy, to the application of legal rules. That is, if fact materiality is to be a decisive factor in the prosecution of deceptive sex, then the embodied experiences and perspectives of gender non-conforming people must be counted as material, that is, they must be acknowledged to matter.

This question of fact materiality also poses a problem for feminism given its law reform and ethical preference for a subjective, that is a complainant-centred, understanding of consent. After all, this amounts to an insistence that, if consent is to be good, information considered important to cisgender women must be disclosed. This position fails to consider the costs associated with disclosing gender history and therefore fails to accord gender non-conforming people care and concern. Of course, in thinking through this question of fact materiality, it might be objected that the right not to associate (not have sex) must trump the right to do so, and that this is especially so in the context of sexual intimacy.[4] However,

3 *R v EB* [2006] EWCA Crim 2945, *Assange v Swedish Prosecution Authority* [2011] EWHC 2849 (Admin), *R v Bingham* [2013] EWCA Crim 823, *R (on the application of F) v DPP* [2013] EWHC 945 (Admin).

4 S F Colb, 'Is There a Moral Duty to Disclose That You're Transgender to a Potential Partner?' *Verdict* 6/18/15 available at https://verdict.justia.com/2015/06/18/is-there-a-moral-duty-to-disclose-that-youre-transgender-to-a-potential-partner (last accessed: 13/2/17).

this gives rise to further difficulties, ones which the gender identity fraud cases serve to dramatise.

Of course, the right not to associate must trump the right to associate in the context of sexual coercion. However, in relation to deceptive sex the matter is more complex. In relation to deceptive sex, and the real issue in these cases proves to be non-disclosure of information and therefore omission, particular problems arise. In the first place, the deception claim relies on the view that what is not disclosed is inconsistent with the facts cisgender people assume. Such a claim is clearly false in the case of a transgender man because no gap exists between his actual and assumed gender identity. Alternatively, the claim of deception may pertain to facts about gender beyond the fact of gender identity. Putting to one side the problem that the relevance of such facts appears limited to their capacity to call gender identity into question, and therefore raises an issue concerning the bona fides of the claim, the difficulty here lies in the notion that people have, or ought to have, a right to know such facts. It is far from clear that a transgender man, who makes no false representation, is under an ethical obligation to disclose highly personal facts about his gender history. Surely, his right to privacy ought to trump, especially given the costs disclosure entails, a cisgender right notionally founded on sexual autonomy, but which is tantamount to nothing less than a right to define him against his will.

Turning to the question of sexual autonomy, which underwrites liberal consent, feminism, or at least those kinds of feminism that overtly favour prosecution, must face up to the fact of agentic choice. While it remains heretical in some quarters to problematise sexual offence allegations, we must be prepared to discuss what it means to say that consent is absent in gender identity fraud cases. This is true in two senses. First, the consent/non-consent dyad cannot be thought apart from the 'privilege of unknowing' (Sedgwick, 1988, 1993), that is, from a cultural and psychological process whereby heterosexual cisgender people learn not to see, or otherwise sense, transgender and queer difference, and the repudiation of one's own bodily experience once it relays the presence of gendered and/or sexual otherness. In other words, and in the present context, it is inadequate to treat non-consent claims as unproblematic assertions of truth.

Second, the cases offer themselves as studies in gender ambiguity or dissonance, and therefore we might consider whether a conclusion of non-consent conceals more than it reveals. In other words, rather than thinking of gender ambiguity in terms of non-consent and deception, we might instead consider the possibility that it is constitutive of desire itself, at least in some cases. That is, we ought to consider the possibility that complainant desire is a 'because of', rather than an 'in spite of', desire. Ultimately, we must be prepared to accept the possibility that the punitive state is being used, not so much 'to protect sexual autonomy against fraudulent solicitation of sex, but rather to protect gender norms and compulsory heterosexuality' (Gross, 2008, p. 165).

Turning to judicial instantiation of an act/omission distinction as a basis for establishing non-consent, as well as part of the mens rea of adult sexual offences committed by way of deception, the book highlighted how the distinction, one long-subject to criticism within criminal law jurisprudence (Ashworth, 1989; Elliot and Ormerod, 2008; Herring, 2015, Chapter 2), fails in two senses. First, it fails to provide a convincing justification for the differential allocation of defendants. This adds weight to existing criticisms of reliance on the distinction. Second, and more revealingly in the present context, it draws attention to the 'definitional problem' (Rosenberg, 2014, p. 393) and how slippage between active deception and non-disclosure of information proves especially notable in the context of questions of gender identity. In this sense, use of the distinction is not only objectionable in terms of its analytical porosity, but also because it fails in its stated aim to limit the reach of the criminal law to conduct only. As we saw, especially in Chapter 5, gender performance can prove enough to take a defendant beyond the legality of omission, thereby rendering the distinction effectively meaningless in the context of gender non-conforming defendants and increasing their exposure to criminal sanction.

Another important theme that emerges from considering gender identity fraud cases, and their legal resolution, is the theme of harm and, more particularly, how we understand the harm concept. This issue is an important one both for feminism, where gendered harms assume particular significance, and more generally within criminal justice debates about setting appropriate limits to the operation of criminal law. In the present context, the question of harm proves important in two senses. First, an issue arises as to whether we are actually in the territory of harm, given Feinberg's distinction between 'harm' and 'offense' (Feinberg, 1985), and if we are, whether a threshold of harm has been crossed justifying criminalisation. Second, we need to reflect on whether the (ideological) source of an experience of harm matters in terms of the significance we attach to it. This issue is especially important given that complainant harms are pleasurable acts reimagined and are intelligible as harms only in the context of the operation and interplay of cisnormativity, transphobia and homophobia and, of course, the more importance we attribute to such harms, the greater our complicity in embedding these norms and phobias. Moreover, and in developing this issue of harm, future calculations of harm must give due weight to the transgender side of the ledger. After all, it should be abundantly clear by now that the 'choice' not to disclose gender history is not simply a matter of privacy. It is a matter of what privacy secures, not just an inner life, but psychic and physical preservation.

Finally, gender identity fraud cases cause us to re-evaluate the concept of deception, or at least the means through which it is satisfied. As noted above, it can certainly not exist where assumed and actual gender identity tally. Nor can it be present in circumstances where a gender non-conforming person remains unaware of the importance of any gap. However, even where a gap exists and where a person is aware both of this fact and its importance to the other sexual party, a conclusion of deception also requires that we accept that an obligation to disclose personal information exists, or ought to exist. As a matter of law, it is only active deception that founds liability, albeit the judiciary have muddied the distinction between act and omission in their treatment of gender identity fraud cases. In terms of normative ethics, the book has argued that if such an obligation ought to exist, it should only do so in circumstances where harms associated with non-disclosure outweigh those associated with disclosure. The burden of proof must rest with those who favour prosecution and/or insist on characterising omission as unethical.

In one sense, discussion of the concepts of consent, harm and deception in the context of gender identity fraud, and their relevance both to feminism and to the operation of criminal justice, lead, almost inevitably, to the question of ethics, to reflection on an ethical relation to the other. While there will be those, including some feminists, who support prosecution on the kinds of facts the gender identity fraud cases disclose, it remains a truism that conclusions of non-consent, harm and deception only make sense when approached through the lens of cisnormativity. If we are to be(come) 'ethically gendered' (Serano, 2013, p. 259) we must recognise that the phrase, 'against my will', popularised by Susan Brownmiller so long ago (Brownmiller, 1975), is, in the present context, transmogrified. That is, at least in relation to transgender defendants, the victim/perpetrator dyad becomes complicated by the fact that claims of sexual violation are themselves founded on a prior violence, the denial of self-determination.

It is appreciated that the book's refusal to view sexual autonomy in absolute terms, and, more particularly, its refusal to concede that complainant ignorance ought necessarily to establish non-consent, will be uncomfortable reading for some. But if we are to do justice to/in these kinds of cases we must be prepared to face difficult questions, and perhaps learn to live with, if we are unable to overcome, feelings of discomfort. For sex, gender and sexuality are complicated affairs and the desire that flows between them, an unruly child. While every women has the right to choose who she becomes sexually intimate with, we should not conclude that this requires others to disclose intimate facts about their bodies and lives, and especially not in circumstances where undisclosed 'facts' assume importance only because of a prior ontological violence. Moreover, we must, in circumstances of desire-led intimacy, recognise agentic choice. We must not pretend our desires, and the pleasures we derive from them, are not our own, no matter how much we, or the legal system, may wish to disown them.

Turning to queer legal theory, and while recognising its more obvious sympathy with the defendants in the cases considered, it must engage, more explicitly, with law. After all, gender non-conforming youth, especially those designated female at birth, are especially vulnerable to state prosecution at this historical moment. Of course, it is important to offer critiques of liberal law, of the way it regulates and represents gender and sexual outsiders. However, resistance, as Zanghellini argues (2009), cannot be confined to discursive analyses, ones which observe law from a distance. Rather, queer legal struggle must also take place on the field of law, within its interstices. This book has sought to do this in two senses. First, through providing a series of queer-informed legal arguments that might be deployed both in actual criminal cases and in broader law reform struggles and second, through the writing of an academic counter-judgment to *McNally*, one which has illustrated how, despite constraints of legal method, custom and precedent, queer judgment is not only desirable, but possible.

To conclude, it is hoped this book has achieved three things. First, that is has provided a wedge against, and a legal resource to help challenge, future prosecutions. Second, that it has laid the ground for serious reflection on the question of ethical characterisation of desire-led intimacy between cisgender and gender non-conforming people, including reflection on the setting of any obligations and, as importantly, upon who should bear them. Finally, that it has contributed to queer and feminist legal theory, the former through the deployment of queer arguments and values on one specific sexual political terrain, and through its call to embrace normative arguments and struggle on behalf of gender non-conforming youth, the latter through highlighting how gender identity fraud cases offer fertile ground for thinking, not only about the legally constructed categories of sex, gender and sexuality, but also, and correspondingly, about how we conceive of the legally constructed categories, and sexual offence triumvirate, of consent, harm and deception.

## Postscript

On 20 July 2017 I submitted the book manuscript to the publishers. On the same day Judge Stockdale handed down a six and a half year prison sentence to Gayle Newland at Manchester Crown Court.[5] Sadly, it seems unlikely that Gayle's case will mark the end of gender identity fraud prosecutions in the UK. Rather, the attrition against gender non-conforming young people looks likely to continue unabated. Each of us must consider our complicity in this state of affairs.

5 J Humphries 'Gayle Newland to be Sentenced for Posing as Man to Dupe Friend into Sex with Fake Penis' *The Liverpool Echo* 20/7/17 available at www.liverpoolecho.co.uk/news/liverpool-news/gayle-newland-sentenced-posing-man-13358713 (last accessed: 20/7/17).

# References

## A


Abate, M A, *Tomboys: A Literary and Cultural History* (Philadelphia, PA: Temple University Press, 2009).

Abrams, K, 'From Autonomy to Agency: Feminist Perspectives on Self-Direction' (1999) 40 *William and Mary Law Review* 805.

Ahmed, S, *The Cultural Politics of Emotion* (Edinburgh: Edinburgh University Press, 2004).

Albrecht, G and Levy, J, 'Constructing Disabilities as Social Problems' in G Albrecht (ed.), *Cross National Rehabilitation Policies: A Sociological Perspective* (London: Sage, 1981) pp. 11–32.

Alexander, L, 'The Moral Magic of Consent' (1996) 2(3) *Legal Theory* 165.

Anderson, M J, *Carl Linnaeus: Father of Classification* (Berkeley Heights, NJ: Enslow Publishers, 1997).

Appiah, K A and A Gutmann, *Color Conscious: The Political Morality of Race* (Princeton, NJ: Princeton University Press, 1998).

Archbold, *Criminal Pleading Evidence and Practice* (London: Sweet & Maxwell, 2010).

Archard, D, *Sexual Consent* (Boulder, CO: Westview, 1998).

Aries, P, *Centuries of Childhood: A Social History of Family Life* (New York: Random House, 1965).

Arnett, J J, 'Learning to Stand Alone: The Contemporary American Transition to Adulthood in Cultural and Historical Context' (1998) 41(5) *Human Development* 295.

Ashworth, A, 'The Scope of Criminal Liability for Omissions' (1989) 105 *Law Quarterly Review* 424.

Ashworth, A, *Principles of the Criminal Law* (Oxford: Oxford University Press, 2009).

Ashworth, A and Horder, J, *Principles of Criminal Law* (7th edn) (Oxford: OUP, 2013).

Ashworth, A and Roberts, J V, *Sentencing Guidelines: Exploring the English Model* (Oxford: Oxford University Press, 2013).

Austin, J, *How To Do Things With Words* (eds J O Urmson and M Sbisa) (Cambridge, MA: Harvard University Press, 1955).

Austin, J, *Philosophical Papers* (Oxford: Oxford University Press, 1961).


## B


Baeten, J M, 'Antiretroviral Prophylaxis for HIV Prevention in Heterosexual Men and Women' (2012) 367(5) *The New England Journal of Medicine* 399.

Baker, D, *The Right Not to be Criminalised* (Aldershot: Ashgate, 2011).

Balkin, J M, (ed.) *What Roe v Wade Should Have Said: The Nation's Top Legal Experts Rewrite America's Most Controversial Decision* (New York: New York University Press, 2005).

Ball, C A, 'Sexual Ethics and Postmodernism in Gay Rights Philosophy' (2002) 80 *North Carolina Law Review* 371.

Bamforth, N, *Sexuality, Morals and Justice: A Theory of Lesbian and Gay Rights Law* (London: Cassell, 1997).

Becker, H S, 'Whose Side Are We On?' (1967) 14(3) *Social Problems* 239.

Berenson, K R and Andersen, S M, 'Childhood Physical and Emotional Abuse by a Parent: Transference Effects in Adult Interpersonal Relationships' (2006) 33 *Personality and Social Psychology Bulletin* 1509.

Bergelson, V, 'Sex, Lies and Law: Rethinking Rape-by-Fraud' in C Ashford, A Reed, and N Wake (eds) *Legal Perspectives on State Power: Consent and Control* (Newcastle upon Tyne: Cambridge Scholars Publishing, 2016) pp. 152–184.

Berger, P L and Luckmann, T, *The Social Construction of Reality* (New York: Anchor Books, 1966).

Bernstein, E, 'The Sexual Politics of "New Abolitionism"' (2007) 18(3) *Differences* 128.

Bernstein, E, 'Carceral Politics as Gender Justice? The "Traffic in Women" and Neoliberal Circuits of Crime, Sex, and Rights' (2012) 41(3) *Theory and Society* 233.

Bettcher, T M, 'Evil Deceivers and Make-Believers: On Transphobic Violence and the Politics of Illusion' (2007) 22(3) *Hypatia* 43.

Bettcher, T M, 'Trans Identities and First-Person Authority' in L J Shrage (ed.) *You've Changed: Sex Reassignment and Personal Identity* (New York: Oxford University Press, 2009) pp. 98–120.

Blos, P, *The Adolescent Passage: Developmental Issues* (New York: International Universities Press, 1979).

Blunt, W, *Linnaeus: the Compleat Naturalist* (London: Frances Lincoln, 2001).

Bohlander, M, 'Mistaken Consent to Sex: Political Correctness and Correct Policy' (2007) 71 *Journal of Criminal Law* 412.

Bok, S, *Secrets: On the Ethics of Concealment and Revelation* (London: Vintage Books, 1998).

Booth, D, 'Nietzsche on the Subject as Multiplicity' (1985) 18 *Man and World: International Philosophical Review* 121.

Bornstein, K, *Gender Outlaw: On Men, Women, and the Rest of Us* (New York: Routledge, 1994).

Bornstein, K, 'Gender Terror, Gender Rage' in S Stryker and S Whittle (eds) *Transgender Studies Reader* (vol 1) (Abingdon, Oxfordshire: Routledge, 2006) pp. 236–243.

Brandt, R, 'The Real and Alleged Problems of Utilitarianism' in T Carson and P Moser (eds) *Morality and the Good Life* (New York: Oxford University Press, 1997) pp. 373–383.

Bronnitt, S, 'Rape and Lack of Consent' (1991) 16 *Australian Criminal Law Journal* 289.

Brown, W, *States of Injury: Power and Freedom in Late Modernity* (Princeton, NJ: Princeton University Press, 1995).

Brownmiller, S, *Against Our Will: Men, Women and Rape* (New York: Simon and Schuster, 1975).

Bryden, D P, 'Redefining Rape' (2000) 3 *Buffalo Criminal Law Review* 317.

Burke, L K and Follingstad, D R, 'Violence in Lesbian and Gay Relationships: Theory, Prevalence, and Correlational Factors' (1999) 19(5) *Clinical Psychology Review* 487.

Butler, J, *Gender Trouble: Feminism and the Subversion of Identity* (London: Routledge, 1990).

Butler, J, 'Imitation and Gender Insubordination' in D Fuss (ed.) *Inside/Out: Lesbian Theories, Gay Theories* (London: Routledge, 1991) pp. 13–31.

Butler, J, *Bodies That Matter: On the Discursive Limits of Sex* (London: Routledge, 1993).

Butler, J, *Undoing Gender* (New York: Routledge, 2004).

Buxton, R, 'Private Life and the English Judges' (2009) 29(3) *Oxford Journal of Legal Studies* 413.


## C


Cahill, A J, *Overcoming Objectification: A Carnal Ethics* (New York: Routledge, 2011).

Califia, P, *Sex Changes: The Politics of Transgenderism* (2nd edn) (San Francisco, CA: Cleis Press 2003).

Callander, D, Newman, C E and Holt, M, 'Is Sexual Racism Really Racism? Distinguishing Attitudes Toward Sexual Racism and Generic Racism Among Gay and Bisexual Men' (2015) 44(7) *Archives of Sexual Behavior* 1991.

Card, R, *Criminal Law* (20th edn) (Oxford: Oxford University Press, 2012).

Cardozo, B, *Selected Writings of Benjamin Nathan Cardozo: The Choice of Tycho Brahe* (ed. M E Hall) (New York: Fallon Publishers, 1947).

Carmody, M, 'Sexual Ethics and the Erotics of Consent' in P Cowling and P Reynolds (eds) *Making Sense of Sexual Consent* (Farnham, Surrey: Ashgate, 2004) pp. 45–56.

Carmody, M and Carrington, K, '*Preventing Sexual Violence?*' (2000) 33(3) *Australian and New Zealand Journal of Criminology* 341.

Carson, T L, *Lying and Deception: Theory and Practice* (Oxford: Oxford University Press, 2010).

Cavanagh, S, 'Touching Gender: Abjection and the Hygienic Imagination' in S Stryker and A Z Aizura (eds) *The Transgender Studies Reader 2* (Abingdon, Oxfordshire: Routledge, 2013) pp. 426–442.

Cavarero, A, *Relating Narratives: Storytelling and Selfhood* (trans P A Kottman) (London: Routledge, 2000).

Chalmers, J and Leverick, F, 'Fair Labelling in Criminal Law' (2008) 71(2) *Modern Law Review* 217.

Chamallas, M, 'Consent, Equality and the Legal Construction of Sexual Conduct' (1988) 61 *South California Law Review* 777.

Chinkin, C, 'A Critique of the Public/Private Dimension' (1999) 10(2) *European Journal of International Law* 387.

Clements-Nolle, K, Marx, R and Katz, M, 'Attempted Suicide Among Transgender Persons: The Influence of Gender-Based Discrimination and Victimization' (2006) 51(3) *Journal of Homosexuality* 53.

Cohen, M S et al, 'Prevention of HIV-1 Infection with Early Antiretroviral Therapy' (2011) 365(5) *The New England Journal of Medicine* 493.

Cohen, S, *Folk Devils and Moral Panics: The Creation of the Mods and Rockers* (London: MacGibbon & Kee, 1972).

Cohen-Kettenis, P T and Pfafflin, F, *Transgenderism and Intersexuality in Childhood and Adolescence: Making Choices* (Thousand Oaks, CA: Sage, 2003).

Colb, S F, 'Is There a Moral Duty to Disclose that You're Transgender to a Potential Partner?' *Verdict* 18 June 2015.

Coleridge, S T, *Biographia Literaria* (vol 2) (London: Clarendon Press, 1907).

Comstock, G, 'Dismantling the Homosexual Panic Defence' (1992) 2 *Law and Sexuality* 81.

Connell, R W, *Masculinities* (Sydney: Allen & Unwin, 1995).

Cover, R, 'Violence and the Word' (1986) 95 *Yale Law Journal* 1601.

Cowan, S, 'Gender is no Substitute for Sex: A Comparative Human Rights Analysis of the Legal Regulation of Sexual Identity' (2005) 13 *Feminist Legal Studies* 67.

Cowan, S, 'Freedom and Capacity to make a Choice: A Feminist Analysis of Consent in the Criminal Law of Rape' in V Munro and C Stychin (eds) *Sexuality and the Law* (Abingdon, Oxfordshire: Routledge, 2007) pp. 51–72.

Cowan, S, 'The Heart of the Matter: A Queer Feminist Critique of Fraudulent Consent and Criminalisation' *Oxford Journal of Legal Studies* (2018) forthcoming.

Cromwell, J, *Transmen and FTMs: Identities, Bodies, Genders & Sexualities* (Chicago, IL: Chicago University Press, 1999).

Currah, P, 'Transgender Rights Without a Theory of Gender?' (2017) 52(3) *Tulsa Law Review* 441.

## D

Davies, M, 'Feminism and the Idea of Law' (2011) 1 *feminists@law* 1.

Davies, M, 'The Law Becomes Us: Rediscovering Judgment' (2012) 20 *Feminist Legal Studies* 167.

Davy, Z, *Recognizing Transsexuals: Personal, Political and Medicolegal Embodiment* (Farnham, Surrey: Ashgate, 2011).

Dean, T, 'Homosexuality and the Problem of Otherness' in T Dean and C Lane (eds) *Homosexuality and Psychoanalysis* (Chicago, IL: Chicago University Press, 2001) pp. 120–143.

Derrida, J. *Of Grammatology* (trans. G C Spivak) (Baltimore, MD: Johns Hopkins University Press, 1977).

Derrida, J, *Writing and Difference* (London: Routledge, 2001).

Doig, G and Wortley, N, 'Conditional Consent? An Emerging Concept in the Law of Rape' (2013) 77(4) *Journal of Criminal Law* 286.

Dougherty, T, 'Sex, Lies and Consent' (2013) 123 *Ethics* 717.

Douglas, M, *Purity and Danger* (London: Routledge, 1966).

Dreger, A, *Hermaphrodites and the Medical Invention of Sex* (Cambridge, MA: Harvard University Press, 2000).

Dripps, D, 'Beyond Rape: An Essay on the Difference Between the Presence of Force and the Absence of Consent' (1992) 92 *Columbia Law Review* 1460.

Duncan, S, 'Law's Sexual Discipline: Visibility, Violence & Consent' (1995) 22 *Journal of Law and Society* 326.

## E

Elliot, T and Ormerod, D, 'Act and Omissions – A Distinction Without a Defence' (2008) 39 *Cambrian Law Review* 40.

Ellison, L and Munro, V E, 'Breaking the Boundaries? Sexual Consent in the Jury Room' (2006) 26(3) *Legal Studies* 303.

Ellison, L and Munro, V E, 'Of "Normal Sex" and "Real Rape": Exploring the Use of Socio-Sexual Scripts in (Mock) Jury Deliberation' (2009) 18(3) *Social Legal Studies: An International Journal* 291.

Ellison, L and Munro, V E, 'Getting to (Not) Guilty: Examining Jurors' Deliberative Processes in, and Beyond, the Context of a Mock Rape Trial' (2010) 30(1) *Legal Studies* 74.

Ellison, L and Munro, V E, 'Better the Devil You Know? "Real Rape" Stereotypes and the Relevance of a Previous Relationship in (Mock) Juror Deliberation' (2013) 14 *International Journal of Evidence and Proof* 299.

Enke, F, 'The Education of Little Cis: Cisgender and the Discipline of Opposing Bodies' in S Stryker and A Z Aizura (eds) *The Transgender Studies Reader 2* (Abingdon, Oxfordshire: Routledge, 2013) pp. 234–247.

Estrich, S, 'Rape' (1986) 95(6) *Yale Law Journal* 1087.

Estrich, S, *Real Rape* (Cambridge, MA: Harvard University Press, 1987).

**F**

Falk, P, 'Rape by Fraud and Rape by Coercion' (1998) 64 *Brooklyn Law Review* 39.

Farmer, L, *Making the Modern Criminal Law: Criminalization and Civil Order* (Oxford: Oxford University Press, 2016).

Feinberg, J, *Harm to Others* (Oxford: Oxford University Press, 1984).

Feinberg, J, *Offense to Others* (Oxford: Oxford University Press, 1985).

Feinberg, J, *Harm to Self* (Oxford: Oxford University Press, 1986).

Feinberg, J, *Harmless Wrongdoing* (Oxford: Oxford University Press, 1988).

Feinberg, L, *Transgender Warriors: Making History from Joan of Arc to Ru Paul* (Boston, MA: Beacon Press, 1996).

Finch, E and Munro, V E, 'Juror Stereotypes and Blame Attribution in Rape Cases Involving Intoxicants' (2005) 45(1) *British Journal of Criminology* 25.

Fineman, M A and A P Romero, *Feminist and Queer Legal Theory: Intimate Encounters, Uncomfortable Conversations* (Farnham, Surrey: Ashgate, 2009)

Finnis, J M, 'Bland: Crossing the Rubicon' (1993) 109 *Law Quarterly Review* 329.

Fisk, N, 'Gender Dysphoria Syndrome: The How, What and Why of a Disease' in D R Laud and P Gandy, *Proceedings of the Second International Symposium on Gender Dysphoria Syndrome* (Stanford, CA: University Medical Center, 1973) pp. 7–14.

Fleming, J G, *Law of Torts* (8th edn) (Sydney: Law Book Company, 1992).

Fletcher, G, *Rethinking Criminal Law* (Oxford: Oxford University Press, 1978).

Foucault, M, *The Order of Things: An Archaeology of the Human Sciences* (London: Tavistock, 1970).

Foucault, M, *The Archaeology of Knowledge* (New York: Harper & Row, 1972).

Foucault, M, *Discipline and Punish: The Birth of the Prison* (London: Penguin, 1977).

Foucault, M, 'Two Lectures' in C Gordon (ed.) *Power/Knowledge: Selected Interviews and Other Writings, 1972–1977* (New York: Pantheon, 1980a).

Foucault, M, *Power/Knowledge: Selected Interviews and Other Writings, 1972–1977* (New York: Pantheon, 1980b).

Foucault, M, *The History of Sexuality vol 1: An Introduction* (London: Penguin, 1981).

Foucault, M, *Michel Foucault: Politics, Philosophy and Culture – Interviews and Other Writings, 1977–1984* (ed. L D Kritzman (trans A Sheridan)) (New York: Routledge, 1988).

Foucault, M, 'How Much Does It Cost to Tell the Truth' in M Foucault (ed.) *Foucault Live Semiotext(e)* (New York: Columbia University Press, 1989) pp. 233–256.

Foucault, M, 'Polemics, Politics and Problematizations' in P Rabinow (ed.) *Essential Works of Foucault, vol 1: Ethics* (New York: The New Press, 1998).

Franke, K, 'Theorizing Yes: An Essay on Feminism, Law and Desire' (2001) 101 *Columbia Law Review* 181.
Fried, C, 'Privacy: A Moral Analysis' in F D Schoeman (ed.) *Philosophical Dimensions of Privacy: An Anthology* (Cambridge: Cambridge University Press, 1984) pp. 203–222.
Furedi, F, *Moral Crusades in an Age of Mistrust: The Jimmy Savile Scandal* (Basingstoke, Hampshire: Palgrave Macmillan, 2013)
Fuss, D, *Essentially Speaking: Feminism, Nature and Difference* (New York: Routledge, 1990).

## G

Gadbin-George, G, 'To Quote or Not to Quote: "Literature in Law" in European Court Decisions and Legal English Teaching' (2013) 64 *ASP: La Revue du GERAS* 75.
Gardner, J, 'The Wrongness of Rape' in J Gardner, *Offences and Defences: Selected Essays in the Philosophy of Criminal Law* (Oxford: Oxford University Press, 2007), Chapter 1.
Gardner, J and Shute, S, 'The Wrongness of Rape' in J Horder (ed.) *Oxford Essays in Jurisprudence* (Oxford: Oxford University Press, 2000).
Garland, D, *Punishment and Modern Society: A Study in Social Theory* (3rd edn) (Oxford: Oxford University Press, 1990).
Gavison, R, 'Feminism and the Public/Private Distinction' (1992) 45 *Stanford Law Review* 1.
Geertz, C, 'Local Knowledge: Fact and Law in Comparative Perspective' in C Geertz *Local Knowledge: Further Essays in Interpretive Anthropology* (New York: Basic Books, 1983) pp. 167–234.
GenderPAC, *The First National Survey of Transgender Violence* (Washington, D.C., MA: GenderPAC, 1997).
Giddens, A and Pierson, C, *Making Sense of Modernity: Conversations with Anthony Giddens* (Palo Alto, CA: Stanford University Press, 1998).
Glazebrook, P, 'Criminal Omissions' (1960) 76 *Law Quarterly Review* 386.
Goffman, E, *The Presentation of Self in Everyday Life* (New York: Doubleday, 1959).
Gooren, L J G, Zhou, J N, Hofman, M A and Swaab, D F, 'A Sex Difference in the Human Brain and its Relation to Transsexuality' (1995) 378 *Nature* 68.
Gotell, L, 'Reassessing the Place of Criminal Law Reform in the Struggle Against Sexual Violence: A Critique of the Critique of Carceral Feminism' in A Powell, N Henry and A Flynn (eds) *Rape Justice: Beyond the Criminal Law* (New York: Palgrave Macmillan, 2015) pp. 53–71.
Govier, E, Diamond, M, Wolowiec, T and Slade, C, 'Dichotic Listening, Handedness, Brain Organization and Transsexuality' (2010) 12 *Intl J Transgenderism* 144.
Green, J, 'Predator?' *San Francisco Bay Times*, 22 Feb 1996.
Green, J, 'Look! No, Don't!: The Visibility Dilemma for Transsexual Men' in S Stryker and S Whittle (eds) *The Transgender Studies Reader* (Abingdon, Oxfordshire: Routledge, 2006) pp. 499–508.
Greenberg, D F, *The Construction of Modern Homosexuality* (Chicago, IL: Chicago University Press, 1988).
Greenberg, J A, *Intersexuality and the Law: Why Sex Matters* (New York: New York University Press, 2012).
Greer, G, *The Whole Woman* (New York: Doubleday, 1999).
Gross, A, 'Democratia, Etniut VeKhukatiut BeIsrael: Bein "HaMedina Ha Yehudit" Ve'HaMedina HaDemocratit' ('Democracy, Ethnicity and Constitutionalism in Israel: Between the "Jewish State" and the Democratic State') (2000) 2 *Israeli Soc* 647.

Gross, A, 'Gender Outlaws Before the Law: The Courts of the Borderland' (2009) 32(1) *Harvard Journal of Law & Gender* 165.

Gross, A, 'Rape by Deception and the Policing of Gender and Nationality Borders' (2015) 24 *Tulane Journal of Law and Sexuality* 1.

Gross, H, 'Rape, Moralism and Human Rights' [2007] *Criminal Law Review* 220.

Gruber, A, 'Rape, Feminism, and the War on Crime' (2009) 84 *Washington Law Review* 581.

## H

Halberstam, J, 'F2M: The Making of Female Masculinity' in L Doan (ed.) *The Lesbian Postmodern* (New York: Columbia University Press, 1994) pp. 210–228.

Halberstam, J, *Female Masculinity* (Durham, NC: Duke University Press, 1998).

Halberstam, J, *In a Queer Time and Place: Transgender Bodies, Subcultural Lives* (New York: New York University Press, 2005).

Hale, B, 'Maccabaean Lecture in Jurisprudence: A Minority Opinion' (2008) 154 *Proceedings of the British Academy* 319.

Hale, C J, 'Leatherdyke Boys and their Daddies: How to have Sex without Women and Men' in R J Corber and S Valocchi (eds) *Queer Studies: An Interdisciplinary Reader* (Melbourne: Blackwell, 2003) pp. 61–70.

Halley, J, Kotiswaran, P, Thomas, C and Shamir, H, 'From the International to the Local in Feminist Legal Responses to Rape, Prostitution/Sex Work, and Sex Trafficking: Four Studies in Contemporary Governance Feminism' (2006) 29 *Harvard Journal of Law and Gender* 335.

Harrison, K, *Sexual Deceit: The Ethics of Passing* (Lanham, MD: Lexington Books, 2013).

Hart, H L A, *Law, Liberty and Morality* (Palo Alto, CA: Stanford University Press, 1964).

Hart, H L A and Honore, A, *Causation in Law* (2nd edn) (Oxford: Oxford University Press, 1985).

Henderson, L, 'What Makes Rape a Crime?' (1988) 3 *Berkeley Women's Law Journal* 193.

Herring, J, 'Mistaken Sex' [2005] *Criminal Law Review* 511.

Herring, J, 'Human Rights and Rape: A Reply to Hyman Gross' [2007] *Criminal Law Review* 228.

Herring, J, *Great Debates in Criminal Law* (3rd edn) (London: Palgrave Macmillan, 2015).

Herring, J and Madden-Dempsey, M, 'Why Sexual Penetration Requires Justification' (2007) 27(3) *Oxford Journal of Legal Studies* 467.

Heyes, C, *Self-Transformations: Foucault, Ethics and Normalized Bodies* (Oxford: Oxford University Press, 2007).

Heyman, S, 'Foundations of the Duty to Rescue' (1994) 47 *Vanderbilt Law Review* 673.

Hill, D and Willoughby, B, 'The Development and Validation of the Genderism and Transphobia Scale' (2005) 53 *Sex Roles* 531.

Hobbes, T, *Leviathan* (Oxford: Oxford University Press, 2008).

Hollway, W, 'Recognition and Heterosexual Desire' in D Richardson (ed.) *Theorising Heterosexuality* (Buckingham: Open University Press, 1996).

Home Office, *Setting the Boundaries: Reforming the Law on Sexual Offences*, vol 1 (London: HMSO, 2000).

Horder, J, 'Consent, Threats and Deception in Criminal Law' (1999) 10(1) *King's College Law Journal* 104.

Hungerford-Welch, P, *Criminal Procedure and Sentencing* (8th edn) (Oxford: Routledge, 2014).

Hunt, A, Fractious Rivals: 'Moral Panics and Moral Regulation' in S Hier (ed.) *Moral Panic and the Politics of Anxiety* (Abingdon, Oxfordshire: Routledge, 2011) pp. 53–70.

Hunter, R, 'An Account of Feminist Judging' in R Hunter, C McGlynn and E Rackley (eds) *Feminist Judgements: From Theory to Practice* (Oxford: Hart Publishing, 2010) pp. 30–43.

Hunter, R, 'The Power of Feminist Judgments?' (2012) 20 *Feminist Legal Studies* 135.

Hunter, R, McGlynn, C and Rackley, E (eds) *Feminist Judgements: From Theory to Practice* (Oxford: Hart Publishing, 2010).

Husak, D, *Overcriminalisation: The Limits of the Criminal Law* (Oxford: OUP, 2008).

## I

Istar, A, 'Couple Assessment: Identifying and Intervening in Domestic Violence in Lesbian Relationships' (1996) 4(1) *Journal of Gay and Lesbian Social Services* 93.

## J

Jagose, A, *Queer Theory: An Introduction* (New York: New York University Press, 1997).

Jagose, A, 'The Trouble with Antinormativity' (2015) 26(1) *Differences* 26.

Jareborg, N, 'What Kind of Criminal Law Do We Want?' in A Snare (ed.) *Beware of Punishment* (Oslo: Pax Forlag, 1995) pp. 17–36.

Jefferson, T, 'Masculinities and Crime' in M Maguire, M Morgan and R Reiner (eds) *The Oxford Handbook of Criminology* (2nd edn) (Oxford: Clarendon Press, 1997).

Jeffreys, S, *Gender Hurts: A Feminist Analysis of the Politics of Transgenderism* (Abingdon, Oxfordshire: Routledge, 2014).

Jenkins, P, *Intimate Enemies: Moral Panics in Contemporary Great Britain* (New York: Aldine de Gruyter, 1992).

## K

Karaian, L, 'The Troubled Relationship of Feminist and Queer Legal Theory to Strategic Essentialism: Theory/Praxis, Queer Porn, and Canadian Anti-Discrimination Law' in M A Fineman, J E Jackson and A P Romero (eds) *Feminist and Queer Legal Theory: Intimate Encounters, Uncomfortable Conversations* (Farnham: Ashgate, 2009) pp. 375–394.

Kennedy, D, *A Critique of Adjudication: Fin de Siecle* (Cambridge, MA: Harvard University Press, 1997).

Keogh, P, Reid, D and Weatherburn, P, *Lambeth LGBT Matters: The Needs and Experiences of Lesbians, Gay Man, Bisexual and Transgender Men and Women in Lambeth* (Lambeth: Sigma Research, 2006).

Keown, J, 'Restoring Moral and Intellectual Shape to the Law after Bland' (1997) 113 *Law Quarterly Review* 481.

Kirby, V, 'Transgression: Normativity's Self-Inversion' (2015) 26(1) *Differences* 96.

Kristeva, J, *The Powers of Horror: An Essay on Abjection* (trans L Roudiez) (New York: Columbia University Press, 1982).

Kruijver, F P M, Zhou, J N, Pool, C W, Hofman, M A, Gooren, L J G and Swaab, D F, 'Male-To-Female Transsexuals have Female Neuron Numbers in a Limbic Nucleus' (2000) 85 *J Clin Endocr Metab* 2034.

## L

Lacey, N, 'Unspeakable Subjects, Impossible Rights: Sexuality, Integrity and Criminal Law' (1998) 11 *Canadian Journal of Law and Jurisprudence* 47.

Laird, K, 'Rapist or Rogue? Deception, Consent and the Sexual Offences Act 2003' (2014) 7 *Criminal Law Review* 492.

Lamble, S, 'Queer Necropolitics and the Expanding Carceral State: Interrogating Sexual Investments in Punishment' (2013) 24(3) *Law & Critique* 229.

Laplanche, J and Pontalis, J B, 'Appendices: [Vocabulaire de la psychanalyse]' (1972) 48 *Yale French Studies* 179.

Laqueur, T, *Making Sex: Body and Gender from the Greeks to Freud* (Cambridge, MA: Harvard University Press, 1990).

Latham, J R, 'Trans Men's Sexual Narrative-Practices: Introducing STS to Trans and Sexuality Studies' (2016) 19(3) *Sexualities* 347.

Laurie, G, *Genetic Privacy: A Challenge to Medico-Legal Norms* (Cambridge: Cambridge University Press, 2002).

Law Commission, *Consent in Sex Offences: A Policy Paper: Appendix C of Setting the Boundaries* vol 2 (London: Home Office, 2000).

Lieber, C, et al, 'America's Churning Races: Race and Ethnic Response Changes between Census 2000 and the 2010 Census' (Center for Administrative Records Research and Application, Working Paper: US Census Bureau, 2014a).

Lieber, C, et al, 'Dynamics of Race: Joining, Leaving and Staying in the American Indian/Alaska Native Race Category between 2000 and 2010' (Center for Administrative Records Research and Application, Working Paper: US Census Bureau, 2014b).

Lindquist Dorr, L, *White Women, Rape, and the Politics of Race in Virginia 1900–1960* (Chapel Hill, NC: University of North Carolina Press, 2004).

Lyotard, J F, *The Postmodern Condition: A Report on Knowledge* (trans. G Bennington) (Minneapolis, MN: University of Minnesota Press, 1984).

Lyotard, J F, *The Lyotard Reader* (London: Blackwell, 1989).

## M

MacKinnon, C, *Toward a Feminist Theory of the State* (Cambridge, MA: Harvard University Press, 1989).

McGregor, J, *Is It Rape? On Acquaintance Rape and Taking Women's Consent Seriously* (Aldershot: Ashgate, 2005).

McNay, L, *Gender and Agency: Reconfiguring the Subject in Feminist and Social Theory* (Oxford: Polity Press, 2000).

Madden-Dempsey, M and Herring, J, 'Rethinking the Law's Response to Sexual Penetration: On Theory and Context' in C McGlynn and V Munro (eds) *Rethinking Rape Law: National, International and European Perspectives* (Abingdon, Oxfordshire: Routledge, 2010) pp. 30–44.

Malkani, B, 'Article 8 of the European Convention on Human Rights and the Decision to Prosecute' (2011) 12 *Criminal Law Review* 943.

Marjury, D, 'Introducing the Women's Court of Canada' (2006) 18 *Canadian Journal of Women & the Law* 1.

Marks, J, *Human Biodiversity: Genes, Race, & History* (New York: Aldine de Gruyter, 1995).

Martin, B, 'Sexualities Without Genders and Other Queer Utopias' (1994) 24(2–3) *Diacritics* 104.

Martin, D L, 'Retribution Revisited: A Reconsideration of Feminist Criminal Law Reform Strategies' (1998) 36 *Osgoode Hall Law Journal* 151.

Mellor, D H, *The Facts of Causation* (London: Routledge, 1995).

Messerschmidt, J W, *Masculinities and Crime: Critiques and Reconceptualisation* (Lanham, MD: Rowman, 1993).

Meyer, A, 'The Moral: Rhetoric of Childhood' (2007) 14(1) *Childhood* 85.

Miles, J, 'Sexual Offences: Consent, Capacity and Children' [2008] *Archbold News* 6.

Mill, J S, *Utilitarianism* (Indianapolis, IN: Hackett Press, 1979).

Miller, W I, *The Anatomy of Disgust* (Cambridge, MA: Harvard University Press, 1997).

Mills, C, 'Passing: The Ethics of Pretending to be What You Are Not' (1999) 25(1) *Social Theory & Practice* 29.

Moore, A, 'Shame on You: The Role of Shame, Disgust and Humiliation in Media Representations of "Gender Fraud" Cases' (2016) 21(2) *Sociological Research Online* 10.

Moore, M S, *Act and Crime: The Philosophy of Action and Its Implications for Criminal Law* (London: Clarendon, 1993).

Moore, M S, *Causation and Responsibility: An Essay in Law, Morals, and Metaphysics* (Oxford: Oxford University Press, 2009).

Moran, L 'Violence and the Law: The Case of Sado-Masochism' (1995) 4 *Law and Critique* 225.

Moran, L, *The Homosexuality of Law* (London: Routledge, 1996).

Moran, L, 'Review of R. Hunter, C. McGlynn and E. Rackley (eds) Feminist Judgments: From Theory to Practice (Oxford: Hart Publishing, 2010)' (2012) 75(2) *Modern Law Review* 287.

Morgan, W, 'Law and Change: Identifying Evil for what it is: Tasmania, Sexual Perversity and the United Nations' (1994) 19 *Melbourne University Law Review* 740.

Morton, J, *Transgender Experiences in Scotland: Research Summary* (Edinburgh: Scottish Transgender Alliance, 2008).

Munro, V, 'Concerning Consent: Standards of Permissibility in Sexual Relations' (2005) 25(2) *Oxford Journal of Legal Studies* 335.

## N

Nagel, T, 'Concealment and Exposure' (1998) 27(1) *Philosophy and Public Affairs* 3.

Namaste, V, *Invisible Lives: The Erasure of Transsexual and Transgendered People* (Chicago, IL: Chicago University Press, 2000).

Nestle, J, (ed.) *The Persistent Desire: A Femme-Butch Reader* (Los Angeles, CA: Alyson Publications 1992).

Nestle, J, Wilchins, R A and Howell, C, *GenderQueer: Voices from Beyond the Sexual Binary* (New York: Alyson Books, 2002).

Nietzsche, F, *On the Genealogy of Morals* (New York: Vintage Books, 1969).

Norrie, A, *Crime, Reason & History* (London: Butterworths, 2001).

Nourse, M, 'Law and Literature – The Contribution of Lord Denning' (2005) 17(1) *The Denning Law Journal* 1.

Nye, J L, 'The Gender Box' (1998) 13 *Berkeley Women's Law Journal* 226.

## O

Okin, S M, *Justice, Gender and the Family* (New York: Basic Books, 1989).

Ormerod, D, *Smith and Hogan's Criminal Law* (13th edn) (Oxford: Oxford University Press, 2011).

## P

Packer, H L, *The Limits of the Criminal Sanction* (Stanford, CA: Stanford University Press, 1968).
Parker, E A, 'Sexual Violence as Derivatization' in G Foster (ed.) *Desire, Love, & Identity: A Textbook for the Philosophy of Sex and Love* (Don Mills, Toronto: Oxford University Press, 2017).
Pateman, C, 'Feminist Critiques of the Public/Private Dichotomy' in S I Benn and G F Gaus (eds) *Public and Private in Social Life* (New York: St. Martin's Press, 1983) pp. 281–303.
Paterson, A, *The Law Lords* (London: Palgrave Macmillan, 1982).
Phillips, A, *Missing Out: In Praise of the Unlived Life* (London: Penguin, 2013).
Plummer, K, *The Making of the Modern Homosexual* (New York: Barnes & Noble, 1981).
Polaszek, A, *Systema Naturae 250 – The Linnaean Ark* (Boca Raton, FL: CRC Press, 2010).
Posner, R, 'The Right to Privacy' (1978) 12 *Georgia Law Review* 393.
Posner, R, *Sex and Reason* (Cambridge, MA: Harvard University Press, 1992).
Prosser, J, *Second Skins: The Body Narratives of Transsexuality* (New York: Columbia University Press, 1998).
Pundik, A, 'Coercion and Deception in Sexual Relations' (2015) 28 *Canadian Journal of Law and Jurisprudence* 97.

## R

Rabinow, P (ed.) *Essential Works of Foucault, vol 1: Ethics* (New York: The New Press, 1998).
Rackley, E, 'The Art and Craft of Writing Judgments: Notes on the Feminist Judgments Project' in R Hunter, C McGlynn and E Rackley (eds) *Feminist Judgements: From Theory to Practice* (Oxford: Hart Publishing, 2010) pp. 44–56.
Rackley, E, 'Why Feminist Legal Scholars Should Write Judgments: Reflections on the Feminist Judgments Project in England and Wales' (2012) 24(2) *Canadian Journal of Women & the Law* 389.
Raj, S, 'Disturbing Disgust: Gesturing To the Abject in Queer Cases' in A Dwyer, M Ball and T Crofts (eds) *Queering Criminology* (London: Palgrave Macmillan, 2016) pp. 82–101.
Raymond, J, *The Transsexual Empire: The Making of a She-Male* (Boston, MA: Beacon Press, 1979).
Reed, B, Rhodes, S, Schofield, P and Wylie, K, *Gender Variance in the UK: Prevalence, Incidence, Growth and Geographic Distribution* (Ashtead, Surrey: Gender Identity, Research and Education Society, 2009).
Rich, A, 'Compulsory Heterosexuality and Lesbian Existence' (1980) 5 *Signs: Journal of Women in Culture and Society* 631.
Ricoeur, P, *Freud and Philosophy: An Essay on Interpretation* (New Haven, CT: Yale University Press, 1970).
Ridolfi, K, 'Law, Ethics, and the Good Samaritan: Should There be a Duty to Rescue?' (2000) 7 *Santa Clara Law Review* 957.
Robinson, K H, *Innocence, Knowledge and the Construction of Childhood: The Contradictory Nature of Sexuality and Censorship in Children's Contemporary Lives* (Abingdon, Oxfordshire: Routledge, 2013).

Robson, R, *Lesbian Outlaw: Survival Under the Rule of Law* (Ithaca, NY: Firebrand Books, 1992)

Robson, R, *Sappho Goes to Law School* (New York: Columbia University Press, 1998).

Rodger, A, 'The Form and Language of Judicial Opinions' (2002) 118 *Law Quarterly Review* 226.

Rogers, J, 'The Effect of "Deception" in the Sexual Offences Act 2003' (2013) 4 *Archbold Review* 7.

Rosenberg, R, 'Between Killing and Letting Die in Criminal Jurisprudence' (2014) 34 *Northern Illinois University Law Review* 391.

Ross, W D, *The Right and the Good* (Oxford: Oxford University Press, 1930).

Rottnek, M, *Sissies and Tomboys: Gender Nonconformity and Homosexual Childhood* (New York: New York University Press, 1999).

Rubenfeld, J, 'The Riddle of Rape-by-Deception and the Myth of Sexual Autonomy' (2013) 122 *Yale Law Journal* 1372.

Rubin, G, 'Thinking Sex: Notes for a Radical Theory of the Politics of Sexuality' in C Vance (ed.) *Pleasure and Danger* (New York: Routledge & Kegan Paul, 1984).

Rubin, G, 'Of Catamites and Kings: Reflections on Butch, Gender, and Boundaries' in S Stryker and S Whittle (eds) *The Transgender Studies Reader* (New York: Routledge, 2006) pp. 471–481.

Rubin, H, 'Phenomenology as Method in Trans Studies' (1998) 4(2) *GLQ: A Journal of Lesbian and Gay Studies* 263.

## S

Sandland, R, 'Between "Truth" and "Difference": Poststructuralism, Law and the Power of Feminism' (1995) 3 *Feminist Legal Studies* 3.

Sandland, R, 'Feminism and the Gender Recognition Act 2004' (2005) 13 *Feminist Legal Studies* 43.

Sarat, A, Cambra, H, Smith, S and Truax, O, 'Law and Lies: An Introduction' in A Sarat (ed.) *Law and Lies: Deception and Truth-Telling in the American Legal System* (New York: Cambridge University Press, 2015) pp. 1–31.

Sarat, A and Kearns, T R, (eds) *Law's Violence* (Ann Arbor, MI: University of Michigan Press, 1995).

Sawicki, J, *Disciplining Foucault: Feminism, Power and the Body* (New York: Routledge, 1991).

Scanlon, T M, *What We Owe to Each Other* (Cambridge, MA: Harvard University Press, 1998).

Schoeman, F D, 'Privacy and Intimate Information' in F D Schoeman (ed.), *Philosophical Dimensions of Privacy: An Anthology* (London: Cambridge University Press, 1984) pp. 403–418.

Schulhofer, S, *Unwanted Sex: The Culture of Intimidation and the Failure of Law* (Cambridge, MA: Harvard University Press, 1998).

Sedgwick, E, 'Privilege of Unknowing' (1988) 1 *Genders* 102.

Sedgwick, E, *The Epistemology of the Closet* (New York: Penguin, 1990).

Sedgwick, E, *Tendencies* (Durham, NC: Duke University Press, 1993).

Segal, L, *Straight Sex: The Politics of Pleasure* (London: Virago, 1994).

Seidman, S, *Difference Troubles: Queering Social Theory and Sexual Politics* (New York: Cambridge University Press, 1997).

Serano, J, *Whipping Girl: A Transsexual Woman on Sexism and the Scapegoating of Femininity* (Berkeley, CA: Seal Press, 2007).

Serano, J, *Excluded: Making Feminist and Queer Movements More Inclusive* (Berkeley, CA: Seal Press, 2013).

Sharpe, A, *Transgender Jurisprudence: Dysphoric Bodies of Law* (London: Cavendish, 2002).

Sharpe, A, 'Endless Sex: The Gender Recognition Act 2004 and the Persistence of a Legal Category' (2007a) 15(1) *Feminist Legal Studies* 57.

Sharpe, A, 'A Critique of the Gender Recognition Act 2004' (2007b) 4(1) *Journal of Bioethical Inquiry* 33.

Sharpe, A, *Foucault's Monsters and the Challenge of Law* (Abingdon, Oxfordshire: Routledge, 2010).

Sharpe, A, 'Transgender Marriage and the Legal Obligation to Disclose Gender History' (2012) 75(1) *Modern Law Review* 33.

Sharpe, A, 'Criminalising Sexual Intimacy: Transgender Defendants and the Legal Construction of Non-Consent' (2014) *Criminal Law Review* 207.

Sharpe, A, 'Expanding Liability for Sexual Fraud through the Concept of "Active Deception": A Flawed Approach' (2016) 80(1) *Journal of Criminal Law* 28.

Shelley, C A, *Transpeople: Repudiation, Trauma, Healing* (Toronto: University of Toronto Press, 2008).

Sherwin, E, 'Infelicitous Sex' (1996) 2 *Legal Theory* 209.

Shiner, L, 'Reading Foucault: Anti-Method and the Genealogy of Power-Knowledge' (1982) 21 *History and Theory* 382.

Sidgwick, H, *The Methods of Ethics* (New York: Dover Press, 1966).

Simester, A P, Sullivan, G R, Spencer, J R and Virgo, G, *Criminal Law: Theory and Doctrine* (4th edn) (Oxford: Hart Publishing, 2010).

Simester, A P, Spencer, J R and Virgo, G, *Criminal Law: Theory and Doctrine* (5th edn) (Oxford: Hart Publishing, 2013).

Skilton, R H, 'Shakespeare and the Supreme Court' (1991) 21(4) *The Gargoyle* 4.

Slater, J, 'HIV, Trust and the Criminal Law' (2011) 75 *Journal of Criminal Law* 309.

Smart, C, *Feminism and the Power of Law* (London: Routledge, 1989).

Smith, A M, 'The Regulation of Lesbian Sexuality through Erasure: The Case of Jennifer Saunders' in K Jay (ed.) *Lesbian Erotics* (New York: New York University Press, 1995) pp. 164–179.

Spade, D, *Normal Life: Administrative Violence, Critical Trans Politics and the Limits of Law* (New York: South End Press, 2011).

Spivak, G C, 'The Problem of Cultural Self-Representation' interviewed by Walter Adamson in S Harasym (ed.) *The Post-Colonial Critic: Interviews, Strategies, Dialogues, Gayatri Chakravorty Spivak* (London: Routledge, 1990) pp. 50–58.

Statham, B, 'The Homosexual Advance Defence: "Yeah, I killed him, but he did worse to me" Green v R' (1999) 20(2) *University of Queensland Law Journal* 301.

Steensma, T D, Biemond, R, de Boer, F and Cohen-Kettinis, P T, 'Desisting and Persisting Gender Dysphoria after Childhood: A Qualitative Follow-Up Study' (2011) 16(4) *Clinical Child Psychol Psychiatry* 499.

Steensma, T D, McGuire, J K, Kreukels, B P C, Beekman, A J and Cohen-Kettenis, P T, 'Factors Associated with Desistence and Persistence of Childhood Gender Dysphoria: A Quantitative Follow-Up Study' (2013) 52(6) *Child and Adolescent Psychiatry* 582.

Steinberg, V L, 'A Heat of Passion Offense: Emotions and Bias in "Trans-Panic" Mitigation Claims' (2005) 25(1) *Boston College Third World Law Journal* 1.

Stember, C, *Sexual Racism: The Emotional Barrier to an Integrated Society* (New York: Harper & Row, 1978).

Stevenson, R L, *The Strange Case of Dr Jekyll and Mr Hyde*, (Munich: Deutscher Taschenbuch Verlag, 1986).

Stone, S, 'The Empire Strikes Back: A Posttranssexual Manifesto' in S Stryker and S Whittle (eds) *The Transgender Studies Reader* (Abingdon, Oxfordshire: Routledge, 2006) pp. 221–235.

Stotzer, R L, 'Violence Against Transgender People: A Review of United States Data' (2009) 14(3) *Aggression & Violent Behavior* 170.

Stryker, S, 'Transgender Studies: Queer Theory's Evil Twin' (2004) 10(2) *GLQ: A Journal of Lesbian and Gay Studies* 212.

Stychin, C F, 'Unmanly Diversions: The Construction of the Homosexual Body (Politic) in Law' in C F Stychin, *Law's Desire: Sexuality and the Limits of Justice* (London: Routledge, 1995a) pp. 117–139.

Stychin, C F, *Law's Desire: Sexuality and the Limits of Justice* (London: Routledge, 1995b).

Sullivan, N, *A Critical Introduction to Queer Theory* (New York: New York University Press, 2003).

## T

Tadros, V, *Criminal Responsibility* (Oxford: Oxford University Press, 2005).

Temkin, J, 'Towards a Modern Law of Rape' (1982) 45 *Modern Law Review* 399.

Thomas, K, 'Beyond the Privacy Principle' (1992) 92(6) *Columbia Law Review* 1431.

Tomsen, S, '"He Had to Be a Poofter or Something": Violence, Male Honour and Heterosexual Panic' (1998) 3 *Journal of Interdisciplinary Gender Studies* 44.

Thomson, J, *The Realm of Rights* (Cambridge, MA: Harvard University Press, 1990).

*Time Magazine*, 'The Transgender Tipping Point' 29 May 2014.

Trans People of Color Coalition, *Addressing Anti-Transgender Violence* (Washington, D.C., MD: TPOCC, 2015).

Tuerkheimer, D, 'Sex Without Consent' (2013) 123 *Yale Law Journal Online* 335.

Turner, W B, *A Genealogy of Queer Theory* (Philadelphia, PA: Temple University Press, 2000).

## V

Valdes, F, 'Afterward & Prologue: Queer Legal Theory' (1995) 83 *California Law Review* 344.

Valverde, M, *Sex, Power & Pleasure* (Cambridge, MA: New Society Publishers, 1987).

van de Burg, W, 'Law and Ethics: The Twin Disciplines' (2010) Erasmus Working Paper Series on Jurisprudence and Socio-Legal Studies No 10–02.

Vance, C, (ed.) *Pleasure and Danger* (New York: Routledge & Kegan Paul, 1984).

## W

Warner, M, 'Introduction: Fear of a Queer Planet' (1991) 29 *Social Text* 3.

Warner, M, *The Trouble with Normal: Sex, Politics and the Ethics of Queer Life* (Boston, MA: Harvard University Press, 2000).

Wasserstrom, R, 'Privacy: Some Arguments and Assumptions' in R Bronaugh (ed.), *Philosophical Law* (Westport, CT: Greenwood Press, 1978).

Waters, E, Jindasurat, C and Wolfe, C, *Report from the National Coalition of Anti-Violence Programs: Lesbian, Gay, Bisexual, Transgender, Queer, and HIV-Affected Hate Violence in 2015* (New York: NCAVP, 2016).

Weait, M, *Intimacy and Responsibility: The Criminalisation of HIV Transmission* (Abingdon, Oxfordshire: Routledge, 2007).

Weeks, J, *Sexuality and its Discontents: Meanings, Myths and Modern Sexualities* (London: Routledge and Kegan Paul, 1985).

Weeks, J, *Against Nature: Essays on History, Sexuality and Identity* (London: Rivers Oram, 1991).

Wertheimer, A, 'Consent and Sexual Relations' (1996) 2 *Legal Theory* 89.

Wertheimer, A, *Consent to Sexual Relations* (Cambridge: Cambridge University Press, 2003).

West, R, 'A Comment on Consent, Sex, and Rape' (1996) 2 *Legal Theory* 233.

Whittle, S, Turner, L and Al-Alami, M, *The Equalities Review: Engendered Penalties: Transgender and Transsexual People's Experiences of Inequality & Discrimination* (London: Press for Change, 2007).

Wilchins, R A, 'What Does it Cost to Tell the Truth?' in S Stryker and S Whittle (eds) *The Transgender Studies Reader* (Abingdon, Oxfordshire: Routledge, 2006) pp. 547–551.

Wilde, O, *The Importance of Being Earnest* (London: Bloomsbury, 2014).

Wilkinson, S, 'Why Lying Is Worse Than Merely Misleading' (2000) 13 *Philosophy Today* 6.

Williams, G, 'Convictions and Fair Labelling' (1983) 42 *Cambridge Law Review* 85.

Williams, G, 'Criminal Omissions – the Conventional View' (1991) 107 *Law Quarterly Review* 87.

Williams, R, 'Deception, Mistake and Vitiation of the Victim's Consent' (2008) 124 *Law Quarterly Review* 132.

World Professional Association of Transgender Health, *Standards of Care for the Health of Transsexual, Transgender and Gender Nonconforming People* (7th Edn) (Minneapolis, MN: WPATH, 2012).

Wren, B, 'Early Physical Intervention for Young People with Atypical Gender Identity Development' (2000) 5 *Clin Child Psychol Psychiatry* 220.

## Z

Zanghellini, A, 'Queer, Antinormativity, Counter-Normativity and Abjection' (2009) 18(1) *Griffith Law Review* 1.

Zelizer, V, *Pricing the Priceless Child: The Changing Value of Children* (Princeton, NJ: Princeton University Press, 1994).

Zucker, K J, 'Gender Identity Disorder' in D A Wolfe and E J Mash (eds) *Behavioral and Emotional Disorders in Adolescents: Nature, Assessment, and Treatment* (New York: Guildford Press 2006) 535–562.

Zucker, K J and Cohen-Kettenis, P T, 'Gender Identity Disorder in Children and Adolescents' in D L Rowland and L Incrocci (eds) *Handbook of Sexual and Gender Identity Disorders* (London: John Wiley & Sons, 2008) 376–422.

# Index

For Product Safety Concerns and Information please contact our EU representative GPSR@taylorandfrancis.com
Taylor & Francis Verlag GmbH, Kaufingerstraße 24, 80331 München, Germany

www.ingramcontent.com/pod-product-compliance
Ingram Content Group UK Ltd.
Pitfield, Milton Keynes, MK11 3LW, UK
UKHW021303190926
475701UK00009B/624
*9780367280246*